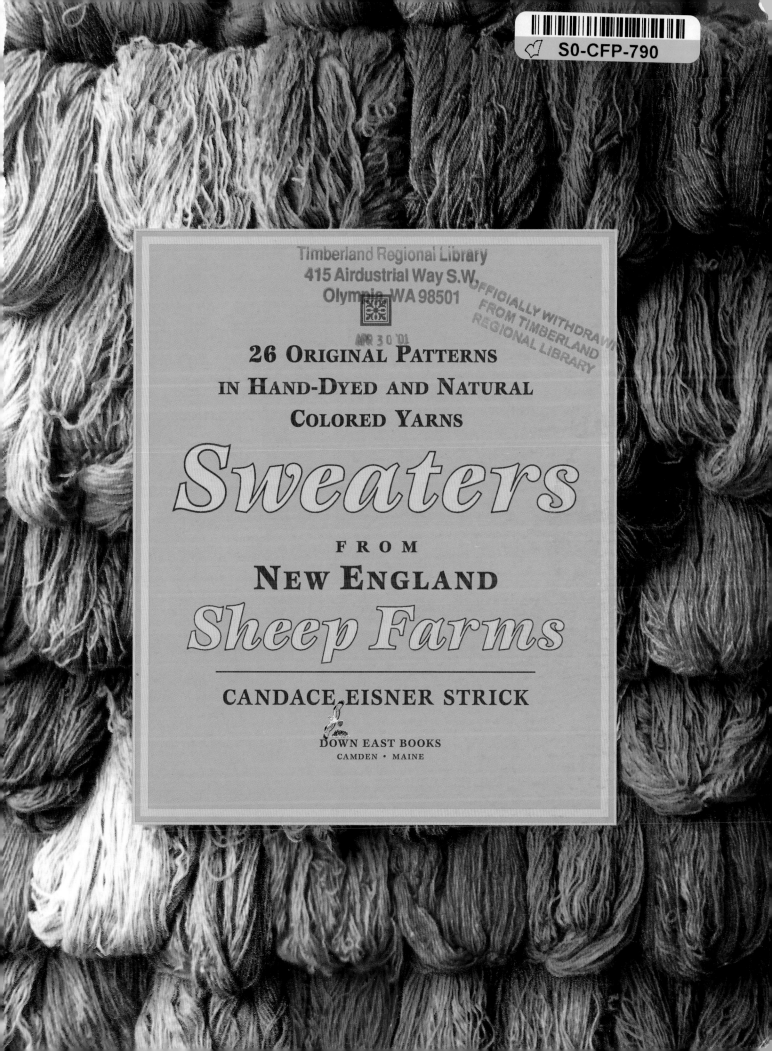

26 ORIGINAL PATTERNS IN HAND-DYED AND NATURAL COLORED YARNS

Sweaters

FROM
NEW ENGLAND
Sheep Farms

CANDACE EISNER STRICK

DOWN EAST BOOKS
CAMDEN · MAINE

FOR KEN ~

As always, forever.

FOR NATHANIEL, LIAM, AND NOAH ~

Time is the most precious thing you have.
Use it to follow your heart, pursue your passions,
and, above all, for the joy of creation.

ISBN 0-89272-446-3

Library of Congress Catalog Card Number: 99-72213

SWEATER PHOTOGRAPHS BY LYNN KARLIN
TITLE PAGE PHOTO COURTESY OF NANNEY KENNEDY

PRINTED IN HONG KONG

5   4   3   2   1

Down East Books
P. O. Box 679
Camden, ME 04843

Contents

Introduction

There are two things in this world that I dearly love. One is yarn; the other is my home in New England. Having lived only in New England and being taught to knit at the age of three, I have been happily immersed in both all my life.

I am a confessed yarn addict and feel absolutely no guilt in stating this fact. I just love yarn and knitting. I have a closet full of beautiful skeins and a head full of ideas for knitting them. There is always something new out there that catches my fancy, and so my collection continues to grow at a faster rate than what I use up. Zero population growth does not apply to my yarn closet. It's a good thing that yarn is easily compressed. I must confess that at times I hear strange sounds coming from the closet. If I dare to open the doors, I find that a terrible chain reaction of cascading skeins and cones has taken place, and I must once more do some creative rearranging to accommodate the chaos. In spite of this, I have a complete and accurate inventory in my brain, even remembering where I bought a certain hank and what the weather was like on that particular day!

There is a saying about heating with wood that goes something like this: "It warms you three times—once when you chop it, once when you stack it, and once again when you burn it." A skein of yarn is a beautiful object that can warm you and give you pleasure many times over. Spending time in yarn stores gives me enormous amounts of pleasure. I can caress the yarn, smell it, look at it, and dream about what to knit with it. When I finally do knit the yarn, it gives all of the previous pleasures plus a beautiful and useful garment when I am finished. I could change around that little ditty about wood and apply it to yarn, adding a fourth pleasure: once when you look at it, once when you buy it, once when you knit with it, and again every time you wear it!

I love New England, and even though I have traveled to other parts of the country and to Europe, I have no desire to live anywhere else. With a short drive through a few New England states, I can hike in the mountains or spend a day at the ocean. The weather is always changing, and just when you think you can't stand another day of heat and humidity, you are rewarded with a cold front rushing through, dropping temperatures and making you reach for a sweater. Fall is spectacular, winter is magical. Spring is a promise of what is to come (but I must confess that the deer flies where I live make it almost impossible to enjoy it). Summer is mellow and lazy, and the fresh fruits and vegetables are its rewards.

I love the architecture and traditional handcrafts of New England. One of the best places to see both is at Sturbridge Village, a re-created working village of the 1830s, located in Sturbridge, Massachusetts. Here, costumed interpreters go about their daily business of the day appropriate to their occupation of the era. I can stand at the carding mill and watch a water-powered carding machine turning out fluffy white rovings of wool, then walk over to one of the beautiful old houses and watch someone spin it on a great wheel. The potter's wheel will mesmerize me as he turns out dishes, pitchers and cups. Hand-dyeing is done during the summer at Sturbridge Village, using traditional native plants to color the yarn. There are several looms set up in the houses, with traditional coverlets and blankets in progress.

I used to think that I was born in the wrong era, loving all of these handcrafts as I do, and wanting only to spend my entire day doing them. However, after last winter, when we were without electricity for three days, I've changed my thinking. I can still do these wonderful things and enjoy the benefits of central heat and good lighting!

It was only natural that I should end up writing about the two things I love so much. My first book—*Sweaters from a New England Village*—is a collection of sweaters inspired by the beautiful yarns still being produced in the historic New England town of Harrisville, New Hampshire. The concept of this second book actually evolved from my search for people and companies to supply me with yarn for an entirely different book idea I was developing. I came across Sonja Fuller's ad in the back of a magazine and sent her my usual form letter, but was rewarded with a unique and personal encounter. I had never even considered using hand-dyed yarn in a project, but after seeing Sonja's, I was totally enthralled with the idea. As I started delving into this particular genre, I was astonished to learn how many people out there were actually growing their own wool and dyeing it. I wanted to see it all, but knew that for practicality's sake, I would have to limit the amount of miles I was willing to travel. I therefore settled on doing research just through the New England states.

A good place to start looking further was at the yearly New Boston, New Hampshire, sheep and wool festival. After spending the day there, I could not believe that I had missed out on such a wonderful thing for so many years. Here was yarn that was totally different from anything I had ever seen at a store, luring me into booths with the promise of possessing it! There were fantastic hanks of hand-dyed yarn as well as natural shades ranging from creamy white to deep chocolate brown—all produced by New England fiber farmers who were more than willing to talk to me. Any time I travel, I've always visited local yarn stores, but now I'd discovered that a sheep and wool festival opened up whole new possibilities for buying not only yarn, but roving, accessories, finished garments, and even sheep and other fiber-producing animals! The people were interesting and fun to talk to, and while I was happily occupied looking at everything, my husband Ken was enthralled with watching the border collies do their sheep trials. Here was the perfect way to spend a day! A few weeks later, the Cummington, Massachusetts, sheep and wool festival yielded another fun and valuable day, and I soon compiled a list of people who were willing to be interviewed and have me design with their yarn.

The people I interviewed for this book are artists, and their work is labor intensive and time consuming. Because of this, they use only the finest fiber—most of it grown under their own discerning and watchful eye. The resulting fiber is the product of years of careful research and breeding. Starting with only the very best, then adding their wonderful colors to it, these amazing fiber artists create hanks of exquisite beauty.

Working with hand-dyed yarn is an experience not to be missed, and there is never a dull moment. The colors will sometimes abruptly change or meld ever so slightly into something else, the luxurious fiber slipping through your fingers is sensuous and pleasing, and the finished garment is like no other in the world. People who have only knit with commercially dyed yarn may have to adjust to all this excitement. Some people worry when they see that the yarn is not a flat, even color, thinking that the garment will come out looking blotchy or uneven. Relax! One of the beauties of hand-dyed yarn is that the colors change imperceptibly throughout the hank, giving the finished garment a sense of movement and added richness of color.

Most knitters go through an evolution in their knitting lifetime by exploring new ideas and challenges, even finding that their tastes in color and design can change considerably over the years. If you have never worked with hand-dyed yarn before, consider this the beginning of your evolution. Endless possibilities will present themselves. For one thing, your fiber-buying potential will be greatly expanded! New designs will creep into your life to accommodate this new yarn, and new pleasures will be had with each individual combination of fiber you use. Don't pass up buying a beautiful skein because you don't know what to do with it at that particular moment; take it home and make it part of your life. In due time a marvelous idea will present itself to you, and you will be as richly rewarded (and warmed) as if you had chopped a cord of wood!

Acknowledgments

It has been my greatest pleasure to travel through New England in search of yarn. The goods these travels have yielded have far surpassed my wildest dreams. I have met fiber artists who are more possessed than I am, working and dyeing to their hearts' content, never minding that they are not yet millionaires from their hours of toil. Their yarns and techniques have astounded and inspired me, and I have come home from each interview with a new outlook on my life and work. All have patiently explained their processes, as well as opening their homes, studios, and lives to me. They have generously provided me with yarn, helping me in any way I have asked. I am indebted to them beyond words, for without them, this book (and the garments) would not have been possible. They are true artists; their hanks are their works of art. Thank you, Loranne Carey Block, Alice Field, Sonja Fuller, Nanney Kennedy, Linda MacMillan, Ellen Minard, Heather Minto, and Margrit Pilcher.

My good friends have always provided me with encouragement, advice, and laughter. For years of friendship I thank Steve and Edith Daigle, Lenore Grunko and Patrick McGlamery, Dody and Mitch Knight, Dahlia Popovits, Carolyn Terhune, Donna McLaughlin, and Ilze Mueller.

My family is my best fan club and advertising committee: my father and stepmother, Raymond and Edna Eisner; my sisters, Judith Eisner and Ardeth Millner; and my three sons, Nathaniel, Liam, and Noah, who think that the only way their mother has fun is by knitting.

Thanks to Meg Swansen, Ann Feitelson, Charlene Schurch, and Joan Shrouder, my fellow knitwear designers who have unselfishly helped and advised me, and to Phyllis and Bob Fishberg, owners of The Wool Connection in Avon, Connecticut, who generously offered me anything in their store for use in the book's production.

At Down East Books, I thank Tom Fernald for having faith in me again, and Karin Womer for all her warm assurance, patience, hard work, and insight.

Our sweater photographs were made in Cushing, Maine. Thanks go to Joe and Judy Miller and Gary and Ida Clarke for allowing us to tramp around their farms. Amber Bonarrigo, John Elliott, Jill Grindle, Kimberly Mullin, Bev Nolan, and Kenneth Strick were our models, and Annie Geller Chapman our model consultant—they all did a wonderful job.

And lastly, more than thank-you goes to my husband Ken, for always being by my side. He has been a help in every part of this book, short of actually knitting the sweaters (even though I begged him on this one!). Throughout the traveling and research he has been my chauffeur, second pair of ears, and devoted companion. At home he winds yarn, proofreads, solves computer problems, and gives advice, all with patience and good humor. With him, anything is possible. His generosity has given me the opportunity to pursue my dreams, his love and devotion have healed my broken bones, and his dancing will always make me smile.

Substituting Commercial Yarns

All the garments in this book were made with hand-dyed yarn. The colors are custom and unique, and most skeins are one-of-a-kind. Using anything other than the particular yarn called for will change the appearance of the finished product. However, all of the designs in this book certainly may be made using commercial yarns. There is a huge variety out there, and yarn store owners are very knowledgeable and willing to help their customers substitute one kind for another.

Some of the yarns from the New England farms I visited are custom spun according to exact instructions and therefore may not *exactly* match the weight and diameter of most commercial yarns. Just comparing two yarns in your hands is not a reliable guide; even though they may look to be the same thickness, they can produce very different gauges when knit up. It is therefore imperative that a swatch be knit and the gauge carefully calculated. To help you make yarn substitutions, if you wish to do so, I have carefully compared these specialty yarns with some of the best commercial yarns, and have summarized that information under "Yarn Sources" below. However, I urge all knitters to make at least one sweater using the extraordinary yarns available from the fiber artists profiled in these pages.

When substituting one yarn for another, the two most important things to take into consideration are yardage and gauge. The total amount of yarn needed is the number of yards in one skein multiplied by the number of skeins required. For example, a sweater calling for six skeins, each skein having 280 yards and weighing four ounces, means the sweater will need 1680 yards/24 ounces. Another yarn may be put up in four-ounce skeins that have only, say, 240 yards per skein. For the same sweater you would need seven skeins/28 ounces. Therefore, do not rely on weight, but always figure out actual yardage.

Metric and English Equivalents

As some yarn labels give information in metric and others in English measurements, it's a good idea to be able to do the math to convert from one measurement system to the other.

Most yarns are put up in either 100-gram or 50-gram increments. One ounce is equal to about 28.57 grams. To figure ounces from grams, divide the total gram weight by 28.5. That will yield the information that a 100-gram skein is about 3.5 ounces, and the 50-gram one is about 1.75 ounces.

American wool is usually put up in skeins of two or four ounces. To figure grams from ounces, you need to multiply the total weight by 28.5. A two-ounce skein thus weighs about 57 grams, and a four-ounce skein weighs about 114 grams.

A meter is equal to about 39 inches. Therefore, one yard equals .914 meters. To convert yards to meters, you must multiply the total yardage by .914. To convert meters to yards, you must divide the total number of meters by .914. A skein of 200 yards would measure about 183 meters. A skein of 200 meters would measure about 219 yards.

Conversions at a glance

ounces = grams ÷ 28.57
grams = ounces x 28.57
inches = centimeters ÷ 2.54
yards = meters ÷ 1.0936
centimeters = inches x 2.54
meters = yards x 1.0936

Handy equivalents

.75 ounce = 21.5 grams
1 ounce = 28.5 grams
1.5 ounces = 43 grams
1.75 ounces = 57 grams
3.5 ounces = 100 grams

Gauge

You probably don't want to hear it all again, but enough cannot be said about the importance of gauge. The same yarn can be knit in a wide variety of gauges just by changing needle size. When you are substituting a yarn for one listed in this book, it is doubly important to knit a swatch to make sure your gauge matches the suggested one. If the gauge is the same, it is safe to make the substitution. Bear in mind, however, that going up or down several needle sizes will produce a fabric that is significantly looser or more tightly woven than what the original fabric was intended to be, and this will affect the way the garment drapes on the body.

If the gauge on your test swatch does not match, the garment is not going to be the same finished dimensions as are listed in the pattern. This can sometimes work to your advantage—if, for instance, you would like the garment to be a wee bit smaller or larger. Make sure you do your math, however, so there will be no hideous surprises!

To figure gauge: Make a swatch at least four inches by four inches. Carefully mark off four inches square. Count the number of stitches both horizontally (stitches) and vertically (rows) within your marks. Divide each amount by four. This is the number of stitches/rows per inch.

Divide the total number of stitches in the sweater by the number of stitches per inch to figure the total width of the garment. For instance, if your gauge is 6 stitches per inch and there are 240 stitches called for, the finished measurement will be 40 inches. If your gauge is off just by one half a stitch (5.5 stitches per inch), the finished measurement will grow to 43.6 inches. If your gauge is 5.75 stitches per inch (this would be 23 stitches per 4 inches), the finished measurement will be 41.7 inches.

Vertical gauge is not quite as important as horizontal, as you can add a row or two to even things out in most sweaters. The danger comes in where particular patterns must be matched in certain places, such as at the shoulders. If your vertical gauge is off and you've had to add or subtract a few rows, things will not match up. This may not be the worst thing in the world, but it certainly is something to take into consideration.

Yarn Sources

In order to make the task of substituting yarns a little easier, I have divided the hand-dyed yarns I used into three categories. If you wish to use one of the recommended commercial yarns listed on pages 8 and 9, or to switch one hand-dyed for another, make sure they are listed in the same category.

CATEGORY 1 is basically a worsted-weight yarn, and yarns in this list knit up to roughly 4.5 to 5 stitches per inch in Stockinette Stitch on #7 needles.

CATEGORY 2 is basically a double-knitting weight and knits up to about 6 stitches per inch in Stockinette Stitch on #5 needles.

CATEGORY 3 is a bulky weight and knits up in Stockinette Stitch to about 3 to 4 stitches per inch on #10 needles.

Some of the hand-dyed yarns, however, fall between these three categories. I have made a note next to those that do. I have classified the commercial yarns in the same way. Also bear in mind that gauge can be greatly affected by how each individual knitter knits. *Always knit a swatch in the suggested stitch as indicated in the pattern, adjusting needle size to get the desired gauge.*

Below I have listed the hand-dyed yarns used for the patterns in this book, identifying them by category and giving addresses of the farms where they can be obtained. After that, I give a second list of comparable commercial yarns, again identified by category.

hand-dyed yarns

CATEGORY 1.

WORSTED WEIGHT. GAUGE 4.5 TO 5 STS/INCH IN STOCKINETTE STITCH WITH #7 NEEDLES.

Bear Hill Farm
(4 OZ/280 YD SKEINS)

SONJA FULLER
13 BEAR HILL RD.
BOZRAH, CT 06334
(860) 889-1719

Meadowcroft Farm
(3.5 OZ/200 YD SKEINS)
Note: This yarn is just a slight bit heavier than the others in Category 1.

NANNEY KENNEDY
45 HOPKINS RD.
WASHINGTON, ME 04574
(207) 845-2587
nanney@kieve.org

Oak Grove Yarns
(CORMO—1.5 OZ/100 YD SKEIN;
ANGORA—1.75 OZ/150 YD SKEIN)

LINDA MACMILLAN
BOX 531 PINE BANKS RD.
PUTNEY, VT 05346
(802) 387-5934
oakgrove@sover.net

Watson Farms
(4 OZ/230 YD SKEIN)

HEATHER MINTO
455 NORTH RD.
JAMESTOWN, RI 02835
(401) 423-0005
FAX (401) 423-2554

CATEGORY 2.

DOUBLE-KNITTING WEIGHT. GAUGE ABOUT 6 STS/INCH IN STOCKINETTE STITCH ON #5 NEEDLES.

Ellen's Half-Pint Farm
(ALPACA—80 YD/OZ,
FALKLAND WOOL—84 YD/OZ, SKEINS WOUND
    INDIVIDUALLY FOR EACH ORDER;
MERINO/SILK—13.5 OZ/1675 YD SKEIN)
Note: The merino/silk is a bit lighter in weight than the standard Category 2. Because of the silk content, it tends to be less lofty than a 100% wool.

ELLEN MINARD
85 TUCKER HILL RD.
NORWICH, VT 05055
(802) 649-5420
ellens@together.net

Snowstar Farm
(4 OZ/320 YD SKEIN)

LORANNE CAREY BLOCK
63 LOVEREN MILL RD.
ANTRIM, NH 03440
(603) 588-2552

Morehouse Farm
(2 OZ/175 YD SKEIN)
Note: This 2-ply Merino is a bit lighter weight than a standard double-knitting weight.

MARGRIT PILCHER
RD 2, BOX 408
RED HOOK, NY 12571
(914) 758-6493

CATEGORY 3.

BULKY WEIGHT. GAUGE 3 TO 4 STS/INCH ON #10 NEEDLES.

Foxhill Farm
(4 OZ /145 YD SKEIN)

ALICE FIELD
BOX 6 MAPLE ST.
LEE, MA 01238
(413) 243-2558

commercial yarns

The following commercial yarns may be substituted for the yarns I used in the original sweaters. I have classified them into the same three weight categories as the hand-dyed yarns listed above. Most of these yarns are readily available in yarn stores, or directly from the source.

Mountain Colors

PO BOX 156
CORVALLIS, MT 59828
(406) 777-3377

A beautiful selection of luscious colors, various plies, and fiber blends.

CATEGORY 1: Their 4/8's wool (250 yd/4 oz skein) is available in almost all yarn shops.

CATEGORY 3: The 3-ply Montana Wool (150 yd/4 oz skein) comes in the same luscious colors as the 4/8's wool.

Heneke Enterprises, Inc.

HENEKE WOOL FASHIONS
630 NO. BLACK CAT RD.
MERIDIAN, ID 83642
(208) 888-3129
FAX (208) 888-2776

These folks raise Merino sheep and alpacas at their ranch. The yarn is splendid, comes in a wide variety of natural shades as well as dyed colors, and in many different blends. It is also available in yarn shops.

CATEGORY 2: Merino 2-ply fingering yarn (260–290 yd/2 oz skein).

Dale of Norway, Inc.

N16 W233390 STONERIDGE DR.,
SUITE A
WAUKESHA, WI 53188
(800) 441-DALE
betsdale@execpc.com

This well-known brand is available in almost all yarn shops. Dale offers a variety of different weights, colors, and fiber content. Although the colors are not variegated, they may be substituted, with different results of course, for some of the variegated yarns called for in this book.

CATEGORY 2: Tiur, a mohair/wool blend (115m/50 gm ball).

CATEGORY 2: Heilo (100 m/50 gm skein).

Knitting Traditions

BETH BROWN-REINSEL
PO BOX 421
DELTA, PA 17314
(717) 456-7950
knittradit@aol.com

Here is wealth of authentic British wool in both dyed and breed-specific natural colors. The yarns are imported from small woolen mills, and are only available through Beth.

CATEGORY 1: Creskeld Wensleydale Aran in dyed colors (133 yd/100 gm skein).

CATEGORY 1: Creskeld Breed Specific Aran in natural colors (133 yd/100 gm skein).

CATEGORY 2: 5-ply Guernsey (246 yd/100 gm skein). A tightly spun multi-ply yarn that is excellent for showing texture, as in the Madder Gansey.

Plymouth Yarn Company, Inc.

PO BOX 28
BRISTOL, PA 19007
(215) 788-0459
FAX (215) 788-2269

Plymouth has a huge variety of yarn in almost every yarn store.

CATEGORY 1: Galway (230 yd/100 gm skein).

CATEGORY 1: Cleckheatons Country 8-ply (105 yd/50 gm skein). Non-variegated.

CATEGORY 1: Cleckheatons Tapestry (110 yd/50 gm skein) is a variegated version of the Country 8-ply listed above.

CATEGORY 1: Gjestal Naturspun No. 3 (200 m/100 gm skein) A natural color worsted weight just a slight bit heavier than most yarns in Category 1, this would make a good substitute for Meadowcroft's yarn.

CATEGORY 1 OR 2: Gjestal Naturspun No. 2 (300 m/100 gm skein), a lighter-weight cousin to the yarn listed above, could fit either category, depending on needle size.

CATEGORY 2: Indiecita Alpaca (220 yd/100 gm skein). Non-variegated.

Rowan Yarns

WESTMINSTER FIBERS, INC.
5 NORTHERN BLVD., SUITE 4
AMHERST, NH 03031
(800) 445-9276

Rowan yarns can be found almost everywhere, and there is wide selection. At this writing, no variegated colors are available.

CATEGORY 1: Magpie Aran (140 m/100 gm skein), in both natural and dyed colors, is a good choice.

CATEGORY 2: Rowan Designer DK Wool (115 m/50 gm skein).

Harrisville Designs

PO BOX 806
HARRISVILLE, NH 03450
(800) 338-9415

The famous Harrisville mill, made more famous by my first book *Sweaters from a New England Village* (Down East Books, 1996), produces a palette of beautiful yarns. The yarn is available in some yarn shops, or directly from the manufacturer.

CATEGORY 1: 2-ply Highland yarn (200 yd/100 gm skein), while not a variegated yarn, is a heathery blend of colors.

Tahki Imports, Ltd.

11 GRAPHIC PLACE
MOONACHIE, NJ 07074
(201) 807-0070
FAX (201) 807-9386

Represented in all yarn stores, this company offers many different lines of yarn that make easy substitutions.

CATEGORY 1: Limbo (135 yd/50 gm skein), a variegated yarn, is available in a wide variety of colors. While it is a bit finer in weight than the other Category 1 yarns, it is possible to go up a needle size or two and match the gauge.

CATEGORY 1: Sable (140 yd/50 gm ball) is a luscious blend of Merino wool and French angora.

Froehlich

Check with your favorite yarn store or mail order source about availability of this beautiful Swiss yarn. Froehlich offers a wide variety of naturally processed, buttery soft wool.

CATEGORY 2: Tolle Wolle (160 m/50 gm skein) is variegated by plying different shades, creating a subtle change of numerous colors.

CATEGORY 3: Swiss Chalet, while heavier than the Tolle Wolle, is a wee bit lighter weight than a true bulky.

Sirdar

FLANSHAW LANE
ALVERTHORPE, WAKEFIELD WF2 9ND
WEST YORKSHIRE, ENGLAND
TELEPHONE: 01924 371501

I have knit the Morehouse Farms "His" sweater in Sirdar's Balmoral yarn and found the horizontal gauge to be exactly the same. The vertical gauge, however, is fewer rows per inch than the Morehouse Farm yarn.

CATEGORY 2: Balmoral (127 yd/50 gm skein)— a luxurious blend of wool, alpaca, and silk—is a true double-knitting weight.

SPECIAL NOTE:
Substitutions for Oak Grove Yarns
The Cormo blend yarns from Oak Grove have a unique spin. The following commercial yarns are similar. While I was not sent a sample of these, I have seen them in yarn stores. Both are **CATEGORY 1**: Cascade Pastaza (132 yd/100 gm skein); Classic Elite Montera (127 yd/100 gm skein).

"The little work-tables of women's fingers
are the play-ground of women's fancies,
and their knitting-needles are fairy-wands
by which they transform a whole room
into a spirit-isle of dreams."
—RICHTER

This little saying was on the inside cover of an old crochet book that my friend Dahlia lent me (*The Art of Crocheting*, Butterick Publishing Co. Ltd, 1901). It's great fun to think of a whole convention of knitters happily transforming the convention hall into sweet dreams, wildly fantasizing (I wonder about what?) while their fingers fly over the "fairy wands"!

General Directions and Useful Techniques

- **Read through all directions before beginning knitting.** (Note that references to charts and yarn colors are printed in capital letters whenever the directions call for starting a *new* chart or changing to a *new* yarn color.)

- **Sizes.** Most patterns give several sizes. Instructions are given for the sizes separated by dashes (S–M–L). When only one figure is given, it applies to all sizes.

- **Measurements** given are for finished size. This is what the garment actually measures in inches. Measurements are given in inches; to convert inches to centimeters, multiply by 2.54.

- **Needle sizes** given are for American sizes. Canadian and metric equivalents are listed below. Note that sizes do not always correspond exactly between one measurement system and another.

AMERICAN	CANADIAN	METRIC
0	14	2
1	13	2.5
2	11	3
3	10	3
4	9	3.5
5	8	4
6	7	4.5
7	7	4.5
8	6	5
9	5	5.5
10	4	6

For length measurements of circular needles:

16-inch = 40-centimeter
24-inch = 60-centimeter
32-inch = 80-centimeter needles.

- **Check your gauge** before beginning. Make sure you knit a large enough swatch (at least four inches, or ten centimeters, square) and measure it carefully on a flat surface. A variance of even half a stitch can mean the difference of several inches over many hundred stitches. If your gauge does not correspond to the one given, try adjusting needle size up or down. If the project is to be knit in the round, knit your test gauge in the round also. This can be done easily on double-pointed needles. When the test piece is finished and bound off, cut it vertically between needles 1 and 3 to yield a flat swatch. (See page 6 for more information about making and measuring a test swatch to test your gauge.)

- **Fair Isle** is a method of knitting that uses two colors in each row. Both colors are carried across the entire row.

Working with two colors can produce an uneven fabric if the yarns are carried across the back too tightly. Carry all unused yarn loosely across the back of the work, spreading stitches on the needle to their true width. Yarns carried for more than four or five stitches should be woven in with the working yarn. This prevents large loops of yarn that could catch on your fingers as you put on and take off the sweater.

- **Intarsia** is a method of knitting that uses small sections of color. The yarn is not carried across the entire row as in Fair Isle method, but is just dropped behind the work when not in use. In order to avoid a hole at each color change, the yarns must be linked together by twisting them around each other at each color junction. Small balls of yarn can be used, but lengths of yarn are easier to handle and untangle.

- **Knit in any ends** left from color changes as you go along. This saves tedious darning in of ends at the completion of the sweater.

- **Casting On.** There are many methods of casting on, but the one that I have found to be consistently the best is the Cable Edge Cast-On. This produces a firm but elastic edge with no holes between the stitches. Make a loop on the left-hand needle, insert the right-hand needle through this loop from front to back, pull the loop through as if to knit but turn the loop and put it on the left-hand needle. Continue casting on, but from now on insert the right-hand needle *between* the two stitches.

- **Decreasing.** Two methods are used; one produces a decrease that slants to the left; the other slants to the right. Both methods eliminate one stitch at a time.

  SSK—This method slants to the left. Slip two stitches knitwise, one at a time, to right needle, then insert point of left needle into the front of both these stitches and knit them together.

  K2 together—This method slants to the right. Insert the right needle as usual through two stitches and knit them together.

- **Increasing.** Two different methods are used in the patterns. If a specific one is called for, the directions will indicate which method to use. Where there is no indication, use whichever method you prefer.

  (1) **Knit into the stitch below** the next stitch on the needle, then knit the stitch as usual. This makes one new stitch.

(2) *Make 1 (M1):* With the right-hand needle, lift the running strand between two stitches and place it on the left-hand needle. Knit (or purl) through the back of this loop

- *Joining Rounds.* Before joining, make sure that the stitches are not twisted around the needles. It is very easy to overlook this, so after working the first round, check again that all stitches are lying correctly.

Knitted Seam for Shoulders

This method is used to join the shoulders on most of the patterns in this book. This makes a flat, almost invisible seam and allows the design of a charted sweater to continue uninterrupted over the seam. This method is worked as follows:

With each set of shoulder stitches on a double-pointed needle, turn entire sweater inside out, right sides together. Hold the right-front shoulder needle and the right-back shoulder needle together in your left hand. Using any color of yarn that was used in the sweater, insert a third needle through the first stitch on both needles, and knit. Repeat with the next stitch, and then pass the first stitch over the second as you would normally do in a cast-off. Continue in this manner of casting off until all the stitches are used. Break the yarn and pass it through the last stitch.

Holding the shoulders right side to right side produces a seam on the inside of the garment. Holding the shoulders wrong side to wrong side and working the seam the same way produces a ridge on the outside of the sweater. The latter method is useful if a ridge is part of the design pattern.

Reading the Charts

Every square on a chart represents a stitch. Every horizontal row of squares represents a row or round. When knitting in the round, charts are always read from right to left, bottom to top. When knitting back and forth, right-side rows are read from right to left, wrong-side rows are read from left to right; bottom to top.

All symbols for charts are explained in the key. For twists and cables, I have purposely chosen diagonal lines to represent the direction that the stitch will lean toward. Front crosses and cables slant to the left; back crosses and cables slant to the right. (Amy Detjen, an expert knitter who took one of my classes on crosses and cables, made up this little ditty as a reminder: "Don't be left out in front; I'll be right back." Each time I turn a cable or cross, I silently chant this. If I've done it wrong, I know immediately, not six inches later!) *However,* twists in which two stitches switch places do *not* follow this rule. They are worked without a cable needle.

A twist that leans to the right is worked through the front, and a twist that leans to the left is worked through the back.

Keeping your place on a chart is the crux of the issue. I have found Post-It notes to be most helpful. I put them directly above the current row. This shows the portion of the chart that has already been completed as well as the row that is being worked. If all work is done in relation to the last completed row, mistakes are easier to spot. The notes pull off cleanly and can be reused a number of times. I also like to use a clipboard with a sliding ruler, but this is slightly less portable. Magnetic boards also work well.

Knitting Backward (or, from Left to Right)

Regular knitting involves working the stitches from the left needle onto the right needle. Knitting backward involves working the stitches from the right needle onto the left needle. The main advantage to this technique is that you do not need to turn your work in order to work a purl row. Stockinette Stitch can be produced by working back and forth on straight needles with the right side facing at all times. The idea of knitting backward is to create a purl stitch by executing it on the right side. This is a useful technique to use when working short rows where constant turning would slow down your progress. You'll find this technique very handy when knitting the scalloped borders on the Sienna Tunic (page 120), Peach Cropped Pullover (page 123), or Amethyst Cardigan (page 126).

In order to learn how to create a purl stitch on the right side, it is helpful to study how the stitch is created on the wrong side in the traditional way. Begin by practicing on a small swatch of about twenty stitches, working a foundation of a few rows in Stockinette Stitch. With a purl row facing you, purl a stitch, stopping halfway through the process. Turn your work to the right side and study what the stitch looks like—where the yarn is going, where it is coming from, and what the loops look like. Turn your work back to the wrong side and complete the stitch. Do this *many* times, then try the backward-knitting method from the instructions that follow.

All the stitches will be on your right-hand needle, the right side of the work will be facing you, and the yarn will be controlled by your right hand. Insert the left-hand needle through the *back* of the first stitch on the right needle. Wrap the yarn *over* the left needle and draw it through the stitch, sliding the right needle out of the old stitch. Remember that the stitches are being removed from the right needle and put on the left needle.

This might seem a bit awkward at first, and you might forget how to do it the next day. After a bit of practice, though, it will become second nature and part of your standard repertoire.

LEFT TO RIGHT: MEADOWCROFT GANSEY (PAGE 77),
LILY POND PULLOVER (PAGE 112) IN TWO COLORWAYS—
DESERT NIGHTS WITH NAVY BLUE, LILY POND WITH PALACE.

The Patterns

LEFT TO RIGHT: VENETIAN BEEHIVES (PAGE 30),
"HERS" WHITE FISHERMAN PULLOVER (PAGE 36),
AND "HIS" MOREHOUSE FARM PULLOVER (PAGE 40).

FACING PAGE: OAK GROVE TESSELATION (PAGE 107) AND CAMDEN GANSEY (PAGE 75). BELOW: TURKISH ROSE (PAGE 82) AND BEAR PAW BARN JACKET (PAGE 61).

ABOVE: FOXHILL FARM TRELLIS JACKET (PAGE 86).
RIGHT: ROCKPORT GANSEY (PAGE 71) IN LIGHT
AND DARK COLORS.

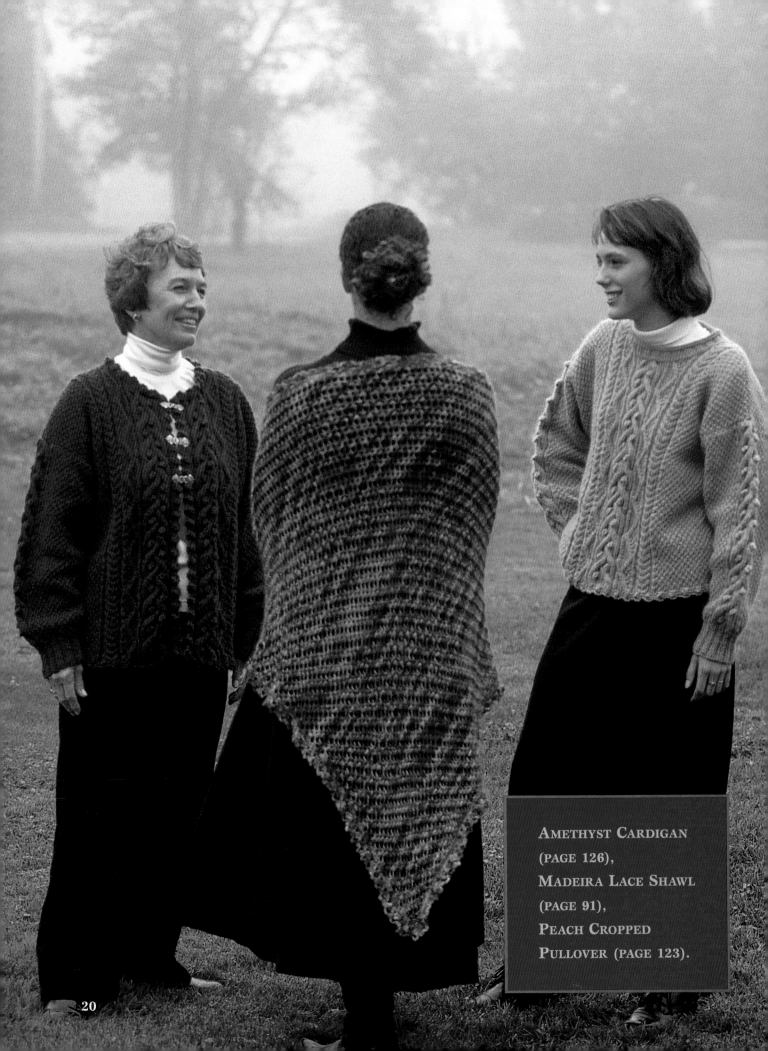

AMETHYST CARDIGAN
(PAGE 126),
MADEIRA LACE SHAWL
(PAGE 91),
PEACH CROPPED
PULLOVER (PAGE 123).

20

CHILD'S JESTER
SWEATER
(PAGE 92).

FACING PAGE: SONJA'S SONG—ALTERNATE COLORWAY SHOWN IN INSET PHOTO—(PAGE 116), ELLEN'S ALPACA SWEATER (PAGE 94). ABOVE: SILK AND JEWELS (PAGE 97).

LEFT: SIENNA TUNIC (PAGE 120) AND HEATHER'S GRAY CABLED PULLOVER (PAGE 56). BELOW: JADE CABLED PULLOVER (PAGE 102), INDIGO (PAGE 50), AND MADDER GANSEY (PAGE 47).

INDIGO FLAMMEGARN SOCKS (PAGE 53). SHEEP MITTENS (PAGE 66).

MARGRIT PILCHER

Morehouse Farm

MILAN • NEW YORK

Morehouse Farm is a scant twenty-one miles from the northwest border of Connecticut, so I am stretching the title of this book—and the New England border—a bit to include Margrit Pilcher's unique and famous yarn. I first discovered a skein of Morehouse Farm yarn at my local yarn store many years ago, and fell in love with it. When the concept for this book first came to mind, I knew that I wanted Morehouse Farm yarn to be a part of it.

To get to Milan from Connecticut there are two ways: highway or back roads. To see Connecticut at its finest, one must drive the back roads. I contentedly knitted my way through all the little towns and villages while Ken drove and kept a running commentary on the sites so I could look up every now and then to notice the charming attractions.

Once you are over the border of New York state, the landscape changes dramatically to wide-open fields and rolling meadows. A few minutes after we crossed into New York, we pulled into the driveway of Morehouse Farm, home of Margrit and Albrecht Pilcher and their award-winning purebred Merino sheep—five hundred of them!! Margrit—a no-nonsense, straight-shooting kind of person—met us with a friendly smile and hearty handshake. We went for a walk around the farm, and our education on sheep farming began immediately. Margrit can reel off facts and figures faster than I can recall the birth dates of my children! She is a wealth of information and knowledge, someone who knows exactly what she is doing. It is obvious why Morehouse Farm is such a success.

Our tour was briefly interrupted while Margrit crossed the street to chase her favorite peacock back to the farm. His mate was on the roof of the barn, screeching in distress. Last year one of the peacocks was killed while crossing the road; now Margrit takes no chances. Assorted chickens were scratching around the yard, Margrit admiring each one.

We stopped at the lambing shed, which had a two-foot-thick layer of straw on the floor. Each day during lambing season, a new layer of straw is spread over the old, dirty layer, providing a clean place for the birthing process and the new babies. After lambing season is over and the straw has started to decompose a little, it is shoveled out and spread over the fields for fertilizer. Each part of the shed is used for a different stage in the lambing process, almost like a walk-through sheep maternity ward. The expectant ewes are

MARGRIT'S WELL-STOCKED SHOP. CANDACE STRICK.

brought in the door on one side, ushered to a different part of the barn for each phase of their birthing process, then are finally lead out through the door on the other side when all is finished.

Lambing takes place twice a year, September through October and January through February, usually with about sixty to one hundred lambs born in each season. It's a breeze in September, Margrit says, but harder in the winter because of the weather. Workers usually take two-hour shifts at night, but Margrit is out there more. "I have no trouble falling asleep anytime, anywhere," she admits, "so staying up during the night is not a hardship for me."

The winter born lambs are usually ready for market in the spring. "Ready for market?" I asked. "You mean, for lamb chops?" My mind had held images only of wool before

27

this, but Margrit assured me that Merino lambs do make excellent eating. The sheepskins are also processed and sold, and Margrit told me about a South American musical instrument made from sheep hooves that she's been eager to make, but can't find a butcher to cut the hooves for her. She also sells the skulls to people who like to hang them on their walls. So it seems that every part of the sheep is used.

We continued our tour up a hillside to where some sheep were grazing. Margrit pointed in about four different directions, telling us which "mob" of sheep were where. (The image of a bunch of angry sheep popped into my mind!) "Mob" is a term Margrit picked up from either an Australian or New Zealand worker they employed in the past.

The Pilchers own about forty acres. They use twenty-five for pasture and lease another seventy acres across the street. While they don't make much of their own hay, they do need the acreage for grazing. The land is vast and rolling; five hundred sheep could be anywhere, but Margrit seemed to know exactly where to find them.

We heard a huge guard dog barking madly in the meadow. He is a Maremma, a barely domesticated breed that is used to keep coyotes from killing the sheep. Without guard dogs, the Pilchers estimate that they would lose about three sheep a day. Margrit was wary of the dog, warning us that he can leap the fence and *will* bite people. I turned around and headed back to safer ground while Margrit sought out the farm manager to ask him to make sure the dog stayed put. Coyote predation is a big problem in this area, and in spite of the dogs, they still manage to kill sheep. The farm's resident llama is useful to a certain extent, as it will chase a coyote from the field. However, when a coyote has already gotten a sheep on the other side of the pasture and is eating it, the llama will ignore the predator.

Back in the safety of the dooryard of the 1790 farmhouse, we saw a guinea hen trying to sit on more than two dozen eggs. Margrit scolded her, threatening to take all those eggs unless she was successful in hatching at least one! Two of the farm's nine cats lazed on the picnic table. Crossing the yard to tour the shop, we passed a huge black walnut tree. I asked Margrit if she uses the nut shells for dyeing, and she shot me a strange look! Entering the shop, I understood why I got that look. There is no need to do anything to the natural color of Margrit's yarn; it is perfect just the way it is.

I could happily spend two or three hours in that shop. All serious knitters know the chain of events when we enter

such a place. I look at one hank and fall in love. I pick it up to fondle it. I need to possess it; I need to knit with it. If I am planning to do a sweater with several colors, I gather up other skeins as well, holding them together in great woolen bouquets. The shop offers six natural colors of the yarn, but the farm raises only two colors of sheep: white and black. To get the pure white, the fleeces are sorted for the brightest of the whites. To get the dark chocolate brown, the "black" fleeces are sorted for the darkest parts. The in-between shades are made by mixing proportions of white and dark. There are also three shades of ragg wool available. This is made by plying a strand of white with a strand of dark.

Now I knew why Margrit had insisted she did not want to crossbreed: "Mix and match is not for me. My yarn is pure Merino, and I only sell registered purebreds." This yarn is too soft to describe, and the joy of knitting with it is a rare pleasure to be savored.

The shop is filled with sample items: beautiful sweaters, hats, mittens, scarves, and shawls, all designed by Margrit. There are kits, buttons, and accessories. And there *are* some skeins of colored wool, most of them dyed by Margrit—in the basement, she murmured, using chemical dyes. They are rich and beautiful, but dyeing is not one of her favorite activities. There are also seductive skeins of a variegated yarn dyed by a woman in Red Hook, New York.

Reluctantly, I left the cubbies to gaze through the plate

BAGS OF FLEECE SIT NEAR THE LARGE SKIRTING TABLE WHERE MARGRIT SORTS THE RAW WOOL. CANDACE STRICK.

glass windows that stretch across the back wall of the shop. Here I saw huge bales of sorted fleece waiting to be shipped out for washing. The white goes to Pennsylvania; the black to Vermont. The washed fiber then goes to one of three spinning mills for carding and spinning. Margrit explained how there are actually two separate parts of this business, the farm end and the design end. In order to keep track of what is profitable, the design part of the business, which is the finished yarn, buys the wool from the farm. The farm is the more expensive end of the enterprise. It would be far more economical for Morehouse Designs to buy the wool from another source, but the farm itself attracts large numbers of people to the shop. "The sheep are the nickels and dimes of this business. I couldn't do it with just one hundred animals," Margrit explained.

Close to the shop is the ram barn, where we eyed the prize-winning studs munching hay, their curling horns framing their faces. Margrit chided them to go out where it is cooler. Pointing out one ram with a sawed-off horn, Margrit told how she found two rams that had been butting one another and eventually got caught in each other's horns. The rams could not untangle themselves. It was a hot day, and they were getting exhausted. With no one around to help, Margrit knew she

CUD-CHEWING TIME IN THE BARNYARD. CANDACE STRICK.

couldn't untangle them herself, so she solved the problem by sawing off the tangled horn with a piece of piano wire. There is no bravado in the way she tells the story; it was just something that needed to be done and she was the only one around to do it. She approaches everything with a matter-of-fact attitude. "I'm realistic about farming. I have very little sympathy for the complaining end of it. Farming is a business—you either make it, or you don't."

We entered the house for tea and more talk, and I knew I had found a kindred spirit when I saw a large two-section cage housing ten cockatiels on one side and two parrots on the other.

When I asked Margrit if she loves birds as much as sheep, her smile told it all. She offered me a cockatiel to take home; I seriously considered it for the next hour while Margrit unfolded the history behind this amazing farm and those who run it. Both animal lovers, Albrecht and Margrit bought the farm in 1977, thinking that they would like to raise some kind of animals, maybe dogs. They ended up buying four prize-winning Merino sheep, and knew they had found what they wanted.

At that time, nobody else in the area was raising Merino sheep. Margrit took her concerns to an agricultural question-and-answer seminar at Cornell University. She wanted to know how to feed this breed of sheep for maximum wool growth. The professor who answered her question told her not to bother with Merinos, to leave them to the Aus-

tralians. Rather than deter Margrit, his remarks made her even more determined to succeed with this venture. The Pilchers took their sheep to Salt Lake City, to the biggest sheep show in the country. Margrit recalls how they were snubbed when they arrived. "We were from the wrong part of the country with the wrong breed of sheep. No one would talk to us." As it turned out, the Pilchers had the sixth highest-selling ram at the auction. "That was a real coup for us. Ever since then, we have been on the map."

The same professor who told Margrit years ago to forget about Merinos wanted to visit Morehouse Farm once he got wind of this incredible Merino success. During his visit he said he wanted to make New York state the Merino capital of the world, whereupon Margrit quietly reminded him about the remark he had made to her a few years ago.

The Pilchers now employ a full-time farm manager who lives on the premises. Don't be confused by this; the Pilchers do not sit around with their feet up eating bonbons all day! Albrecht works in New York City, and Margrit gets up at four in the morning to go to the "green market" in the city three days a week, September through May. She sets up by eight o'clock, and sells everything from the farm—"skeins, skins, and skulls," she laughs. Between market days, she designs and knits, runs the shop, fills yarn orders, attends ewes in labor, and takes care of the hundreds of other details of the daily farm business. Her energy is exuberant and overflowing.

Born in Switzerland, Margrit was educated in the United States. She liked it here better and decided to stay. Before she was a sheep farmer she was a graphic designer in New York City. "If I were back in Switzerland and shifted careers like this, people would think I was absolutely crazy!" she admits.

Margrit is definitely not crazy. She is a woman who knows what she wants and how to succeed at it. Her goal was to produce the finest Merino wool around. With aplomb, grace, intelligence, and plenty of hard work, she has.

Today, as I was taking care of my cockatiel and parrot, I noticed that it is time to give the cages a thorough cleaning—not one of my favorite jobs. Besides, I have a million other things that need to be done. Then I thought about how Margrit would approach this task. Why, she would just roll up her sleeves and get started! After all, it needs to be done, and who else is going to do it?

Venetian Beehives

The unusual beehive motif for this sweater comes from a six-teenth-century Venetian embroidery pattern, found in The New Carolingian Modelbook: Counted Embroidery Patterns from Before 1600, by Kim Brody Salazar writing as Ianthé d'Averoingne, Outlaw Press, 1995. The entire sweater is knit in the round, with steeks for the armholes and neck openings. All directions for steeking are written within the pattern. (Pictured on page 14.) Directions for a matching hat appear on page 33.

YARN

Morehouse Farm 2-ply Merino wool (2 oz/175 yd skeins)

COLOR	SMALL	MED.	LARGE
A. Chocolate	6	6	7
B. Charcoal	3	3	4
C. Silver	2	2	3
D. Oatmeal	2	2	3
E. White	2	2	3

NEEDLES

#3, #5, and #6 circular (24- or 32-inch); #6 circular (16-inch); #3 and #5 double-pointed. (See page 10 for equivalent metric and Canadian needle sizes.)

GAUGE

24 sts and 29.5 rnds = 4 inches worked in pattern on #6 needle.

FINISHED SIZES (IN INCHES)

Small	41.5
Medium	45
Large	48.25

(For information on converting measurements and skein weights to metric equivalents, see page 6.)

Patterns

Stockinette Stitch: Knit every round

Braid

Rnd 1: *K1 Color B, K1 Color E*; repeat between *s.
Rnd 2: Bring both colors forward. *P1 B, P1 E*; repeat between *s, bringing the next color *over* the previous color. (The two strands of yarn will get twisted around each other as your rnd progresses. The next rnd, however, will untwist them.)
Rnd 3: *P1 Color B, P1 Color E*; repeat between *s, bringing the next color *under* the previous color.

HEM: With #3 needle and COLOR B, cast on 225–243–261 sts. Place a marker and join round. Work in Stockinette Stitch for 3 inches. Purl 1 rnd, knit 1 rnd, increasing 25–27–29 sts evenly spaced. (250–270–290 sts.)

BORDER: Work the 3 rnds of Braid (see column 1). Change to #5 needle and remove marker.

Knit 1 st in COLOR A ("seam" st), place a marker, work rnd 1 of CHART A over the next 123–133–143 sts, working the 16-st repeat 7–8–8 times, then the first 11–5–15 sts of the repeat, place a marker, knit 1 st in COLOR A ("seam" st); repeat between *s. All rnds begin and end here.

Work the remaining 17 rnds of Chart A, keeping the 2 seam sts marked off on either side in Color A.

Work another 3 rnds of Braid, continuing the Braid pattern across the seam sts.

Knit 1 rnd all in COLOR B, including the seam sts.

BODY: Change to #6 needle and begin working CHART B (page 34) Hereafter, all seam sts are worked in Color A.

Beginning with rnd 1–64–55, knit the first seam st, *work the 32-st repeat 3–4–4 times, then work the first 27–5–15 sts of the repeat, work 1 seam st*; repeat between *s for back.

For size Small, work through the 72 rnds of Chart B, then work rnds 1–29. For sizes Medium and Large, begin at round indicated and work to end of chart, work the entire 72 rnds of the chart, then work rnds 1 through 29.

Divide for armholes and begin steeks: On rnd 30 you will be casting on your steek stitches. These 10 extra sts form a bridge where the armhole openings will be, and allow work to continue in the round. Later on, these steek sts will be cut up the middle to form the armhole openings, trimmed, and hemmed down. The sleeve sts will be picked up around the openings. Work all steeks in alternating colors, reversing the order on each round.

On rnd 30, work to 2 sts before marker, place next 6 sts on a pin (2 sts of front, 2 seam sts, 2 sts of back), place a marker, cast on 10 sts in alternating colors for steek, place a marker, work to 2 sts before next marker, place next 6 sts on a pin (2 sts of back, 2 seam sts, 2 sts of front), place a marker, cast on 10 sts in alternating colors. You will now be working on 119–129–139 sts *each* for front and back. All rnds begin and end at st #5 of the steek you just worked, and this is where all new colors will be joined in. Ends do not need to be worked in anymore, since the steek will be cut and the ends trimmed away.

As you continue Chart B through rnd 72, then rnds 1 through 4, *remember to start both the front and the back 2 sts in from the right edge of the chart. All rnds also will end 2 sts less than the rnds before the armhole break.*

SHAPE NECK: Chart C shows neck shaping for both front and back. The back is worked straight until shortly before the end. *You will begin shaping the back neck while you are still shaping the front neck steek.* Decreases for front and back neck are worked on either side of steek as follows: K2 together, work 10 steek sts, SSK.

Front Neck: Work 5 armhole steek sts. Following rnd 1 of CHART C, work 48–53–57 sts, place middle 23–23–25 sts on a holder for front neck, place a marker, cast on 10 sts in alternating colors for front neck steek, place a marker, work the remaining 48–53–57 sts of front, work armhole steek and 119–129–139 sts of back, work remaining 5 sts of armhole steek. End of rnd. As you work the chart, you will decrease 1 st each side of front neck steek every rnd 7 times, then every other rnd 3 times, then every 3rd rnd 2–2–4 times. Work 3–3–2 rnds even. (36–41–43 sts for shoulders.)

Back neck: *At the same time,* on rnd 17–17–24, work 41–46–48 sts, place middle 37–37–43 sts on holder for back neck, place a marker, cast on 10 steek sts in alternating colors, place a marker, work remaining 41–46–48 sts of back. Decrease 1 st on either side of back neck steek every rnd 5 times.

Last rnd: Following rnd 23–23–28, cast off last 5 steek sts, work sts of front, casting off the 10 steek sts at front neck, cast off 10 steek sts of armhole, work the sts of back, casting off the 10 steek sts at back neck, cast off remaining 5 steek sts of armhole.

CUTTING THE STEEKS: Using the zigzag stitch on a sewing machine, or backstitching by hand, sew through all cast-on and cast-off edges of all steeks. Using a sharp pair of scissors, cut up the middle of the steeks between sts 5 and 6. Trim away ends left from changing colors.

While most directions for steeking call for trimming them down to a 2-stitch width, I prefer the security of keeping them at 5 stitches. Turn back the 5 steek sts, hemming them down by hand using an overcast stitch. Be careful that your stitching does not show through on the right side. When you have finished, work back over the stitches in the opposite direction, forming Xs.

Steam gently.

JOIN SHOULDERS: Use the knitted seam method. (See page 11.)

NECKBAND. *Note: When picking up stitches around openings that have been steeked, use the stitch directly adjacent to the last steek stitch. Insert the needle through both loops of the stitch, draw yarn through, and knit.*

With COLOR B and 16-inch circular #5 needle, starting at the right back shoulder, pick up and knit 7 sts down right back, knit the 37–37–43 sts from back neck holder, pick up and knit 7 sts up left back, pick up and knit 25–25–31 sts down left front, knit the 23–23–25 sts from front neck holder, pick up and knit 25–25–31 sts up right front. Place a marker. (124–124–144 sts.) Work the 3 rnds of Braid. Change to COLOR A and knit 1 rnd. Change to #3 needle. Work in K2, P2 Ribbing for 1–1–1.5 inches. Work 5 rnds in knit. Bind off loosely.

SLEEVES: With #5 circular needle (16-inch) and COLOR B, starting at underarm, place a marker, knit the 2 seam sts, place a marker, knit the next 2 sts from pin, pick up and knit 72–72–79 sts to shoulder seam, pick up and knit 71–71–78 sts to underarm pin, knit the remaining 2 sts from pin. (149–149–163 sts.) All rnds begin and end between the seam sts. The seam sts are always worked in Color A (except when working the Braid rnds), and decreases are done on either side of these sts as follows: Knit 1 seam st, K2 together at beginning of rnd, work to 2 sts before marker, SSK, knit 1 seam st.

Work the 3 rnds of Braid, keeping the underarm sts marked and working them in Color B.

To read Chart D: Work begins on the first stitch on the right-hand edge of the sleeve chart. Work the 32-st repeat until the stitches on the needles are used up. The heavy vertical lines on the chart indicate where to begin the rnd. Always begin the rnd at the vertical line, work through to the end of the repeat, then work the full 32-st repeat until the rnd is completed. When you have completed all 72 rnds of the chart once, begin again at rnd 1, working from the 2nd vertical decrease line that lies to the left of the first decrease line.

Change to #6 needle and commence working CHART D. Work 1 rnd. Beginning on rnd 2, decrease 1 st at beginning and end of every other rnd 17 times, every third rnd 15 times, then every fourth rnd 11–11–14 times. (86–86–92 sts decreased; 63–63–71 sts remain.)

Change to double pointed needles when necessary.

Work 4–9–4 rnds even.

Knit 1 rnd in COLOR B, decreasing 1 st within the rnd. (62–62–70 sts.)

Work Braid over next 3 rnds.

Knit 1 rnd in COLOR B, decreasing 18–14–18 sts evenly spaced. (44–48–52 sts.)

Change to #3 double-pointed needles and COLOR A. Work in K2, P2 Ribbing for 2.5 inches. Bind off loosely in Ribbing pattern.

FINISHING: Turn under bottom hem at purl-row line and slip stitch loosely in place. Weave in all loose ends and steam gently.

Using COLOR B and a tapestry needle, work duplicate stitch over 2 rows up side seam stitches. (See photograph below.) If desired, work the same on sleeve seams.

DUPLICATE STITCH DETAIL.

Lynn Karlin.

MEASUREMENTS IN INCHES

A. 41.5–45–48.25
B. 3
C. 13.5–14.5–16
D. 9.5–9.5–10
E. 17.25–18–19.5
F. 2.5

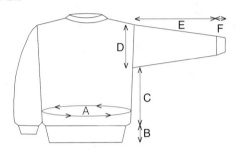

CHART A: **BORDER** *(Pattern Repeat)*

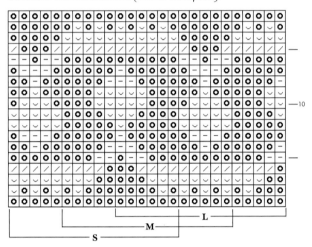

KEY FOR CHARTS

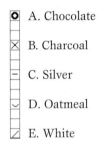

A. Chocolate

B. Charcoal

C. Silver

D. Oatmeal

E. White

Chart C neck-shaping guidelines:

RND 1: BEGIN FRONT NECK SHAPING, SIZES S, M, L.
RND 17: BEGIN BACK NECK SHAPING, SIZES S & M.
RND. 22: BEGIN BACK NECK SHAPING, SIZE L.

CHART C: **NECKLINE** *left*

Sleeve Hat

The matching hat was a total accident. In knitting the Venetian Beehive sweater, I finished one of the sleeves, only to discover that I did not like the way I had shaped it. Rather than rip out all that work, I cut it off about one inch from where the stitches were picked up around the armhole opening. I raveled this back to the picked-up stitches, and knit the sleeve again, this time shaping it more to my liking.

The cut-off sleeve laid around the house for a while, and was always a great source of laughter for those who saw it. The Venetian Beehives sweater became known to my friends as the "three-sleeved sweater." As a joke one day, I put the cut-off sleeve on my head, and to everyone's surprise, it made a great hat! So I added ribbing and finished the end off with a huge pom-pom. Voilà! Nobody laughs at it anymore! (Almost nobody . . .)

To make this hat, you will need one skein of each of the colors listed for the Venetian Beehive sweater, #3 and #6 circular needles (16-inch), and #3 double-pointed needles. It is one size.

With #3 needle and COLOR A, cast on 148 sts. Work in K2, P2 Ribbing for 4 inches. (Brim is worn rolled up.) On the last rnd, increase 1 st. (149 sts.)

Follow the sweater directions for sleeve, size Small, but do not bind off stitches when you are done with the cuff Ribbing. Instead, K2 together, P2 together across the last rnd. Fasten off by drawing yarn through remaining sts.

Make a pom-pom using all the colors. Sew to end of sleeve/hat.

Wear with seam in back.

LYNN KARLIN.

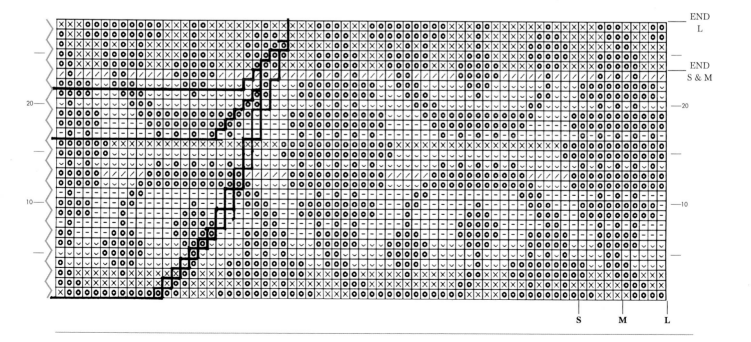

CHART B: **BODY**

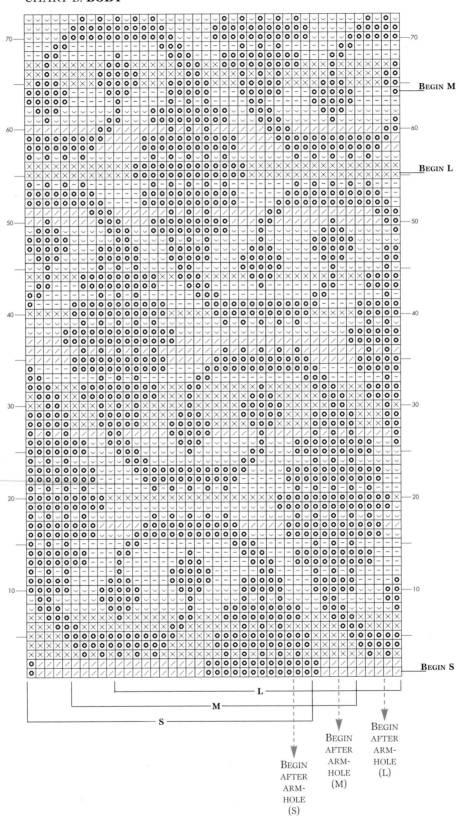

BEGIN M

BEGIN L

BEGIN S

BEGIN
AFTER
ARM-
HOLE
(S)

BEGIN
AFTER
ARM-
HOLE
(M)

BEGIN
AFTER
ARM-
HOLE
(L)

CHART D: **SLEEVE**

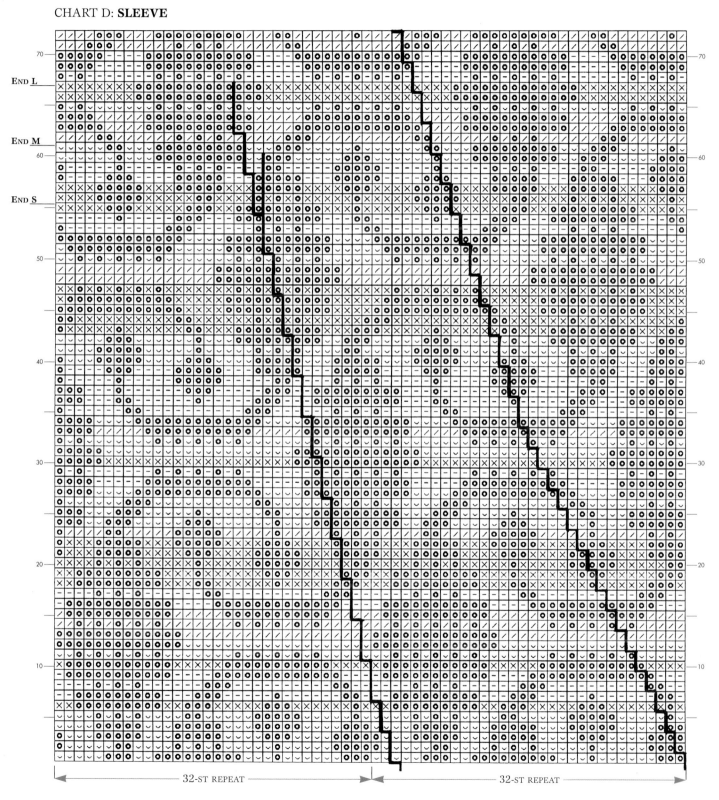

"Hers" White Fisherman Pullover

Knitters are a divided lot. Some refuse to read a chart, others cannot stand to follow the written directions. For both the "his" and "hers" sweaters from Morehouse Farm, I offer you both methods. (Pictured on page 14.)

YARN

Morehouse Farm Merino 2-ply wool (2 oz/175 yd), 11 skeins White

NEEDLES

#4 and #6 single-pointed, #4 double-pointed or circular (16-inch). *(See page 10 for equivalent metric and Canadian needle sizes.)*

GAUGE

27 sts and 37 rows = 4 inches worked over pattern on #6 needles.

FINISHED SIZE

44 inches.

(For information on converting measurements and skein weights to metric equivalents, see page 6.)

ABBREVIATIONS

<u>Kb</u> (knit back)—Knit stitch through back of loop.

<u>Pb</u> (purl back)—Purl stitch though back of loop.

<u>CRp</u> (cable right, purl)—Slip 1 st to cable needle and hold in back of work, K2**b**, purl 1 st from cable needle.

<u>CRk</u> (cable right, knit)—Same as CRp but *knit* 1 st from cable needle.

<u>CLp</u> (cable left purl)—Slip 2 sts to cable needle and hold in front of work, purl 1 st, K2**b** from cable needle.

<u>CLk</u> (cable left, knit)—Same as CLp but *knit* 1 st.

<u>FC4</u> (front cable worked over 4 sts)—Slip 2 sts to cable needle and hold in front of work; knit 2, knit 2 sts from cable needle.

<u>BC4</u> (back cable worked over 4 sts)—Same as FC4 but hold cable needle in back.

<u>BC4b</u> (back cable worked over 4 sts)—Slip 2 sts to cable needle and hold in back of work, K2**b**, K2**b** sts from cable needle.

<u>FC4b</u> (front cable worked over 4 sts)—Same as BC4**b** but hold cable in *front* of work.

*Note: BC4**b** and FC4**b** are the same as FC4 and BC4, except that sts are knit through the back. BC4**b** and FC4**b** are used in the center front panel and FC4 and BC4 are used in the braid cable.*

<u>FT</u> (front twist)—K2 together, then knit 1st again. Slip both sts from needle together.

<u>BT</u> (back twist)—Skip 1 st, knit 2nd st through back of loop, K2 together through the back loop. Slip both sts from needle together.

<u>M1p</u> (make one, purl)—Make one stitch by picking up the horizontal loop between 2 stitches; purl into the *back* of this loop.

Patterns

Cable (Worked over 12 sts.)
Row 1: K2, FC4, BC4, K2
Row 2: Purl 12.
Row 3: Knit 12.
Row 4: Purl 12.
Row 5: FC4, K4, BC4.
Row 6: Purl 12.
Repeat these 6 rows.

Mock Cable (Worked over 4 sts.)
Row 1: Work FT, work BT.
Row 2: Purl.
Row 3: Work BT, work FT.
Row 4: Purl.
Repeat these 4 rows.

Cable Waves (4-st twist separated by 3 sts.)
Row 1: Knit.
Row 2: K3, P2, K5, P2, K3.
Row 3: K2, FT, BT, K3, FT, BT, K2.
Row 4: Purl.
Repeat these 4 rows.

Center Cabled Panel (Worked over 18 sts.)
Row 1: P7, FC4**b**, P7.
Row 2: K7, P4**b**, K7.
Row 3: P6, CRk, CLk, P6.
Row 4: K6, P2**b**, P2, P2**b**, K6.
Row 5: P5, CRk, K2, CLk, P5.
Row 6: K5, P2**b**, P4, P2**b**, K5.
Row 7: P4, CRp, FT, BT, CLp, P4.
Row 8: K4, P2**b**, K1, P4, K1, P2**b**, K4.
Row 9: P3, CRp, P1, BT, FT, P1, CLp, P3.
Row 10: K3, P2**b**, K2, P4, K2, P2**b**, K3.
Row 11: P2, CRp, P2, FT, BT, P2, CLp, P2.
Row 12: K2, P2**b**, K3, P4, K3, P2**b**, K2.
Row 13: P1, CRp, P3, BT, FT, P3, CLp, P1.
Row 14: K1, P2**b**, K4, P4, K4, P2**b**, K1.
Row 15: P1, CLp, P3, FT, BT, P3, CRp, P1.
Row 16: K2, P2**b**, K3, P4, K3, P2**b**, K2.
Row 17: P2, CLp, P2, BT, FT, P2, CRp, P2.
Row 18: K3, P2**b**, K2, P4, K2, P2**b**, K3.
Row 19: P3, CLp, P1, FT, BT, P1, CRp, P3.
Row 20: K4, P2**b**, K1, P4, K1, P2**b**, K4.

Row 21: P4, CLp, BT, FT, CRp, P4.
Row 22: K5, P2**b**, P4, P2**b**, K5.
Row 23: P5, CLp, K2, CRp, P5.
Row 24: K6, P2**b**, P2, P2**b**, K6.
Row 25: P6, CLp, CRp, P6.
Row 26: K7, P4**b**, K7.
Row 27: Same as row 1 but BC4**b**.
Rows 28 through 52: Same as rows 2 through 26.
Repeat these 52 rows.

X-Panels (Worked over 21 sts.)

Work from chart, reading the right-side rows from right to left, and wrong-side rows from left to right.

RIBBING: With #4 single-pointed needles, cast on 138 sts.

Row 1 (right side): P2, (K4, P2) twice, FT, BT, P2, K1b, P2, (K2, P2) five times, K1b, P2, work row 1 of Cable over the next 12 sts, P2, K1b, P2, K2, P2, FT, BT, P2, K2, P2, K1b, P2, work row 1 of Cable over the next 12 sts, P2, K1b, P2, (K2, P2) five times, K1b, P2, FT, BT, (P2, K4) twice, P2.

Row 2: K3, P2, K4, P2, K3, P4, K2, P1b, K2, (P2, K2) five times, P1b, K2, work row 2 of Cable over the next 12 sts, K2, P1b, K2, P2, K2, P4, K2, P2, K2, P1b, K2, work row 2 of Cable over the next 12 sts, K2, P1b, K2, (P2, K2) five times, P1b, K2, P4, K3, P2, K4, P2, K3.

Row 3: P2, (FT, BT, P2) twice, BT, FT, P2, K1b, P2, (K2, P2) five times, K1b, P2, work row 3 of Cable over the next 12 sts, P2, K1b, P2, K2, P2, BT, FT, P2, K2, P2, K1b, P2, work row 3 of Cable over the next 12 sts, P2, K1b, P2, (K2, P2) five times, K1b, P2, BT, FT, (P2, FT, BT) twice, P2

Row 4: (K2, P4) three times, K2, P1b, K2, (P2, K2) five times, P1b, K2, work row 4 of Cable over the next 12 sts, K2, P1b, K2, P2, K2, P4, K2, P2, K2, P1b, K2, work row 4 of Cable over the next 12 sts, K2, P1b, K2, (P2, K2) five times, P1b, (K2, P4) three times, K2.

Row 5: Same as row 1, but work row 5 of Cable.
Row 6: Same as row 2, but work row 6 of Cable.

Note: It is easy to work the Ribbing pattern if you just follow the stitches that have been established. Cables and twists are always turned on right-side rows. Cable is turned on rows 1 and 5; Mock Cables and center 4 stitches are twisted every other row, alternating between FT, BT and BT, FT; the K1b and P1b are kept constant; the 2 little Cable Waves on each end of the needle are twisted FT, BT every 4 rows.

Rows 7 through 12: Work same as rows 1 through 6.
Rows 13 through 23: Work same as rows 1 through 11.
Row 24: (Increase row.) All increases are made in knit stitches by knitting in the row below and then knitting the stitch on the needle as normal. It is very important that stitches are increased in the correct place in order to keep the cables in the correct place for the body.

Following the above directions for row 6, work 7 stitches, increase in the next stitch, work 4 stitches, increase in each of the next 2 stitches, work 16 sts, increase in the next st, work 35 sts, increase in the next st, work 4 sts, increase in the next st, work 35 sts, increase in the next st, work 16 sts, increase in each of the next 2 sts, work 5 sts, increase in the next st, work last 6 sts. (148 sts.)

Change to #6 needles. All cables are kept in pattern as established.

BACK

Note about working from written directions: The Cable Waves and Mock Cables are a repeat of 4 rows; the Cable pattern is a repeat of 6 rows; and the Center Cabled Panel and the X-Panel are repeats of 52 rows. The 4-row patterns will come out even at the completion of the 52 rows of the center panels. The 6-row cable, however, will have to be kept track of separately, since it will not come out even at the completion of the center panel. Any reference to a certain row in the chart is the same as that corresponding row of written directions for the Center Cabled Panel and/or X-Panel.

Note about working from the chart: Follow written directions for establishing the patterns, then keep track of all patterns on the chart. The Cable Waves, Mock Cable, and Cable patterns will be well established by the time you have completed your first run-through of the large 52-row motifs. Simply continue those 4- and 6-row patterns as established while you work the repeats of the large charted motifs.

Row 1 (right side): Work first row of Cable Waves pattern over 15 sts, P2, work first row of Mock Cable over 4 sts, P2, K1b, P1, work first row of X-Panel over next 21 sts, P1, K1b, P2, work first row of Cable over next 12 sts, P2, K1b, work Center Cabled Panel over next 18 sts, K1b, P2, work first row of Cable over next 12 sts, P2, K1b, P1, work first row of X-Panel over next 21 sts, P1, K1b, P2, work first row of Mock Cable over next 4 sts, P2, work first row of Cable Wave Pattern over last 15 sts

Row 2 (wrong side): Follow row 2 of directions and chart, working the sts between patterns as knits, and all K1bs as P1bs, on this and all other wrong-side rows.

Continue in pattern as established for 221 rows (4 complete repeats of chart, plus rows 1 through 13).

On the next row (row 14 of Center Cabled Panel), bind off 50 sts in knit, work middle 48 sts and put on a holder for back neck, bind off in knit the remaining 50 sts.

FRONT: Work 24 rows of Ribbing as for back. Then work body as for back, but for only 195 rows (3 complete repeats of chart plus rows 1 through 39).

Next row (row 40 of chart): Work 65 sts, place middle 18 sts on a holder for front neck. Leave remaining 65 sts on a spare needle. Work each side separately. *Note:* Continue to turn cables as long as possible as you make the neck decreases. See photograph of the model in the hat on page 33 for neckline detail.

Right shoulder: Bind off 3 sts at the beginning of the next row (neck edge), then 2 sts at the beginning of every other row twice, then decrease 1 st at neck edge every other row, 8 times. Work even through row 13 of chart. Bind off remaining 50 sts in knit.

Left shoulder: With wrong side facing, attach yarn to neck edge. Work rows 14 and 15 of chart, then work as for right shoulder.

SLEEVES: With #4 needles cast on 64 sts. Work Ribbing as follows.

Row 1: P2, K2, P2, K1b, P2, work first row of Cable over next 12 sts, P2, K1b, P2, K2, P2, FT, BT, P2, K2, P2, K1b, P2, work first row of Cable over next 12 sts, P2, K1b, P2, K2, P2.

Row 2: K2, P2, K2, P1b, K2, work second row of Cable

over next 12 sts, K2, P1b, K2, P2, K2, P4, K2, P2, K2, P1b, K2, work second row of Cable over next 12 sts, K2, P1b, K2, P2, K2.

Row 3: Continue in pattern as established, working row 3 of Cable and working the center 4 sts as BT, FT.

Rows 4 through 23: Continue in established pattern, repeating the 6 rows of Cable, and alternating the center 4 sts on right side between FT, BT and BT, FT.

Row 24: (Increase row.) Increases are worked the same as the last row of Ribbing on front and back, but on the following stitches: Work 1 st, increase in next st, work 3 sts, increase in next st, work 23 sts, increase in next st, work 4 sts, increase in next st, work 23 sts, increase in next st, work 3 sts, increase in next st, work 1 st. (70 sts.)

Change to #6 needles and work patterns. *Note:* The first and last 6 sts of each row are worked in Cable Wave Pattern.

Row 1 (right side): Knit 6, P2, K1b, P2, work first row of Cable over next 12 sts, P2, K1b, work first row of Center Cabled Panel over next 18 sts, P2, K1b, P2, work first row of Cable over next 12 sts, P2, K1b, P2, K6.

Row 2: K1, P2, K3, work pattern as established to last 6 sts, K3, P2, K1.

Row 3: FT, BT, K2, work pattern as established to last 6 sts, K2, FT, BT.

Row 4: Increase 1 st, purl 6, work pattern as established to last 6 sts, purl 6, increase 1.

Continue in pattern, increasing 1 st each side every fourth row 31 times. (132 sts/124 rows.) *Note:* The increase stitches are added into the outer edges of Cable Wave Pattern. On row 2 of the pattern there will be 5 knits between the 2 purls. The 3 knits next to the Cable stay constant.

Work 16 rows even. (140 rows total.)

Shoulder Strap: At the beginning of the next 2 rows (rows 37 and 38 of Center Cabled Panel) bind off 54 sts, decreasing 2 sts evenly over Cable. (24 sts.)

Keeping first 3 sts and last 3 sts as established (right side—P2, K1b; wrong side—K2, P1b), work middle 18 sts of Center Cabled Panel through row 52, then work rows 1 through 50.

Rows 51 and 52: Bind off 2 sts at beginning of row.

Put remaining 20 sts on a holder.

ASSEMBLING: Mark a 9.75-inch armhole depth with safety pins on both sides of front and back. Sew shoulder strap of sleeve to front and back shoulder, then sew sleeve tops to body, having sides of sleeve even to pins. Sew sleeve seams and side seams.

NECK. *Note:* When knitting sts from holders, always work Kb into the established Kb stitches.

With #4 double-pointed needles or 16-inch circular, knit 48 sts from back-neck holder, pick up and knit 2 sts, knit 20 sts from left shoulder strap holder, pick up and knit 20 sts down left front, knit 18 sts from front neck holder, pick up and knit 20 sts up right front, knit 20 sts from right shoulder strap holder, pick up and knit 2 sts. Place a marker. (150 sts.)

Rnd 1: K12, P2, K1**b**, M1p, P1, K2, (P2 tog) twice, FT, BT, (P2 tog) twice, K2, M1p, P1, K1**b**, P2, K12, P2, K1**b**, P2, K2, P2 tog, P1, FT, BT, P1, P2 tog, K2, P2, K1**b**, (P2 tog) twice, K11, K2 tog, P2, K1**b**, M1p, P1, K2, (P2 tog) twice, FT, BT, (P2 tog) twice, K2, M1p, P1, K1**b**, P1, P2 tog, K10,

(K2 tog) twice, P2, K1**b**, P2, K2, P2 tog, P1, FT, BT, P2 tog, P1, K2, P2, K1**b**, P2. (136 sts—18 sts decreased, 4 sts made.)

Rnd 2: K12, P2, K1b, P2, K2, P2, K4, P2, K2, P2, K1b, P2, K12, P2, K1b, P2, K2, P2, K4, P2, K2, P2, K1b, P2, K12, P2, K1b, P2, K2, P2, K4, P2, K2, P2, K1b, P2.

Rnd 3: Work in Ribbing as established, following row 1 of Cable over the K12s and working BT, FT on center 4 sts of front, back, and shoulder straps.

Rnd 4: Work in Ribbing as established, following row 2 of Cable and working K4 over center 4 sts of front, back, and shoulder straps.

Rnds 5 through 19: Work in Ribbing in established pattern, working Cable in numerical row sequence; working the center 4 sts of back, front, and shoulder straps every other row alternately as FT, BT and BT, FT; and working the rows where they are not twisted as K4s.

Bind off in knit, decreasing 3 sts evenly over each Cable.

FINISHING: Steam lightly. Weave in any loose ends.

MEASUREMENTS IN INCHES

A. 22
B. 2.75
C. 15.25
D. 9.75
E. 15
F. 2.75
G. 3

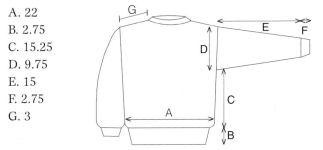

KEY FOR CHARTS

☐	Stockinette Stitch
⬢	Purl on right side; knit on wrong side
▨▨◥◣	Front cable worked over 4 sts (FC4**b**)
▨▨◢◤	Back cable worked over 4 sts (BC4**b**)
BT	Back twist
FT	Front twist
I◥◣	Cable left—knit
—◥◣	Cable left—purl
◢◤I	Cable right—knit
◢◤—	Cable right—purl
I	Knit on right side; purl on wrong side
−	Purl on right side; knit on wrong side
⅄	Knit into back of st on right side; purl into back of st on wrong side

CABLE WAVES	MOCK CABLE	X-PANEL	CABLE	CENTER CABLED PANEL	CABLE	X-PANEL	MOCK CABLE	CABLE WAVES
4-ROW REPEAT	4-ROW REPEAT	52-ROW REPEAT	6-ROW REPEAT	52-ROW REPEAT	6-ROW REPEAT	52-ROW REPEAT	4-ROW REPEAT	4-ROW REPEAT

CHART: **BODY**

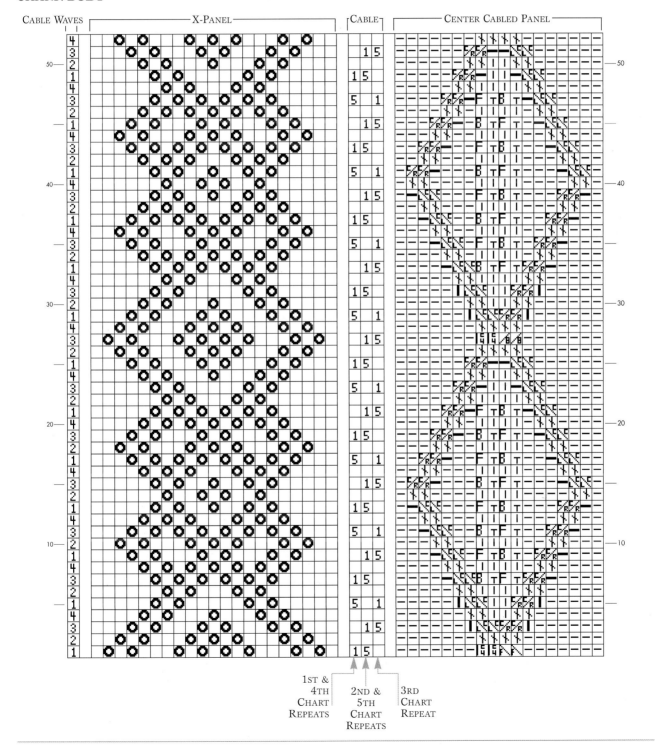

1ST & 4TH CHART REPEATS

2ND & 5TH CHART REPEATS

3RD CHART REPEAT

"His" Morehouse Farm Pullover

Different cables and texture design distinguish this sweater from its female counterpart on page 36. Both sweaters are made from luxury Morehouse Merino wool—so soft you might think it is cotton. I've given both charted and written directions. (Pictured on page 14.)

YARN

Morehouse Farm 2-ply Merino Wool (2 oz/175 yd skeins) 13 skeins Oatmeal.

NEEDLES

#4 and #6 single-pointed, #4 double-pointed or circular (16-inch). *(See page 10 for equivalent metric and Canadian needle sizes.)*

GAUGE

27 sts and 37 rows = 4 inches worked over pattern on #6 needles.

FINISHED SIZE

48.5 inches.

(For information on converting measurements and skein weights to metric equivalents, see page 6.)

ABBREVIATIONS

Kb (knit back)—Knit stitch through back loop.

Pb (purl back)—Purl stitch though back loop.

CRp (cable right, purl)—Slip 1 st to cable needle and hold in back of work, K2b, purl 1 st from cable needle.

CRk (cable right, knit)—Same as CRp but *knit* 1 st from cable needle.

CLp (cable left, purl)—Slip 2 sts to cable needle and hold in front of work, purl 1 st, K2b from cable needle.

CLk (cable left, knit)—Same as CLp but *knit* 1 st.

FC4 (front cable worked over 4 sts)—Slip 2 sts to cable needle and hold in front of work; knit 2, knit 2 sts from cable needle.

BC4 (back cable worked over 4 sts)—Same as FC4 but hold cable needle in back.

BC4b (back cable worked over 4 sts)—Slip 2 sts to cable needle and hold in back of work, K2b, K2b sts from cable needle.

FC4b (front cable worked over 4 sts)—Same as BC4b but hold cable in *front* of work.

Note: BC4b and FC4b are the same as FC4 and BC4, except that sts are knit through the back. BC4b and FC4b are used in the center front panel and FC4 and BC4 are used in the braid cable.

FT (front twist)—K2 together, then knit 1st again. Slip both sts from needle together.

BT (back twist)—Skip 1 st, knit 2nd st through back of loop, K2 together through the back loop. Slip both sts from needle together.

M1p (make one, purl)—Make one stitch by picking up the horizontal loop between 2 stitches; purl into the *back* of this loop.

Patterns

Braid Cable A (Worked over 12 sts.)
Rows 1, 3, and 5: Purl.
Row 2: FC4, K4, BC4.
Row 4: K2, FC4, BC4, K2.
Row 6: K4, BC4, K4.
Repeat these 6 rows.

Braid Cable B (Worked over 12 sts.)
Rows 1 through 5: Same as Braid Cable A.
Row 6: K4, FC4, K4.
Repeat these 6 rows.

Mock Cable (Worked over 4 sts.)
Row 1: Work FT, work BT.
Row 2: Purl.
Row 3: Work BT, work FT.
Row 4: Purl.
Repeat these 4 rows.

Cable Waves (Worked over 17 sts on front and back.)
Row 1 (wrong side): Purl.
Row 2 (right side): Knit.
Row 3, beginning of needle: K5, P2, K5, P2, K3.
Row 3, end of needle: K3, P2, K5, P2, K5.
Row 4, beginning of needle: K4, FT, BT, K3, FT, BT, K2.
Row 4. end of needle: K2, FT, BT, K3, FT, BT, K4.
Repeat these 4 rows.

Center Cabled Panel (Worked over 24 sts.)
Row 1 (wrong side): K10, P4b, K10.
Row 2: P10, BC4b, P10.
Row 3: K10, P4b, K10.
Row 4: P9, CRk, CLk, P9.
Row 5: K9, P2b, P2, P2b, K9.
Row 6: P8, CRk, K2, CLk, P8.
Row 7: K8, P2b, P4, P2b, K8.
Row 8: P7, CRp, FT, BT, CLp, P7.
Row 9: K7, P2b, K1, P4, K1, P2b, K7.
Row 10: P6, CRp, P1, BT, FT, P1, CLp, P6.
Row 11: K6, P2b, K2, P4, K2, P2b, K6.
Row 12: P5, CRp, P2, FT, BT, P2, CLp, P5.
Row 13: K5, P2b, K3, P4, K3, P2b, K5.
Row 14: P4, CRp, P3, BT, FT, P3, CLp, P4.

Row 15: K4, P2b, K4, P4, K4, P2b, K4.
Row 16: P3, CRp, P4, FT, BT, P4, CLp, P3.
Row 17: K3, P2b, K5, P4, K5, P2b, K3.
Row 18: P2, CRp, P5, BT, FT, P5, CLp, P2.
Row 19: K2, P2b, K6, P4, K6, P2b, K2.
Row 20: P1, CRp, P6, FT, BT, P6, CLp, P1.
Row 21: K1, P2b, K7, P4, K7, P2b, K1.
Row 22: P1, CLp, P6, BT, FT, P6, CRp, P1.
Row 23: K2, P2b, K6, P4, K6, P2b, K2.
Row 24: P2, CLp, P5, FT, BT, P5, CRp, P2.
Row 25: K3, P2b, K5, P4, K5, P2b, K3.
Row 26: P3 CLp, P4, BT, FT, P4, CRp, P3.
Row 27: K4, P2b, K4, P4, K4, P2b, K4.
Row 28: P4, CLp, P3, FT, BT, P3, CRp, P4.
Row 29: K5, P2b, K3, P4, K3, P2b, K5.
Row 30: P5, CLp, P2, BT, FT, P2, CRp, P5.
Row 31: K6, P2b, K2, P4, K2, P2b, K6.
Row 32: P6, CLp, P1, FT, BT, P1, CRp, P6.
Row 33: K7, P2b, K1, P4, K1, P2b, K7.
Row 34: P7, CLp, BT, FT, CRp, P7.
Row 35: K8, P2b, P4, P2b, K8.
Row 36: P8, CLp, K2, CRp, P8.
Row 37: K9, P2b, P2, P2b, K9.
Row 38: P9, CLp, CRP, P9.
Row 39: Same as row 1.
Row 40: P10, FC4**b**, P10.
Rows 41 through 76: Repeat rows 3 through 38.
Repeat these 76 rows.

Tree of Life (Worked over 27 sts.)

Work from chart, reading the right-side rows from right to left and the wrong-side rows from left to right.

RIBBING: With #4 needles, cast on 150 sts. Work Ribbing as follows.

Row 1 (wrong side): P3, (K2, P2) 10 times, K2, P1b, K2, P12, K2, P1b, (K2, P2) 2 times, K2, P4, K2, (P2, K2) 2 times, P1b, K2, P12, K2, P1b, K2, (P2, K2) 10 times, P3.

Row 2: K3, (P2, K2) 3 times, P2, FT, P2, (K2, P2) 6 times, K1b, P2, row 2 of Braid Cable A, P2, K1b, (P2, K2) 2 times, P2, row 1 of Mock Cable, P2, (K2, P2) 2 times, K1b, P2, row 2 of Braid Cable B, P2, K1b, P2, (K2, P2) 6 times, BT, P2, (K2, P2) 3 times, K3.

Row 3: Same as row 1, but working row 3 of Braid Cables.

Row 4: Same as row 2 but working row 4 of Braid Cables and working center 4 sts in row 3 of Mock Cable.

Continue in Ribbing pattern as established, working FT near beginning of needle and BT near end of needle, working center 4 sts in Mock Cable in row sequence, and working Braid Cable rows in sequence, remembering to work Braid Cable A for first cable and Braid Cable B for second cable.

Work 27 rows of Ribbing.

Row 28 (right side): Increase row. *Note:* All increases are made in knit stitches by knitting in the row below and then knitting the stitch on the needle as normal. Work Ribbing as established, increasing 14 sts as follows:

Work 10 sts, increase in next st.
Work 2 sts, increase in next st.
Work 8 sts, increase in next st.
Work 3 sts, increase in next st.
Work 3 sts, increase in next st.
Work 6 sts, increase in next st.

Work 3 sts, increase in next st.
Work 66 sts, increase in next st.
Work 3 sts, increase in next st.
Work 6 sts, increase in next st.
Work 3 sts, increase in next st.
Work 3 sts, increase in next st.
Work 8 sts, increase in next st.
Work 2 sts, increase in next st.
Work 10 sts. (164 sts total.)

BACK

Note about working from written directions: The Cable Waves pattern is a repeat of 4 rows; the Braid Cable pattern is a repeat of 6 rows; and the Center Cabled Panel and the Tree of Life pattern are repeats of 76 rows. The 4-row patterns will come out even at the completion of the 76 rows of the large motifs. The 6-row cable, however, will have to be kept track of separately, since it will not come out even at the completion of the center panel. Any reference to a certain row in the chart is the same as that corresponding row of written directions for the Center Cabled Panel and/or Tree of Life pattern.

Note about working from the chart: Follow all written directions for establishing the patterns, then keep track of all patterns simultaneously on the chart. The Cable Waves and Braid Cable patterns will be well established by the time you have completed your first run-through of the 76-row motifs. Simply continue those 4- and 6-row patterns as established while you work the repeats of the large charted motifs.

Change to #6 needles and begin working charts.

Row 1 (wrong side): Work 17 sts in row 1 of Cable Waves Pattern, K2, P2, K2, work row 1 of Tree of Life Pattern over next 27 sts, K2, P1b, K2, work row 5 of Braid Cable, K2, P1b, work row 1 of Center Cabled Panel over next 24 sts, P1b, K2, work row 5 of Braid Cable, K2, P1b, K2, work row 1 of Tree of Life Pattern over next 27 sts, K2, P2, K2, work row 1 of Cable Waves Pattern over next 17 sts.

Row 2: Continue working pattern as established, working FT and BT as established in Ribbing every right-side row. Remember to work Braid Cable A for first cable and Braid Cable B for second cable, and to work appropriate rows 3 and 4 of Cable Waves pattern for beginning of needle and end of needle.

Work the 76 rows of chart 3 times, then work row 1. (229 rows total.)

On next row, bind off the first 55 sts in knit, work pattern over middle 54 sts and place on a holder, bind off in knit remaining 55 sts.

FRONT: Work as for back, but working the 76 rows of chart 2 times, then rows 1 through 57. (209 rows total.)

Next row (row 58 of pattern): Work 69 sts, work middle 26 sts and place on a holder, work remaining 69 sts. Work each side separately from this point.

Right shoulder (row 59): Work 1 row.

Rows 60 through 71: Bind off 3 sts at the beginning of the next row, then 2 sts every other row three times, then 1 st 5 times. (55 sts remain.)

Row 72: Work even. Bind off in knit.

Left Shoulder: Attach yarn at neck edge with wrong side facing. Following Row 59 of pattern, bind off 3 sts at the beginning of the next row, then 2 sts every other row three times, 1 st 5 times. (55 sts remain.)

Work 2 rows even. Bind off in knit.

SLEEVES: With #4 needles, cast on 76 sts. Work in Ribbing as follows:

Row 1: wrong side (P2, K2) 2 times, P1b, K2, P12, K2, P1b, (K2, P2) 2 times, K2, P4, (K2, P2) 2 times, K2, P1b, K2, P12, K2, P1b, (K2, P2) 2 times.

Row 2: (K2, P2) 2 times, K1b, P2, row 2 of Braid Cable A, P2, K1b, (P2, K2) 2 times, P2, row 1 of Mock Cable, (P2, K2) 2 times, P2, K1b, P2, row 2 of Braid Cable B, P2, K1b, (P2, K2) 2 times.

Continue in Ribbing as established, working center 4 sts in row sequence for Mock Cable, and working Braid Cable rows in sequence.

Work 27 rows of Ribbing.

Row 28 (right side): (Increase row—work same as increases in back and front Ribbing).) Increase 10 sts as follows: Cast on 1 st, increase in each of next 2 sts, work 2 sts, increase in each of next 2 sts, work 64 sts, increase in each of next 2 sts, work 2 sts, increase in each of next 2 sts, cast on 1 st. (86 sts total.)

Change to #6 needle and work pattern as follows:

Row 1 (wrong side): P11, K2, P1b, K2, work row 5 of Braid Cable A, K2, P1b, K10, P4b, K10, P1b, K2, work row 5 of Braid Cable B, K2, P1b, K2, P11.

Row 2: K11, P2, K1b, P2, work row 6 of Braid Cable A, P2, K1b, work row 2 of Center Cabled Pattern over next 24 sts, K1b, P2, work row 6 of Braid Cable B, P2, K1b, P2, K11.

Row 3: Work P1, K5, P2, K3 over first 11 sts, continue in pattern as established, work K3, P2, K5, P1 over last 11 sts.

Row 4: Knit 5, FT, BT, K2, work in established pattern to last 11 sts, K2, FT, BT, K5.

Row 5: Purl 1, M1, purl 10 sts, work in established pattern to last 11 sts, purl 10, M1, P1.

Continue in established pattern, increasing 1 st each end of needle every fifth row 33 times and working the increased sts into the established cable wave pattern. (148 sts; total of 155 rows—2 complete charts plus 3 rows.)

Work 1 row.

Shoulder Strap: At the beginning of the next 2 rows (rows 4 and 5) cast off 59 sts, decreasing 3 sts evenly over each braid cable. Work on center 30 sts in pattern, following rows 6 through 70. Place sts on holder.

ASSEMBLING: Mark a 9-inch armhole depth with safety pins on both sides of front and back. Sew shoulder straps of sleeves to front and back shoulders, then sew sleeve tops to body, having sides of sleeve even with pins. Sew sleeve seams and side seams.

NECK: With #4 circular needle or double-pointed needles, and starting at right back, work the 54 sts from back neck holder as follows: K12, P2, K1b, (P2, K2) 2 times, P2, K4, P2, (K2, P2) 2 times, K1b, P2, K12.

Work the 30 sts from left shoulder strap holder as follows: P2, K1b, (P2, K2) 2 times, P2, K4, P2, (K2, P2) 2 times, K1b, P2.

Pick up and knit 22 sts down left front neck.

Work the 26 sts from front neck holder as follows: K1b,

(P2, K2) 2 times, P2, K4, P2, (K2, P2) 2 times, K1b.

Pick up and knit 22 sts up right front neck.

Work the 30 sts from right shoulder strap holder same as for left shoulder strap. Place a marker to mark beginning and end of round. (184 sts.)

Rnd 1: Work row 2 of Braid Cable A over next 12 sts, P2, K1b, (P2, K2) 2 times, P2, row 1 of Mock Cable, P2, (K2, P2) 2 times, K1b, P2, work row 2 of Braid Cable B over next 12 sts, P2, K1b, (P2, K2) 2 times, P2, row 3 of Mock Cable, P2, (K2, P2) 2 times, K1b, (P2, K2) 2 times, P2, work row 2 of Braid Cable A, P2, K1b, (P2, K2) 2 times, P2, row 3 of Mock Cable, P2, (K2, P2) 2 times, K1b, P2, work row 2 of Braid Cable B, (P2, K2) 2 times, P2, K1b, (P2, K2) 2 times, P2, row 3 of Mock Cable, P2, (K2, P2) 2 times, K1b, P2.

Rnd 2: Work in Ribbing as established but *do not* turn any cables or twists. Work Braid Cable as K12; work Mock Cable as K4.

Repeat these 2 rnds 8 times (16 rnds total), working Mock Cables and Braid Cables in row sequence.

Bind off in knit, decreasing 6 sts over each Braid Cable, and decreasing 2 sts over each Mock Cable.

MEASUREMENTS IN INCHES

A. 24.25
B. 3.5
C. 13.25
D. 11
E. 16.5
F. 3.5
G. 3

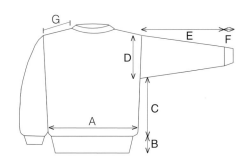

KEY FOR CHARTS

	Stockinette Stitch
	Purl on right side; knit on wrong side
	Front cable worked over 4 sts (FC4**b**)
	Back cable worked over 4 sts (BC4**b**)
BT	Back twist
FT	Front twist
	Cable left—knit
	Cable left—purl
	Cable right—knit
	Cable right—purl
	Knit on right side; purl on wrong side
	Purl on right side; knit on wrong side
	Knit into back of st on right side; purl into back of st on wrong side

CABLE WAVES	TREE OF LIFE	BRAID CABLE B	CENTER CABLED PANEL	BRAID CABLE A	TREE OF LIFE	CABLE WAVES
4-ROW REPEAT	38-ROW REPEAT	6-ROW REPEAT	38-ROW REPEAT	6-ROW REPEAT	38-ROW REPEAT	4-ROW REPEAT

CHART: **BODY**

CHART REPEAT: 1ST 2ND 3RD

CABLE WAVES

TREE OF LIFE

CENTER PANEL

BRAID CABLE

LORANNE CAREY BLOCK

Snow Star Farm

ANTRIM · NEW HAMPSHIRE

Ken and I arrived at Loranne Carey Block's farm in the early afternoon of a sultry day. It had threatened to rain on and off all day, and started just as we got out of the car. The weather did nothing to dampen Loranne's warm and friendly welcome, however. She was in the middle of dyeing two different batches of yarn; one with indigo and one with goldenrod. The two processes are very different, and she launched into an immediate explanation and demonstration, going back and forth between the two porches where it was all taking place.

On the front porch, overlooking the barn and grazing sheep, a huge fifty-five-gallon drum—the indigo dye pot—simmered on a propane burner. In it were eight skeins of yarn hanging straight down. Loranne explained why dyeing

lets the skeins hang in the air for about twenty minutes. If the color is not yet deep enough, she dips the skeins in the dye bath again. The most perfect way to dye with indigo is to do many short dips, ensuring a more even take.

Traditionally, Loranne explained, indigo dyeing was done in urine, which provided the perfect pH level and absence of oxygen. Flinching somewhat, I imagined a woman working over a huge vat of boiling urine. "Did they water it down?" I asked. "No," Loranne answered. "It was pretty intense! Do you know all those beautiful old blue coverlets?" (Yes! I've always admired these at antique shops, running my hands over the threads of colored richness and pattern, longing to possess one.) "They were all dyed with urine indigo!" While the process itself may have been odoriferous, Loranne assured me that the finished skeins did not smell. Very much interested in the historical and traditional approach, Loranne was planning to also dye indigo in this way. She points to a covered pail on the porch where she was collecting urine, then ordered me not to write about it!

While the indigo skeins were hanging, we walked through the house to the back porch, where the goldenrod dye bath simmered, and I was momentarily sidetracked while I took in Loranne's spacious and beautiful log cabin. There is evidence everywhere of her twenty-five-year involvement with yarn and fiber: a great wheel, two huge looms in the loft, posters of knitting, bags of yarn! Graciously, Loranne

A SAMPLING OF SNOW STAR FARM'S COLORFUL YARN PALETTE. LORANNE CAREY BLOCK.

with indigo is such a unique process. There are two crucial factors involved in an indigo bath: the pH level and the absence of oxygen in the water. In an ordinary dye bath, the skeins are periodically stirred around to ensure even distribution of color. With indigo, stirring is not desirable since it adds oxygen to the water.

I knew that indigo yields a rich, dark blue color, but as I peered into the pot I saw only a pale turquoise. Carefully and slowly lifting the skeins from the pot, Loranne told me, with delight in her voice, to watch the color. As the skeins hit the air and the oxidation process began, they magically started turning from yellow-green to the traditional blue! Loranne

said the goldenrod could wait while she gave us a guided tour. Loranne's first loom is a sixty-inch, eight-harness giant. Next to it stands an old barn loom. Although she does not have time for it now, she used to do a lot of weaving in the past, especially when she was resident weaver/textile specialist at the Hancock Shaker Village in Pittsfield, Massachusetts. On the bed in the master bedroom we admired a beautiful plaid blanket, handwoven by Loranne with yarn she hand spun and dyed.

We returned to the goldenrod dye bath, simmering in a stainless steel pot over a propane burner. Loranne gave it a few stirs with a huge, witchlike wooden fork. The pleasant

44

fragrance is sweet and pungent. (The pot was an incredible five-dollar "buy" Loranne found at a garage sale.) After boiling the hand-collected goldenrod to extract the color, Loranne had strained the liquid to remove any plant material. For that particular color, she was using a mordant of alum. The mordant is what helps the dye take to the yarn. Different mordants will yield different colors from the same dye bath, as will pots made from different materials. An iron pot will tend to "sadden" a color; making it look more gray. Loranne is very careful about any chemicals she uses, and often chooses alum because it's harmless. She even mothproofs the natural way, by tucking a bar of lavender soap into her stored skeins of yarn to keep them moth-free and sweet-smelling.

The batch of yarn had been simmering about an hour, and Loranne found that it was not to her liking. She added some powdered iron to the bath, hoping it would turn a bit more green. "I used to use old cookstove parts and horseshoes," she laughs. Iron can be harsh to the yarn, so she adds only the smallest amounts and is careful how long the yarn is exposed to it.

LORANNE LIFTS A HANK OF WOOL DYED WITH BLACK WALNUT. LORANNE CAREY BLOCK.

While the goldenrod continued to simmer, we went back inside for homemade gingerbread and lemonade. Loranne took this opportunity to show me her dye notebooks. Here she has kept a sample of every color and formula she has ever tried, documented with what kind of pot, mordant, and dye she used, as well as it's test for light-fastness. The range of colors she can get from changing just one of these variables is amazing. One of the problems of natural dyes is that they often fade when exposed to light. Loranne does a light test by placing one sample of the yarn in her south window and another sample in the room away from direct light. After an appropriate length of time she compares the two. If the test piece has faded, she alters the dye formula to make it more lightfast. All of the colors she offers have been tested this way.

"I dye like I cook," she said. "I follow recipes but I also use a lot of creative improvisation based on my background in color theory." (Judging from the many cookbooks in the kitchen bookcase and the delicious snack I'd just eaten, I could tell that Loranne also loves to cook.) By keeping precise notes on each new dye recipe, she is able to repeat a color, as well as change it. Starting with an initial visualization of a particular color and staying alert for "pleasant surprises that can occur in the dye pot," Loranne has developed a color spectrum that sings with intensity.

I sat back and admired the view of trees and mountains out the back window. The farm is one mile down a country dirt road. It is peaceful, serene, and unspoiled by any signs of civilization. Loranne is as calm and peaceful as her surroundings, and she talked about her work and her love of color with the obvious content of someone who totally enjoys what she does. While we chatted, Moss, the border collie, ran in and out like he owned the farm, while a cat napped on a bench on the back deck. If there is anywhere for an artist to be inspired, it is surely here.

Loranne was an art major in college and always loved the history and traditional part of everything. When someone asked her to do some rainbow dyeing with her yarn, she brought the dyes home but found herself procrastinating about starting the project. After realizing that she was putting it off because she just wasn't comfortable with using all those chemical dyes, she decided to explore natural dyeing. "I mostly use reds, yellows and blues, using the overdye process to fill in the spectrum," she explained. Some of the indigo skeins she dyed the day of our visit would be put into the goldenrod pot to produce a green. The goldenrod-dyed could just as easily be thrown into the indigo dye pot for another green, for that matter! "I play with the color until I like it," she laughed. By doing a lot of overdyeing, she is able to achieve the fully saturated colors that she loves.

The dyes Loranne uses are a combination of native plants and traditional imported dyes. Showing me her color card, she explained the dye used for each color. The reds come from madder, which is a root, or from cochineal, a bug native to southern climates. Yellows are either from goldenrod, a common roadside plant, or osage orange, a shrubby tree native to the Midwest and Northeast. The gold comes from onion skins, which Loranne saves from her family's daily use. (She explained that they must be combined with iron in order to be lightfast.) Blues are from indigo, and greens are made from indigo/yellow combinations. Purples are a combination or an overdye of indigo and red. The browns are from black walnuts (for a rich, dark color) or butternuts (for a lighter version). "I have proportions and recipes for everything, and surprisingly enough, I can duplicate my colors very closely," Loranne said.

Loranne's yarn has a distinctive, tightly spun twist to it, almost like a traditional gansey yarn. This is the result of careful fleece selection and intensive work and experimentation with the spinnery where she sends her wool. "The way it is spun is the way I would spin it myself," she explained. "I've chosen Corriedale and Romney sheep for the specific characteristics of their wool and have carefully blended proportions of each breed in my yarns." She recently added a heavier weight to her line. It is three-ply, which makes it 50 percent heavier than her other yarn, but still done in the same tight spin.

The next time we inspected the indigo batch we found that some of the skeins showed light patches. Loranne said there are three ways of looking at these particular skeins: they could appeal enormously to some people just the way they are; they could be dipped back into the pot to even out the color; or they could be overdyed with a different color altogether. The final judgment is Loranne's.

Knowing how labor intensive her work is, I was curious about whether Loranne ever found time to knit with her own yarns. She showed me some sweaters she had lovingly knit for her son, Brendan, now twelve. They are obvi-

BRENDAN AND SHEENA SHARE A LICHEN-COVERED BOULDER. LORANNE CAREY BLOCK.

ous treasures to her, and she even has a baby photograph of him wearing one. Brendan is home-schooled, which takes up a good portion of Loranne's day. Like so many other people, she finds it hard to find the time to do everything she wants to do. "When I had a smaller flock, I did a lot of knitting. Now I have portfolios full of ideas, but by the time everything else is done, it's nighttime, and I'm too tired!" Her husband, Richard, a graphic designer, is totally enthused about all of Loranne's projects. He designs all of the yarn labels and helps with the sheep chores and dyeing. Brendan is an accomplished fiddle player and often accompanies his parents to fairs, where he performs.

Loranne recently found a journal from twenty years ago in which she'd written about her dream of having a sheep farm and her own yarn company. That dream is now her life, but the economic reality for her—as for most people in this field—is that it is hard to break even, let alone make a profit. Loranne, however, seems content and at peace with what she does. "I just adore color," she says. "Dyeing brings together art and color, tradition and history, as well as providing an excuse to walk through the woods looking for black walnut trees."

Madder Gansey

The rich, deep color of this yarn comes from the traditional natural dye of madder. Easy textures make it interesting. (Pictured on page 25.)

YARN

Snow Star Farm Yarn 100% wool (4 oz/320 yd), 7 skeins Madder

NEEDLES

#2 and #3 circular (24-inch and-16 inch), #2 and #3 double-pointed. *(See page 10 for equivalent metric and Canadian needle sizes.)*

GAUGE

23 sts and 32 rnds = 4 inches worked over stockinette stitch on #3 needle

FINISHED SIZE

46 inches.

(For information on converting measurements and skein weights to metric equivalents, see page 6.)

ABBREVIATIONS

RT—Right twist. K2 together, knit first stitch again and slip both stitches from needle.

LT—Left twist. Skip first stitch, knit through *back* of second stitch then knit both stitches together through *back*.

SSK—Slip 2 stitches, one at a time, knitwise; insert left needle into the fronts of these two sts and knit them together.

Patterns

Stockinette Stitch: When working in the round, knit every round; when working back and forth, knit the right side, purl the wrong side.

Column (Worked over 5 sts in the round.)
Rnds 1 through 3: K2, P1, K2.
Rnd 4: Purl 5.

V-Panel (Worked over 14 sts in the round.)
Rnd 1 and all odd-numbered rnds: P2, K10, P2.
Rnd 2: P2, K3, RT, LT, K3, P2.
Rnd 4: P2, K2, RT, K2, LT, K2, P2.
Rnd 6: P2, K1, RT, K4, LT, K1, P2.
Rnd 8: P2, RT, K6, LT, P2.

Yoke Pattern (Worked back and forth.)
Row 1 (right side): Knit.
Row 2: K4, *P2, K8*; repeat between *s to the last 6 sts, P2, K4.

Row 3: K3, RT, LT, *K6, RT, LT*; repeat between *s to the last 3 sts, K3.
Row 4: Purl.
Row 5: Knit.
Row 6: K9, *P2, K8*; repeat between *s to the last 11 sts, P2, K9.
Row 7: K8, RT, LT, *K6, RT, LT*; repeat between *s to the last 8 sts, K8.
Row 8: Purl.

V-Panel on Yoke (Worked back and forth.)
Row 1: K2, P10, K2.
Rows 2 through 8: Same as V-panel in the round.

BODY: *The body is worked in the round up to the armholes; therefore, follow all patterns designated as "worked in the round" in the list above.* With #2 needle (24-inch), cast on 120 sts, place a marker, cast on another 120 sts, place a marker. (240 sts.) Join rnd. (The markers divide your work into back and front. The last marker placed is the indication for beginning of rounds.)

Ribbing: Work in K2, P2 ribbing for 2.5 inches. On the last rnd increase 26 sts evenly spaced—13 sts on front, 13 sts back. (266 sts total.)

Purl 1 rnd, knit 1 rnd, purl 1 rnd. Change to #3 needle (24-inch).

Establish patterns: Work the last 3 sts of rnd 1 of Column pattern, *work rnd 1 of V-Panel pattern over the next 14 sts, work rnd 1 of Column over the next 4 sts*, repeat between *s until 2 sts before end of rnd, work the first 2 sts of rnd 1 of V-Panel.

Continue working in numerical rnd sequence of these 2 patterns for 13 inches, ending with a completed rnd 7 of V-Panel, and a completed rnd 3 of Column.

Divide for armholes: Following rnd 8 of V-Panel and rnd 4 of Column, work to 1 stitch before marker, cast off next 3 sts, work to 1 stitch before next marker, cast off 3 sts. (130 sts *each* for front and back.)

FRONT: *Work now progresses back and forth, beginning with a right-side row. Follow all patterns above designated as "worked back and forth." (You may continue to use the circular needle, working back and forth on it. After the first row, place remaining 130 sts for back onto a stitch holder.)*

First Row: Work row 1 of V-Panel and row 1 of Column over the 130 sts of the front. Knit the next 3 rows.

Begin Yoke. Row 1 (right side): K1, P2, K10, P2, K100, P2, K10, P2, K1.
Row 2: P1, K2, P10, K2, P100, K2, P10, K2, P1.
Next row: K1, work row 2 of V-Panel over next 14 sts, work row 1 of Yoke Pattern over next 100 sts, work row 2 of V-Panel over last 14 sts, K 1.

Continue in this established pattern, working the first and last stitch in stockinette stitch, the V-Panel in numerical row sequence over the established 14 stitches on either side of the yoke, and the Yoke Pattern in numerical sequence over the center 100 stitches. Work for 68 rows, ending with a completed row 4 of Yoke Pattern.

Shape Neck: Continuing in established pattern, on a right-side row, work 53 sts, work the middle 24 sts and place on a holder for front neck, work the remaining 53 sts.

Right shoulder: Beginning on the next row (wrong side), decrease 1 st at neck edge every row 4 times. Work 1 row. Decrease 1 st at neck edge on next and then every other row 4 times. Work 3 rows even. Decrease 1 st at neck edge on next and then every fourth row 2 times. (43 sts.)

Work 7 rows even. Place stitches on holder for shoulder.

Left shoulder: Attach yarn at the neck edge. Beginning on row 6 (wrong side) of Yoke Pattern, work as for right shoulder.

BACK: Work as for front until 83 rows of Yoke Pattern have been completed.

Shape back neck: Work 49 sts, work middle 32 sts and place on a holder for back neck, work remaining 49 sts.

Right shoulder: Beginning on next row, decrease 1 st at neck edge every other row 6 times. (43 sts.) Work 1 row even. (You should have completed row 8 of Yoke Pattern.) Place sts on holder for shoulder.

Left shoulder: With right side facing, attach yarn at neck edge and work as for right shoulder.

JOIN SHOULDERS: Use the knitted seam method described on page 11.

NECK: With #2 circular needle (16-inch) and starting at right back shoulder, pick up and knit 11 sts down right back, knit the 32 sts from back neck holder, pick up and knit 11 sts up left back, pick up and knit 23 sts down left front, knit 5 sts from front neck holder, place a marker, knit the middle 14 sts from front neck holder, place a marker, knit the remaining 5 sts from front neck holder, pick up and knit 23 sts up right front to shoulder seam. Place a marker to indicate beginning of rnds. (124 sts.)

Purl one rnd, knit one rnd, purl one rnd.

Rnd 1: Work in K2, P2 ribbing to first marker at front neck, work rnd 1 of V-Panel in the round over the next 14 sts, continue K2, P2 until end of rnd.

Rnds 2 through 7: Work in established ribbing, working the 14 sts of V-Panel in the numerical rnd sequence.

Rnd 8: Work in established Ribbing, working the 14 sts of V-Panel as P2, RT, K1, RT, LT, K1, RT, P2.

Work Rnd 1 again.

Bind off loosely in knit.

SLEEVES: Beginning at middle of underarm cast-offs and using a #3 circular needle (16-inch), pick up and knit 68 sts to shoulder seam, pick up and knit another 68 sts to underarm, place a marker, pick up and knit 1 more st, place a marker. (137 sts.)

This last marked off stitch is the underarm "seam" stitch and is always worked in knit. All decreasing is done on either side of this stitch as follows: *For rnds 4 and 8*, P2 together at beginning of rnd, work to 2 sts before marker, P2 together, knit underarm seam st. *For rnds that are worked on the plain knit part of sleeve*, K2 together at beginning of rnd, work to last 2 stitches before marker, SSK, knit seam stitch.

Purl 1 rnd, knit 1 rnd, purl 1 rnd.

Establish the sleeve pattern as follows, working decreases every fourth rnd.

Rnds 1 and 2: Knit.

Rnd 3: K1, *LT, RT, K6*; repeat between *s, ending LT, RT, K1, knit seam stitch.

Rnd 4 (decrease rnd): P2 together, *K2, P8*; repeat between *s, ending K2, P2 together, knit seam stitch.

Rnds 5 and 6: Knit

Rnd 7: K5, *LT, RT, K6*; repeat between *s, ending LT, RT, K5, knit seam st.

Rnd 8: (decrease rnd) P2 together, P4, *K2, P8*; repeat between *s, ending K2, P4, P2 together, knit seam stitch.

Work these 8 rnds 8 times (64 rnds), working decreases on every fourth rnd, incorporating them into established pattern. (*Note:* The above 8 rnds are written out in order to establish the pattern. With each decrease that is made, you must start the pattern in a different place. From this point on, it is easy to just look at the established pattern and know where to make the twists.)

Knit 3 rnds.

Purl 1 rnd, working decreases on either side of seam st.

Knit 1 rnd, purl 1 rnd, knit 1 rnd.

Next rnd: Knit, working decreases.

Continue working in stockinette stitch for 52 rnds, working decreases every fourth rnd. (69 sts.)

Optional Initials: If you would like to knit initials into the sleeve, select the letters from the alphabet chart. Put them side by side, leaving 2 stitches between each letter. Count the total number of stitches required. Decide where you would like the initials to be, and mark off the stitches required on your needle. Work the letters over the marked stitches, *remembering to work them upside down and from right to left!!* (The lower right-hand corner of the alphabet chart shows an example of how I made the chart for my personal initials.)

Purl 1 rnd, knit one rnd, purl one rnd.

Change to #2 double-pointed needles. Knit one rnd, decreasing 27 sts evenly spaced. (48 sts.)

Work in K2, P2 ribbing for 2.5 inches, working underarm stitch now in ribbing pattern. Bind off loosely in knit.

MEASUREMENTS IN INCHES

A. 46
B. 2.5
C. 14
D. 11.5
E. 15.25
F. 2.5

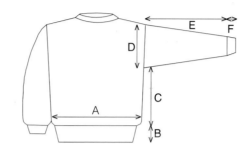

ALPHABET CHART

WORK INITIALS IN PURL ON STOCKINETTE STITCH BACKGROUND.

EXAMPLE OF INITIALS TURNED UPSIDE-DOWN, READY TO BE WORKED INTO SLEEVE.

Indigo

Is it blue on white, or white on blue? It doesn't matter, since the pattern shifts halfway up anyway! Knit this intriguing and easy sweater (pictured on p. 25) using steeks for the armholes and neck openings. The body pattern comes from Latvia, the border is from a Turkish sock pattern (see Sources, p. 128).

YARN

Snow Star Farm 100% pure wool (4 oz/320 yd skeins)

COLOR	SMALL	MEDIUM	LARGE
A. Indigo	3	4	4
B. Natural White	3	4	4

NEEDLES

#3 and #5 circular (24- or 32-inch and 16-inch), #3 and #5 double-pointed. *(See page 10 for equivalent metric and Canadian needle sizes.)*

GAUGE

24 sts and 25 rows = 4 inches worked over pattern on #5 needle.

FINISHED SIZES (IN INCHES)

Small	40
Medium	44
Large	48

(For information on converting measurements and skein weights to metric equivalents, see page 6.)

MEASUREMENTS IN INCHES

A. 40–44–48
B. 2–2–2.5
C. 12.5–12.5–14.5
D. 10.5–10.5–11.5
E. 16.75–16.75–18.75
F. 2–2–2.5

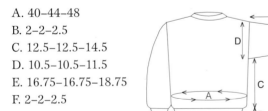

KEY FOR CHARTS

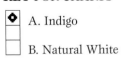

◆ A. Indigo

☐ B. Natural White

Pattern

Stockinette Stitch (Knit every round.)

BODY: With #3 circular needle and Indigo, cast on 240–264–288 sts. Place a marker (referred to as first marker) and join round, being careful not to twist stitches. Purl 1 rnd. Repeat the following 2 rnds for your size 6–6–8 times.

Small and Large: Rnd 1: *K1 White, P1 Indigo, K2 White*; repeat between *s. Rnd 2: *K1 Indigo, P1 Indigo, K1 Indigo, K1 White*; repeat between *s.

Medium: Rnd 1: *K3 White, P1 Indigo*; repeat between *s. Rnd 2: *K1 Indigo, K1 White, K1 Indigo, P1 Indigo*, repeat between *s.

Next 2 rnds: Knit 1 rnd in Indigo, purl 1 rnd in Indigo.

Change to #5 needle and begin CHART A: Work the 12-st repeat of the chart 20–22–24 times around the body of the sweater.

Work the 12 rnds of the chart 5–5–6 times, then rnds 13–26 again.

Rnd 27: Work 120–132–144 sts, place a marker (referred to as second marker), work remaining 120–132–144 sts to first marker.

DIVIDE FOR ARMHOLES AND BEGIN STEEKS: On

CHART B: NECKLINE

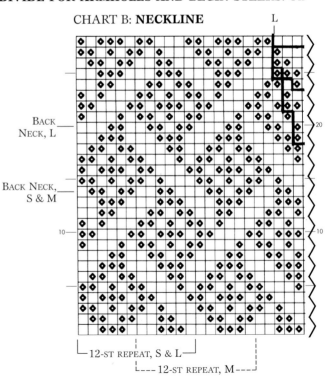

BACK NECK, L

BACK NECK, S & M

12-ST REPEAT, S & L

12-ST REPEAT, M

rnd 28 you will be casting on your steek stitches. These 10 extra stitches form a bridge where the armhole openings will be, allowing work to continue in the round. Later on, these steek stitches will be cut up the middle to form the armhole openings, trimmed, and hemmed down. The sleeve stitches will be picked up around the openings.

Rnd 28: Work to 3 sts before second marker. Place the next 5 sts on a pin. *Place a marker and cast on 10 sts in alternating colors, place a marker.* Work to 3 sts before first marker. Place next 5 sts on a pin. Work between *s. You will now be working on 115–127–139 sts *each* for the front and back. Continue working the steek stitches in alternating colors, reversing the order on each rnd. All rnds begin and end at st #5 of the first steek.

Note that once you have put 5 sts on a pin and started the steek for each armhole opening, those sets of 5 sts will be "missing" from the charted pattern in subsequent rounds. You will need to allow for this in order to continue the established pattern for the rest of the body. Therefore, when following the chart after the armhole break, remember to begin the 12-st repeat 2 sts in from the right-hand side of chart, and end 3 sts before the end of the 12-st repeat when you get to the next armhole steek.

Repeat rnds 29 through 40 three times, then work rnds 29 through 36 once more.

Shape Neck: Start working CHART B at point indicated for your size. Work 47–53–57 sts, place middle 21–21–25 sts on a holder for front neck, place a marker, cast on 10 steek sts in alternating colors, place a marker, work remaining 47–53–57 sts of front, work the 115–127–139 sts of back.

This front neck steek is worked exactly the same as the armhole steeks. Continue working the armhole steeks and the front neck steek as you complete Chart B.

The back is worked straight until shortly before the end.

You will begin shaping the back neck while you are still shaping the front neck. Front neck and back neck decreases are worked as follows: Work to 2 sts before steek, K2 together, work 10 steek sts, SSK, work remaining sts.

Decrease 1 st each side of front neck steek every rnd 6 times, every other rnd 3 times, then every third rnd 2-2-4 times. *At the same time, begin shaping back neck on rnd 15–15–21 as follows:* Work 41–47–49 sts, place middle 33–33–41 sts on holder for back neck, place a marker, cast on 10 steek sts in alternating colors, place a marker, work remaining 41–47–49 sts. Decrease 1 st each side of back neck steek every rnd 5 times.

Rnd 21–21–27: Work the sts of the front, casting off the steek sts of the second armhole. Work the sts of the back, casting off the back neck steek sts. Cast off the steek sts of the first armhole.

Rnd 22–22–28. Work front sts, casting off the steek sts. *Note:* The front is worked one rnd more than the back.

Place the remaining 36–42–44 sts of each shoulder on #5 double-pointed needles.

CUTTING THE STEEKS: Using the zigzag stitch on a sewing machine, or backstitching by hand, sew through all cast-on and cast-off edges of all steeks. Using a sharp pair of scissors, cut up the middle of the steeks between sts 5 and 6. Trim away any ends.

While most directions for steeking call for trimming them down to a 2-stitch width, I prefer the security of keeping them at 5 stitches. Turn back the 5 steek sts, hemming them down by hand using an overcast stitch. Be careful that your stitching does not show through on the right side. When you have finished, work back over the stitches in the opposite direction, forming Xs. Steam gently.

JOIN SHOULDERS: Holding shoulder right side to right

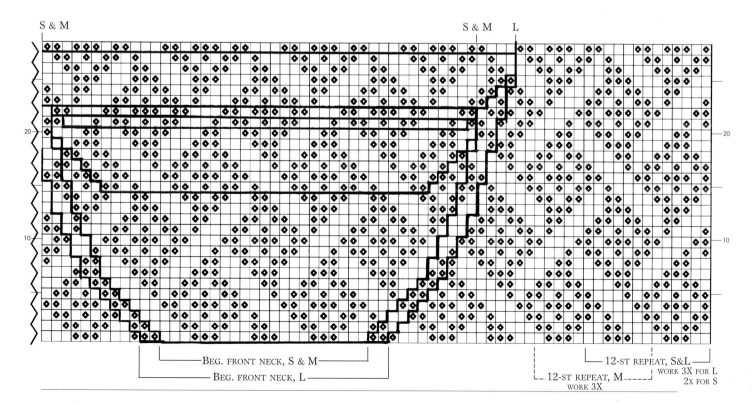

side, join using the knitted seam method (page 11).

Note—Picking Up Stitches: When picking up stitches around openings that have been steeked, use the stitch directly adjacent to the last steek stitch. Insert the needle through *both* loops of the stitch, draw yarn through, and knit.

NECK: With #3 circular (16-inch) and Indigo, starting at right-back shoulder, pick up and knit 6 sts down right back, knit the 33–33–41 sts from back-neck holder, pick up and knit 6 sts up left back to shoulder seam. Pick up and knit 22–22–26 sts down left front, knit the 21–21–25 sts from front-neck holder, pick up and knit 22–22–26 sts up right front. Place marker. (110–110–130 sts.)

With Indigo, purl 1 rnd, decreasing 1 st at beginning of rnd, and 1 st after next shoulder seam. (108–108–128 sts.)

Work the following 2 rnds 5–5–6 times:

Rnd 1: *K1 White, P1 Indigo, K2 White*; repeat between *s.

Rnd 2: *K1 Indigo, P1 Indigo, K1 Indigo, K1 White*; repeat between *s.

Knit 1 rnd in Indigo.

Bind off in purl using Indigo.

SLEEVES. *To Read Sleeve Chart:* Work begins 7 sts before the 12-st repeat. After these 7 sts are worked once, work the 12-st repeat until the end of the rnd. Decreases are shown only at the beginning of the rnd; do not forget to work them at the end of the rnd also. Work the vertical decrease lines in numerical order.

With #5 circular (16-inch) and White, knit the last 2 sts from the underarm pin, pick up and knit 65–65–71 sts to shoulder seam, pick up and knit 64–64–70 sts to pin, knit 2 sts from pin, place a marker, knit the last st from pin, place a marker. (134–134–146 sts.)

The stitch between the markers is the underarm st, and is always knit in Indigo. All decreasing is done on either side of this st as follows: K2 together at beginning of rnd, work to 2 sts before marker, SSK, knit underarm st.

Work rnd 1 of CHART C.

Beginning on rnd 2, decrease 1 st at beginning and end of every second rnd 12 times, every third rnd 10 times, and every fourth rnd 11–11–14 times. Work 2 rnds even. (68–68–74 sts.)

Change to #3 double-pointed needles. With Indigo, knit 1 rnd, decreasing 20–20–18 sts evenly spaced. (48–48–56 sts.)

With Indigo, purl 1 rnd.

Work the following 2 rnds 6–6–8 times, working the underarm stitch in pattern:

Rnd 1: *P1 Indigo, K3 White*; repeat between *s.

Rnd 2: *P1 Indigo, K1 Indigo, K1 White, K1 Indigo*; repeat between *s.

Knit 1 rnd in Indigo.

Bind off in purl, using Indigo.

CHART A: **BODY**

CHART C: **SLEEVE DECREASES**

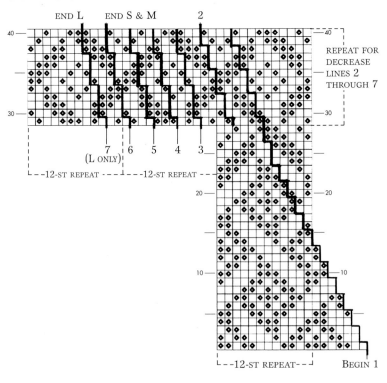

Indigo Flammegarn Socks

Knit these fun socks to keep your toes warm! The variegated yarn will surprise you with its patterns. (Pictured on page 26.)

YARN

Snow Star Farm Sport Weight Wool, 1 skein (4 oz) Indigo Flammegarn. *(For information on converting measurements and skein weights to metric equivalents, see page 6.)*

NEEDLES

1 set #5 double-pointed. *(See page 10 for equivalent metric and Canadian needle sizes.)* Note: These directions are written for 4 needles, with the instep stitches all on 1 needle. If you prefer to work with 5 needles, divide your instep stitches across 2 needles.

GAUGE

6 sts and 8 rnds = 1 inch worked over stockinette stitch.

SIZE

Adult medium. (Length of foot is adjustable.)

ABBREVIATIONS

SSK—Slip 2 sts one at a time to right-hand needle, insert left-hand needle into the fronts of these 2 sts and knit them together.

sl—Slip.

PSSO—Pass slipped stitch over.

Pattern

Stockinette Stitch: Knit every round.

Cuff Pattern. *Note:* When slipping stitches, make sure the yarn is in the back, but slip sts as if you are purling.

Rnds 1 and 2: Purl

Rnds 3 through 6: Sl 1, *K4, sl 2*; repeat between *s to 5 sts before end of rnd, K4, sl 1.

Rnds 7 and 8: Repeat rnds 1 and 2.

Rnds 9 through 12: K2, *sl 2, K4*; repeat between *s to 4 sts before end of rnd, sl 2, K2.

Repeat these 12 rnds for pattern.

SCALLOP CAST-ON: (*Note:* Instead of turning your work to purl the 3 sts as described below, you may find it easier to just knit them backward. See page 11 for instructions on knitting backward.)

Tie a loop on the needle. This is the first stitch. *Cast on 3 *more* sts.

Knit the 3 cast-on sts; purl the 3 sts; knit the 3 sts; purl the 3 sts.

The 3 sts you have just worked are on the left-hand nee-

dle. Slip the second stitch over the first, then slip the third stitch over the first.* You have remaining the original loop, plus one stitch on the top of one scallop.

Repeat between *s 11 times more. You will have a total of 13 sts, including the first loop, and have made 12 scallops.

Next row: *K1, pick up (through the back loop) and knit 3 sts along the top of the scallop.* Repeat between *s 11 times more, K1. (49 sts.)

Join the round.

CUFF: P 1 rnd, decreasing 1 stitch. (48 sts.)

Work 5 rnds of *K1, P1*; repeat between *s.

Work the 12 rnds of Cuff Pattern 5 times. (60 rnds.)

Knit 1 rnd.

Purl 1 rnd.

Next rnd: Knit 36 sts. Slip the next 24 sts onto a double-pointed needle for heel stitches. Slip the remaining 24 sts onto another double-pointed needle for instep sts.

HEEL: Working back and forth, work the following 2 rows 10 times.

Row 1: *Sl 1, K1*; repeat between *s.

Row 2: Sl 1, purl to end.

TURN HEEL

Row 1: K14, sl 1, K1, psso, K1

Row 2: Sl 1, P5, P2 tog, P1.

Row 3: Sl 1 st, knit to within 1 st of gap, sl 1, K1, psso, K1.

Row 4: Sl 1, purl to within 1 st of gap, P2 tog, P1.

Repeat rows 3 and 4 until all stitches are used.

Knit to middle of next row (7 sts.).

GUSSETS: With a new needle, knit the second half of the heel stitches (7 sts), pick up and knit 10 sts along left edge of heel. With a new needle, knit the instep stitches. With a new needle, pick up and knit 10 sts along the right edge of heel, knit the first half of the heel sts.

Work the following 2 rnds until 48 sts remain.

Rnd 1: (Needle 1) knit to last 3 sts, K2 tog, K1; (needle 2) knit the instep sts; (needle 3) K1, SSK, knit to end of needle.

Rnd 2: Knit.

After decreasing is completed, knit even until foot measures 2 inches from end of toe.

TOE: Work the following 2 rnds until 24 sts remain.

Rnd 1: (Needle 1) knit to last 3 sts, K2 tog, K1; (needle 2—instep sts) K1, SSK, knit to last 3 sts, K2 tog, K1; (needle 3) K1, SSK, knit to end of needle.

Rnd 2: Knit.

Now work rnd 1 only until 8 sts remain.

Weave the remaining sts together.

DON AND HEATHER MINTO

Watson Farm

JAMESTOWN · RHODE ISLAND

Don and Heather Minto are living out their dream on a 280-acre farm just this side of paradise. As caretakers of the Watson Farm in Jamestown, Rhode Island, they are responsible for running a working farm owned by the Society for the Preservation of New England Antiquities (SPNEA). Their lifelong dream came true in March 1980. After a five-hour interview with the executive board of the SPNEA, they were offered the job on the spot. Don recalls that it was the first, and only, time in his life (so far) that he was speechless. All he could do was nod his head in agreement.

The Mintos are anything but speechless now. Their profound and deep-rooted love of the land is evident in everything they talk about, and their commitment to their work takes the shape of twelve- to fourteen-hour days. The farm is storybook beautiful and seems to run in complete order. It is home to a flock of forty Romney and Romney-cross sheep, sixty-five cattle, several draft horses, assorted ducks, chickens, and of course, the five resident border collies. All the grain and hay for the animals is grown on the farm. Don and Heather and their three daughters live in the eleven-room 1796 farmhouse. The fields and meadows go right down to the beach of Narragansett Bay. Looking in one direction you see the Jamestown bridge; on the other side is the bridge to Newport. It is a million-dollar view, and this property would have a market value of millions if the SPNEA were not protecting it from development.

Don recalls that when they first arrived to take over operations, the farmhouse had been unoccupied since 1938. There was no electricity or indoor plumbing. The Mintos spent their first year camping in a tent on the grounds and carrying water from the well by hand. SPNEA gradually renovated the house, and they were able to move in. The Society is now responsible for taking care of all the buildings, while the Mintos own all the animals and run the farm. Heather, with a degree in Museum Education, coordinates all the educational programs that go on at the farm and in the local schools. Don, whose degree is in plant soil science and resource management, farms the

land using a rotational grazing system modeled after a method widely used in New Zealand. Watson Farm's grasslands are its greatest resource, and Don explains how proper grazing management can actually improve the land. Rather than being allowed to roam at will across large pastures, the cattle and sheep are moved periodically from one relatively small grazing area to another. This forces them to utilize all the forage in a given area, rather than selectively grazing only their favorite plants, and also allows each grazed section plenty of recovery time before the animals are stocked there again. The Mintos use a system of portable electric fencing to keep the animals within bounds. The border collies help out when needed.

Heather chose to breed Romney sheep because of their fleece's long and lustrous staple. The flock produces more than three hundred pounds of wool a year, which Heather carefully sorts into hundred-pound batches that are sent to Green Mountain Spinnery in Vermont to be carded and spun. Some of the fleece she dyes, and then mixes with the natural fleece to produce unique and beautiful shades of yarn with subtle highlights of color. Just recently the wool from Watson Farms, known as Bay Island Wool, is being knit into sweaters that are marketed at a local shop to commemorate Jamestown's heritage. Fittingly, the symbol of Jamestown is a sheep. Heather coordinates sheep-to-shawl contests as demonstrations for school children to learn about the whole process: from the sheep's back to a useful article of clothing. At home on the farm, she spins, weaves, and knits, wistfully confiding to me that she

THE HISTORIC WATSON FARM HOMESTEAD. CANDACE STRICK.

wishes she had more time for these things. Running the farm, working the garden, raising the children, and doing administrative work for SPNEA takes up most of her day.

When I arrived for my visit, we walked out to the meadow, the five collies racing ahead of us, to see the sheep. Heather's love for her animals showed as she proudly pointed out how beautiful one ewe was, what a gorgeous face another one had. She called softly to the lambs, wanting them to come closer to the fence for me, then commanded Bet, one of the collies, to "go round." Deftly, Bet skipped in-

54

side the fence, running low in a circle, subtly nudging the sheep over. The other four dogs, eager to show their stuff, are commanded to lie down while Bet gets all the glory!

Heather's original interest in raising sheep was to find the right natural colors so she could skip the whole step of dyeing. She started with a black Romney many years ago, when nobody was interested in black sheep. She now has an as-

HEATHER WITH A SAMPLING OF BAY ISLAND WOOLS. CANDACE STRICK.

sortment of white, gray, and black, yielding enough variations in color to do her unique combining process. Being a vegetarian, I asked about marketing the sheep for meat. Heather explained that Romney sheep have the advantage of being useful for both wool and meat. Although she loves her sheep, in any farm operation, one must look at the economics. "I sometimes scold the sheep when they are not cooperating and threaten them that they will be lamb chops soon enough if they don't shape up!" Heather said.

The day I visited Don and Heather was clear and hot. Don was thinking, as usual, about haying. One field was ready to be mowed, but the weather had to be just right for the next couple of days. If cut hay gets rained on for more than one day, it is ruined. "Our life is seasonal, and our work changes according to the season," explained Don "It is a sequence of planting, harvesting, shearing, shipping wool, and weeding." In between there is equipment maintenance: "I spend one-third of my time using the equipment for farming, then another third of my time fixing what broke when I used it!" Don's greatest ambition would be to harness his draft horses to do the work of the power equipment.

Every detail of farming reflects Don's commitment to the land and what will be best for it. He described a weed that was taking over the pastures. It could be eradicated with chemicals, but Don steadfastly refuses to use herbicides. Instead, he was experimenting with an insect that is supposed to slowly eat the stalk and move down into the roots, killing the plant. As we walked through the fields, he pulled up a specimen to show us, and I noticed that even with weeds, he is respectful. As we approached the grazing cattle, I warily

slowed down; were we going to walk right through them? The collies circled the cattle, taking the roundabout way, but Don sauntered through, and I followed. He talked gently to them, admiring them, telling me who's who in the cattle world. The cattle calmly enjoyed their all-organic diet, unaware that they are highly prized for their organic meat.

To live and work on such a beautiful piece of land is an honor for Don. "I would be no happier if I owned this land. After all, no one really owns land." His knowledge of the historical farming practices on this land help him to make decisions about how to farm it today. His educational goal is to teach children to respect the land and what it can do for them. Walking the land, and talking about the land, Don Minto is in total heaven.

Don and Heather absolutely love running Watson Farm, and never once alluded to doing anything different with their lives. I asked them where they might see themselves in ten years, and their answer was, "Right here, doing what we do now. It sustains us and gives us energy. " Don described a recent Father's Day that he spent with his youngest daughter, raking twenty acres of hay with the horses, and singing songs the whole time. Heather and Don both agreed, though, that if the farm operation were scaled down, things wouldn't be quite so hectic. "When we walk down to the beach at sunset, and just stop to look around, we are truly graced to have these moments that make it all worthwhile."

In finishing up our interview, I asked each of them to describe what would be a perfect day on the farm:

Heather—"I would get up early and have some quiet time either reading or writing. All the animals would be where they belong, I would get all my morning chores down before 9 a.m. so I could get into the garden before it got too hot. I could then spend the rest of the day doing spinning, weaving, and sitting on the porch knitting. But first, we'd have to build the porch!"

Don—"I would rise at the first day's light, play my guitar for about half an hour, walk through the fields to greet the morning, check the horses, then eat breakfast. I would like to do all the chores without any equipment breaking down. But a perfect day"—a glance at the sky—"a perfect day would be to get the hay in before it rains."

ONE OF THE ROMNEY LAMBS PEERS ACROSS A SECTION OF PORTABLE ELECTRIC FENCE. CANDACE STRICK.

Heather's Gray Cabled Pullover

Heather Minto creates beautiful colors in her yarns by carding small amounts of dyed wool with the natural colors of the fleece. The textures and cables in this design only serve to enhance the wool's beauty. (Pictured on page 24.)

YARN

Watson Farm Knitting Worsted, 7–8–9 skeins Heather's Gray.

NEEDLES

#5 and #7 single-pointed, #5 circular (16-inch) **or** #5 double-pointed. *(See page 10 for equivalent metric and Canadian needle sizes.)*

GAUGE

22.5 sts and 24 rows = 4 inches, worked in Basket Rib on #7 needles.

FINISHED SIZES (IN INCHES)

Small   40.5
Medium   44.5
Large   48.5

(For information on converting measurements and skein weights to metric equivalents, see page 6.)

SPECIAL ABBREVIATIONS:

See chart key.

BASKET RIB PATTERN

(for front, back, and first 4 rows of sleeve)
Row 1: (RS) *K1, P1*; repeat between *s, end K1.
Row 2: K2, *P1, K3*; repeat between *s, end P1, K2.
Row 3: P2, *K1, P3*; repeat between *s, end K1, P2.
Row 4: *P1, K1*; repeat between *s, end P1.
Row 5: K1, *P3, K1*; repeat between *s.
Row 6: P1, *K3, P1*; repeat between *s.

FRONT: With #5 needles, cast on 107–127–137 sts. Work Bobble Ribbing for body as follows:

Row 1: (K2, P3) 8–10–11 times, (RT, P3) 2 times, (K2, P3) 2 times, (LT, P3) 2 times, (K2, P3) 7–9–10 times, K2.

Row 2: (P2, K3) 21–25–27 times, P2.

Repeat these 2 rows 4–4–5 times.

Next row: Bobbles are made in *every other* P3 space. Beginning in the first–first–second P3 space of ribbing, work in established ribbing, making a bobble in the middle stitch of the P3 space (P1, MB, P1) every other space. Continue across row, making a bobble in every other space and working the RTs and LTs as established.

Work row 2, then work rows 1 and 2 of ribbing 3–3–4 times more.

Increase row (right side): Work in established ribbing, but work the increases in the knit stitches by knitting into the row below the stitch, then knitting the stitch. Increase 3–1–0 sts evenly spaced within the sts *before* the RTs. Work the RTs, *P3, increase 1 st in each of the next 2 sts*, repeat between *s, P3, work through the LTs, increase 3–1–0 sts evenly spaced within the remaining sts. (117–133–141 sts.)

Change to #7 needles.

Begin Chart. The next row is a set–up row (wrong side): Purl 21–29–33 sts, work set–up row from CHART A over the next 75 sts, purl remaining 21–29–33 sts.

Row 1: Work row 1 of Basket Rib pattern over 21–29–33 sts, work row 1 of Chart A over the next 75 sts, work row 1 of Basket Rib over the remaining 21–29–33 sts.

Next rows: Work Basket Rib in numerical row sequence over established 21–29–33 sts on either side of center, work CHART A in numerical row sequence over middle 75 sts. *Note: The 6-row repeat of Basket Rib pattern does not come out even with the 45 rows of the chart. Therefore, each time the chart is repeated, you must be careful to maintain the established row sequence for the Basket Rib pattern.*

Work the 45 rows of Chart A, then repeat rows 6 through 45 twice. Work rows 6 through 8 *again* for Small, 6 through 16 for Medium, and 6 through 24 for Large.

Shape front neck (right side): Following row 9–17–25 of Chart A, work 48–54–58 sts, place middle 21–25–25 sts on holder for front neck, place remaining 48–54–58 sts on a spare needle for other shoulder.

Left Shoulder: Beginning on next row, bind off sts at neck edge every other row as follows: Small—1 st 10 times; Medium and Large—2 sts once, then 1 st 10 times. Work 2–4–4 rows even. Place remaining 38–42–46 sts on holder for shoulder.

Right Shoulder: Attach yarn at neck edge and work row 9–17–25. Beginning on next row, work neck shaping same as for left shoulder, but working only 1–3–3 rows even at end. (Remember to follow *left* side of chart for right shoulder!)

BACK: Work as for front, working the 45 rows of CHART A, then working rows 6 through 45 twice. Work rows 6 through 24 for Small, 6 through 32 for Medium, and 6 through 40 for Large.

Shape back neck: Following row 25–33–41, work 41–45–49 sts, place middle 35–43–43 sts on holder for back neck, attach another ball of yarn and work remaining 41–45–49 sts. Work both sides at the same time. Beginning on next row, decrease 1 st at neck edge every other row 3 times. Place remaining 38–42–46 sts on holders for shoulder.

JOIN SHOULDERS: Use the knitted seam method. (See page 11 for directions.)

NECK: Use #5 circular (16-inch) *or* double-pointed needles. With right side facing and starting at right back shoulder, pick up 6 sts down right back, knit the 35–43–43 sts from back neck holder, pick up and knit 6 sts up left back, pick up and knit 20–26–26 sts down left front, knit the 21–25–25 sts from front neck holder, pick up and knit 20–26–26 sts up right front. Place a marker. (108–132–132 sts.)

Size Small only. Rnd 1: P3, K2, P3, RT, P3, K2, P1, P2 tog, P1, K1, K2 tog, P3 (middle back), K2 tog, K1, P1, P2 tog, P1, K2, P3, LT, (P3, K2) 4 times, (P3, RT) 2 times, [P3, (K2 tog) 2 times] 2 times, P3, LT, (P3, K2) 4 times. (100 sts.)

Sizes Medium and Large only: Rnd 1: (K2 tog) 2 times, P3, K2, P3, (RT, P3) 2 times, [(K2 tog) 2 times, P3] 2 times, (LT, P3) 2 times, K2, P3, (K2 tog) 2 times, (P3, K2) 5 times, P3, RT, [P3, (K2 tog) 2 times] 2 times, P3, LT, (P3, K2) 5 times, P3. (120 sts.)

Rnd 2 *(for all sizes)*: Work in established ribbing, but working the RTs and LTs as K2.

Rnd 3: Work in established ribbing, but working RTs and LTs.

Repeat rnds 2 and 3 once more, then work rnd 2.

Next rnd: Following rnd 3 and beginning in the first P3 space, work a bobble in every other P3 space.

Work rnds 2 and 3 twice more.

Bind off loosely in pattern.

SLEEVES: With #5 needles, cast on 47–57–57 sts. Work Bobble Ribbing for sleeve as follows:

Row 1: (K2, P3) 2–3–3 times, (RT, P3) 2 times, (K2, P3) 2 times, (LT, P3) 2 times, K2, (P3, K2) 1–2–2 times.

Row 2: *P3, K2*; repeat across row.

Repeat these 2 rows 4–4–5 times.

Beginning in the 1st–2nd–2nd P3 space, work in established ribbing but make a bobble in every other P3 space.

Work row 2, then work rows 1 and 2 of ribbing 3–3–4 times more.

Increase row (right side): Working in established ribbing, increase 6–5–5 sts evenly spaced within the first 10– 12–12 sts, work through the RTs, (P3, increase 1 st in each of next 2 sts) 2 times, P3, work through LTs, P3, increase 6–5–5 sts evenly spaced within the remaining 10–12–12 sts. (16–14–14 sts increased, for a total of 63–71–71 sts.)

Change to #7 needles.

Begin Chart. The next row is a set-up row (wrong side): Purl 13–17–17 sts, work the middle 37 sts from set-up row of CHART B, purl 13–17–17 sts.

Row 1: Work row 1 of Basket Rib Pattern over first and last 13–17–17 sts, follow row 1 of Chart B over the middle 37 sts. Chart is followed the same as for Front and Back, following numerical rows of Basket Rib written for each chart repeat.

Increase 1 st each side of sleeve every fourth row 23–25–25 times, working the added sts into established Basket Rib pattern. (109–121–121 sts.)

Work even until entire piece measures 19–20–21 inches, ending with a completed wrong-side row. Bind off loosely in knit, decreasing 2 sts over the center cable, or 1 st over each 4-st cable.

FINISHING: Mark down 10–11–11 inches from shoulder on front and back for armhole depth. Sew sleeve between these markers, matching center cable of sleeve to shoulder seam. Sew sleeve and body seams.

If you would like to steam your sweater and stretch it widthwise to open the cables slightly, hold the iron over the sweater and press the steam button. *Do not* press cables. Pressing the iron directly on the cables will flatten them out and spoil the beautiful three-dimensional effect.

MEASUREMENTS IN INCHES

A. 20.25–22.25–24.25
B. 3–3–3.5
C. 15–16–17
D. 10–11–11
E. 16–17–17.5
F. 3–3–3.5

KEY FOR CHARTS

Cable 4 front. Slip 2 sts to cn and hold in front, then K2 sts from cn.

Cable 4 back. As above, but hold sts in back.

Front Braid Cable. Slip 3 sts to cn and hold in front; K2, sl the purl st from cn back to left needle and purl it, K2 from cn.

Back braid cable. As above, but hold sts in back.

Knit on right side; purl on wrong side.

Purl on right side; knit on wrong side.

Bold symbol means to knit the st when working the 3-st left- or right-cross (below).

Bold symbol means to purl the st as when working the 3-st left- or right-cross (below).

Cable 5 back. Slip 3 sts to cn and hold in back, K2, then K3 sts from cn.

(MB) Make bobble. K, YO, K, YO, K into same stitch, turn work and purl these 5 sts, turn work, knit 3, k2 tog, slip the 3 sts, one at a time, over the k2 st.

Left-cross purl. Slip 2 sts to cn and hold in front, P1, then K sts from cn.

Left-cross knit. As above, but K1 st.

Right-cross purl. Slip 1 st to cn and hold in back, K2, then P st from cn.

Right-cross knit. As above, but K the st from cn.

(LT) Left twist. Skip 1 st, K into the loop behind the 2nd st but do not slip from needle, K both sts tog through the back loop and slip both from needle.

(RT) Right twist. Knit 2 tog but do not slip from needle, K first st, then slip both from needle together.

Knit through the back on right-side rows; purl through the back on wrong-side rows.

CHART A: **BODY**

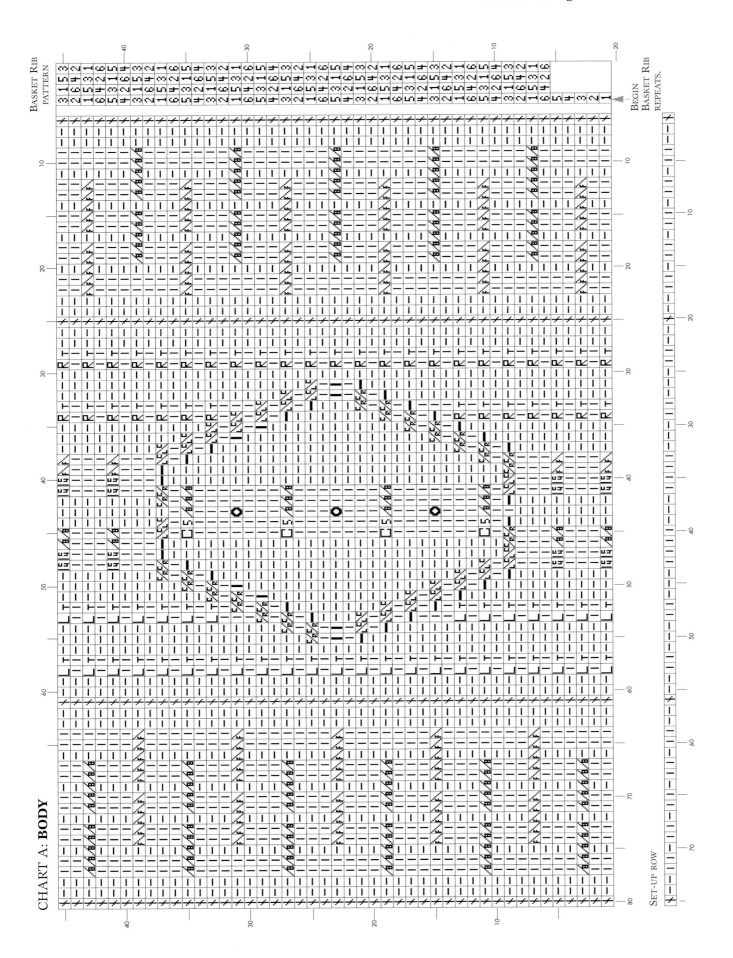

CHART B: **SLEEVE**

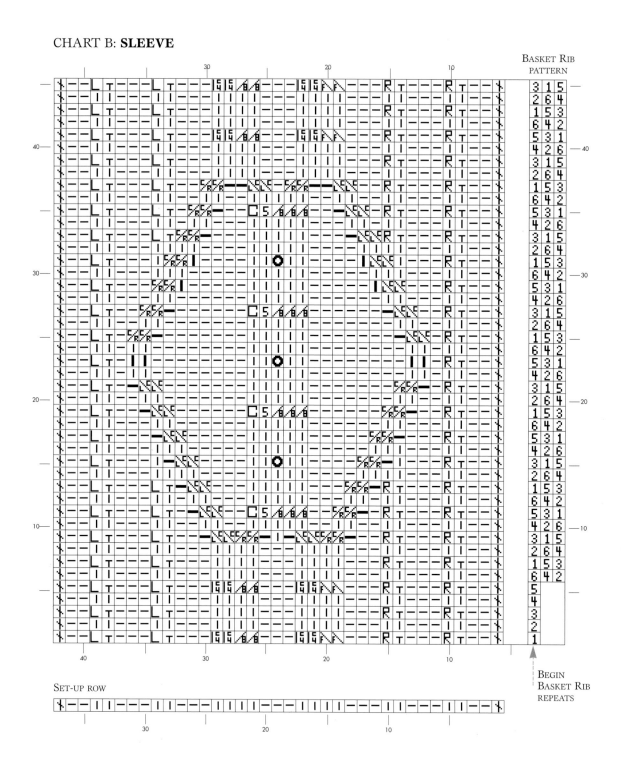

BASKET RIB
PATTERN

SET-UP ROW

BEGIN
BASKET RIB
REPEATS

Bear Paw Barn Jacket

Bear Paw is a traditional quilt pattern adapted for this sweater. The proportions of this garment are generous enough to allow another sweater to be worn under it. (Pictured on p. 17)

YARN

Watson Farm wool (4 oz/230 yd skein)

COLOR	SKEINS
A. Chocolate Brown	5
B. Light Gray	2
C. Creamy White	1

NEEDLES

#7 and #9 single-pointed, #7 circular (24-inch). *(See page 10 for equivalent metric and Canadian needle sizes.)*

GAUGE

8 sts and 11 rows = 2 inches worked over stockinette stitch.

FINISHED SIZE

52.5 inches.

(For information on converting measurements and skein weights to metric equivalents, see page 6.)

BUTTONS

eight ⁷⁄₈-inch.

Pattern

Stockinette Stitch (Knit one row, purl one row.)

Note on working the Bear Paw design: This design is worked using the intarsia method. Each area of color is worked using a separate length of yarn. Where colors meet, it is important to link one color yarn around the other, or you will have a hole at the junction of the colors. You will have many ends of yarn in this pattern; they may be either knitted in as you go along, or woven in along the joining lines after the knitting is completed.

BACK: With #7 needles and COLOR B, cast on 104 sts.

Row 1 (right side): K3, *P2, K2*; repeat between *s, end P2, K3.

Row 2 (wrong side): P3, *K2, P2*; repeat between *s, end K2, P3.

Repeat these 2 rows for 2 inches, ending on a wrong-side row and increasing 1 st on this last row. (105 sts.)

Change to #9 needles and COLOR A. Beginning with a knit row, work stockinette stitch for 70 rows before commencing Chart A.

Using Chart A: *Note that the chart for Left Front also serves as the chart for the Back.* For Back, work the chart right to left to the marked center stitch, then left to right on the same row to complete the other half of the back. Do not repeat the center stitch. (The entire chart will be worked as is for the Left Front.)

Work CHART A, casting off 8 sts at the beginning of rows 33 and 34 (Note that this cast-off edge for row 34 is not shown on chart.)

Neck and Shoulders: On row 98 work 29 sts, place middle 31 sts on a holder for back neck, attach another ball of yarn and work remaining 29 sts. Work 1 more row on both sides. Bind off both sets of shoulder stitches.

POCKET LININGS: (Make 2.) With #9 needles and COLOR A, cast on 22 sts. Beginning with a knit row, work 26 rows of stockinette stitch. Place sts on a holder.

RIGHT FRONT: With #7 needles and COLOR B, cast on 54 sts.

Ribbing: K3, *P2, K2*; repeat between *s to last 3 sts, P3. Repeat this row until ribbing measures 2 inches.

Change to #9 needles and COLOR A. Beginning with a knit row, work stockinette stitch for 28 rows.

Pocket: On row 29, make pocket as follows: Work 18 sts, slip next 22 sts onto a holder. With the right side of the pocket lining facing, knit the 22 sts of the lining. Work the remaining 14 sts of row. Continue working in stockinette stitch for a *total* of 70 rows.

Following CHART B, work Bear Paw design, casting off 8 sts at the beginning of row 34. Work 1 row of COLOR A after Bear Paw design is complete.

Shape Neck: At the beginning of row 83 cast off 6 sts at neck edge. Then cast off at neck edge, every other row: 4 sts once, 2 sts once, and 1 st 5 times. Work even on 29 sts for 2 rows. Bind off for shoulder.

LEFT FRONT: Cast on as for right front, but work ribbing as follows: P3, *K2, P2*, repeat between *s, end K3. Work this row until ribbing measures 2 inches.

Work as for right front, but making pocket on row 29 as follows: Work 14 sts; slip next 22 sts onto a holder; with the right side of pocket lining facing, knit across the 22 sts of lining; knit the remaining 18 sts.

Work CHART A, shaping armhole on row 33.

Shape neck as for right front, but beginning on row 84. After neck shaping is completed, work 1 more row. Bind off for shoulder.

POCKET TOPS: Using #7 needles and COLOR B, and with

right side facing, slip the 22 sts from holder onto the left needle. Knit 1 row, then work the following 2 rows of ribbing for a total of 7 rows, ending with row 1.

Row 1 (wrong side): *P2, K2*; repeat between *s, end P2.
Row 2 (right side): *K2, P2*; repeat between *s, end K2.
Bind off in knit.

Sew pocket linings to inside of sweater using a slip stitch. Tack pocket tops down at edges.

SLEEVES: With #7 needles and COLOR B, cast on 42 sts.
Ribbing/Cuffs: K3,*P2, K2*; repeat between *s, end P3. Repeat this row for 4 inches, increasing 9 sts evenly spaced on the last row. (51 sts.)

Change to #9 needles and work CHART C, increasing 1 st each side of sleeve every third row 11 times, then every fifth row 9 times. (91 sts.) Work the Bear Paw design over the first 25 rows, as shown in the chart, then continue in COLOR A. After increasing is completed, work 6 rows even.

Shape Sleeve Cap: At the beginning of the next 2 rows cast off 8 sts. At the beginning of the next 12 rows cast of 2 sts. Cast off remaining 51 sts.

LEFT FRONT BAND: Using the #7 circular needle and COLOR B, with right side facing and beginning at neck edge, pick up and knit 163 sts. Work back and forth on needle.

Row 1 (wrong side): *P2, K2*; repeat between *s, end P3.
Row 2 (right side): K3, *P2, K2*; repeat between *s.
Repeat these 2 rows for a total of 9 rows. Bind off in knit.

RIGHT FRONT BAND (BUTTONHOLE): Using #7 circular needle and COLOR B, with right side facing and beginning at lower edge, pick up and knit 163 sts. Work back and forth on needle.

Row 1 (wrong side): P3, *K2, P2*; repeat between *s.

Row 2 (right side): *K2, P2*; repeat between *s, end K3.
Repeat these 2 rows for a total of 4 rows.
Row 5. Make buttonholes as follows: Work 3 sts, cast off 3 sts, *work 18 sts (there are 19 sts on the needle counting the one left from the previous cast-off), cast off 3 sts.* Repeat between *s 7 times. Work last 2 sts (8 buttonholes made.)
Row 6: Work in established ribbing, casting on 3 sts over each buttonhole.
Rows 7 through 9: Work in established ribbing.
Bind off in knit.

SHOULDER SEAMS. *Sew* the shoulder seams. (A knitted shoulder seam would be too stretchy for this sturdy jacket.)

COLLAR: Using #7 needles and COLOR B, with right side facing and starting at center of buttonhole band, pick up and knit 36 sts to shoulder seam, pick up and knit 2 sts down right back, knit the 31 sts from back neck holder, decreasing 1 st at center back, pick up and knit 2 sts up left back, pick up and knit 36 sts down left front, ending at middle of button band. (106 sts.)

Row 1 (wrong side): *P2, K2*; repeat between *s, end P2.
Row 2 (right side): *K2, P2*; repeat between *s, end K2.
Repeat these 2 rows for a total of 12 rows.
Purl 1 row.
Knit 1 row.
Bind off in purl.

FINISHING: Sew side seams. Sew sleeve seams, reversing seam for bottom 2 inches of cuff, where it will be rolled up. Pin and sew sleeve to sweater, matching underarm seam to side seam of sweater and aligning middle of sleeve cap with shoulder seam. Sew buttons to band. Steam sweater lightly.

MEASUREMENTS IN INCHES

A. 26.25
B. 2
C. 18.5
D. 11.5
E. 18.5
F. 2

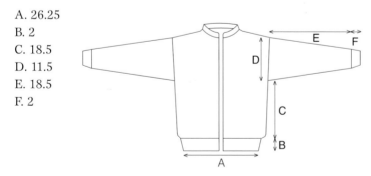

KEY FOR CHARTS

	Chocolate Brown
1	Light Gray
✦	Creamy White

CHART A:
BACK and LEFT FRONT

FOR SWEATER BACK: WORK CHART R TO L THROUGH CENTER BACK STITCH, THEN L TO R. *DO NOT* RE-PEAT CENTER STITCH.

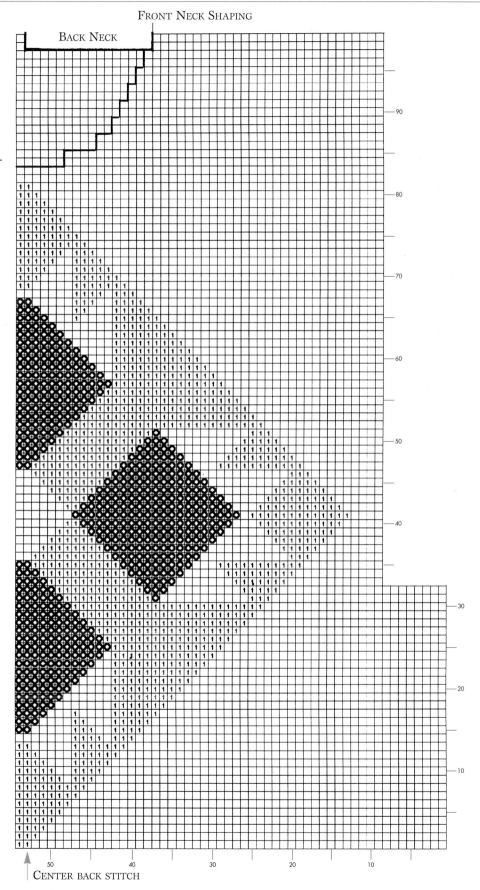

FRONT NECK SHAPING

BACK NECK

CENTER BACK STITCH

CHART B:
RIGHT FRONT

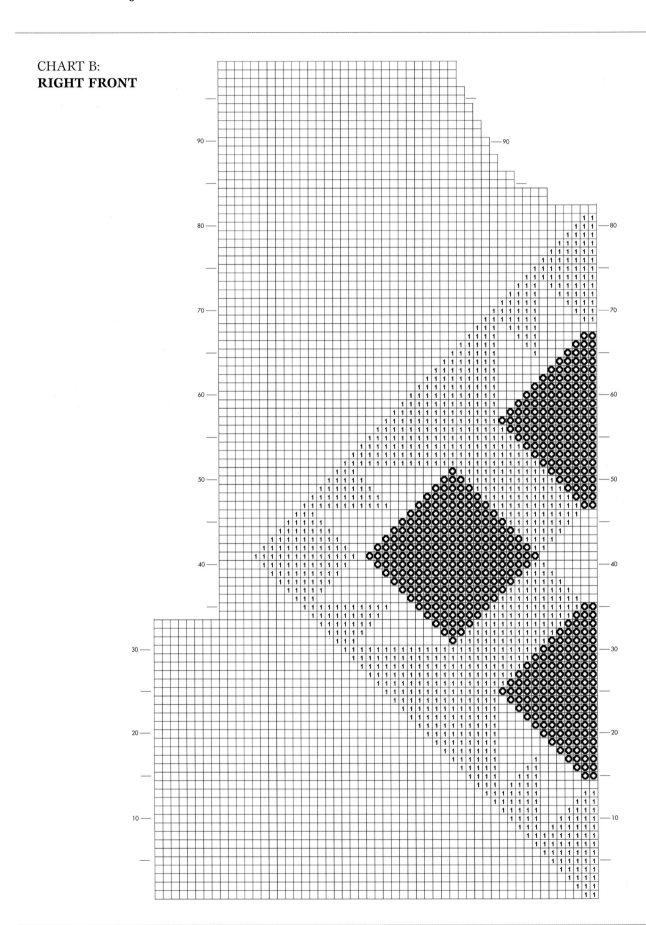

CHART C: **SLEEVE**

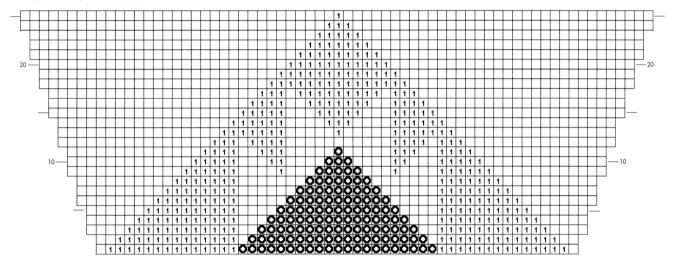

Sheep Mittens

A book about sheep farms would not be complete without something that has a sheep motif!! (Pictured on page 26.)

YARN

Watson Farm Worsted Weight Wool (4 oz/230 yd skein); 1 skein Natural White for pattern, 1 skein Heather's Gray for background.

NEEDLES

1 set double-pointed #3. *(See page 10 for equivalent metric and Canadian needle sizes.)*

GAUGE

6.5 stitches = 1 inch worked over pattern.

LEFT MITTEN: With #3 needles and background color, cast on 50 sts. Divide evenly onto 3 needles and join.

Cuff: Work in K1, P1 ribbing for 2 rnds. Work the 13 rnds of CHART A, working the 10-st repeat 5 times around. Knit one rnd in background color, decreasing 12 sts evenly spaced. (38 sts.) Work 6 rnds of K1, P1 ribbing. Knit one rnd, increasing 8 sts evenly spaced. (46 sts.)

Divide sts as follows: 12 sts on needle #1, 11 sts on needle #2, and 23 sts on needle #3. Needles #1 and #2 have the palm sts, and needle #3 has the back-of-hand sts.

Work the first 7 rnds of the mitten pattern (CHART B), reading the chart from right to left.

Thumb gusset: On the eighth rnd of Chart B, knit the first 18 sts (st 18 is the first outline st for thumb). Work the first row of CHART C by increasing in the first st after the outline st, working the next st, and then increasing in the next st. Returning to Chart B, knit 1 st in pattern (outline for thumb), work to end of rnd.

Continue to follow Chart B plus Chart C, increasing for the gusset (after the first outline stitch and before the second outline stitch) every third round. There will be 2 more sts between the outline stitches after each increase rnd.

When the gusset is completed there will be 13 sts for the thumb, including the outline sts. In the next rnd, slip these sts to a thread, cast on 5 sts, work to end of rnd. (46 sts.)

Shape tip. Begin the decreasing on rnd 41 as follows:
Needle #1: K1, sl1, K1, PSSO, work to end of needle.
Needle #2: Work to 3 sts before end of needle, K2 tog, K1.
Needle #3: K1, sl1, K1, PSSO, knit to 3 sts before end of needle, K2 tog, K1.

Continue to decrease until 7 sts remain for the palm and 7 sts for the back of the hand.

Break yarn, weave sts together.

THUMB: Slip the 13 sts for the thumb onto two needles. With a third needle pick up and knit 7 sts at the inside of the thumb, starting with gray and alternating colors. Work the rest of CHART C, decreasing for the tip as follows:

Needle #1: K1, sl1, K1, PSSO, work to end of needle.
Needle #2: Work to 3 sts before end of needle, K2 together, k1.
Needle #3: Work across the 7 sts.

Repeat the decrease as indicated on the chart until 14 sts remain. Break yarn, run the end through the sts and fasten off.

RIGHT MITTEN: Work as for left mitten until ready to begin Chart B. Divide the sts as follows: 23 sts on needle #1, 11 sts on needle #2, and 12 sts on needle #3. Needle #1 has the back-of hand-sts, and needles #2 and #3 have the palm sts.

Work chart reading from *left to right.*

CHARTS FOR **MITTENS**

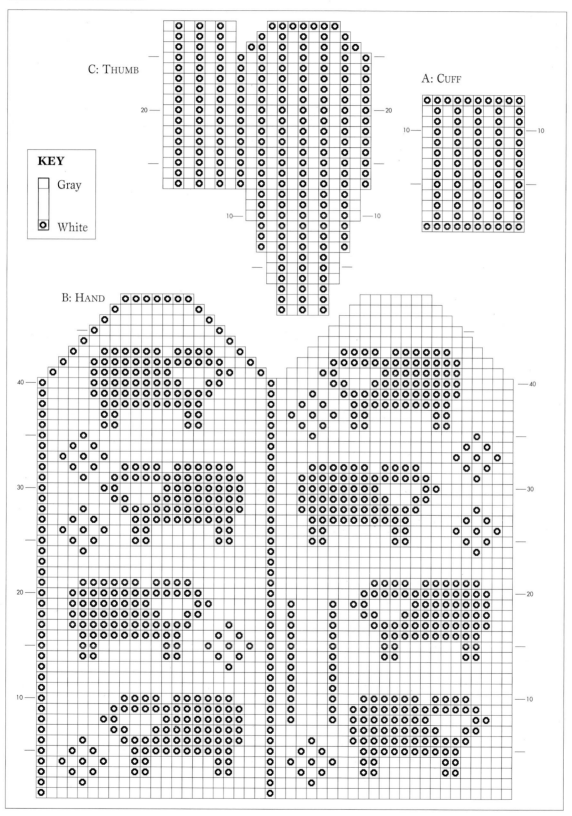

C: THUMB

A: CUFF

KEY

☐ Gray

◉ White

B: HAND

Meadowcroft Farm

WASHINGTON · MAINE

Before I met Nanney, she had sent me some samples of her yarn. Attached to the hank of yarn, appropriately called "Seacolors," was a card that read:

> Inspired by Nature
>> Hand-dyed in Seawaters
>>> Warmed by the Sun
> Grown on the Backs
>> Of Fine-Wooled Sheep and Goats
>>> Still Grazing on the Hills
> Of our Farmstead in Maine.
>>> Remember the Sun, and Enjoy!

I was smitten by the prose on this little card, as well as by the unique yarn to which it was attached. I anxiously awaited the day of our interview, all the while dreaming of gorgeous hand-dyed yarn warming in the sun.

When Ken and I arrived at Meadowcroft after a six-hour

NANNEY BRINGS A WELL-STOCKED AND ATTRACTIVELY LAID-OUT DISPLAY WHEN SHE TRAVELS TO FAIRS AND SHOWS. NANNEY KENNEDY.

ride, the day was cold, overcast, and misting, but we had no doubt that we had arrived at the right place. Right in front of us was a rack filled with dripping hanks of yarn; sheep and angora goats were grazing and bleating in the surrounding meadows. Nanney Kennedy bounded out of the house to greet us, immediately infusing us with warmth and much-needed energy. Nanney is whacky, wild, and wonderful; the air around her fairly crackles with energy. Her love of life is

infectious, and all you can do is sit back and try to take it all in. Her yarns are the perfect expression of her personality— bright bursts of color punctuating a beautiful and harmonious background.

The first thing Nanney explained was why she had a silo sitting on its side in her driveway. It would soon be put upright and used to store the 100 percent organic grain she feeds her animals. Having done postgraduate work in agriculture and resource economics, Nanney is concerned about the future of the land and feels an obligation to preserve it. "I am living at the headwaters of the Damariscotta River, the watershed where I grew up. I'm an organic farmer now, trying to utilize the land appropriately."

Nanney led us into the house, where we were greeted by a few of the resident cats and dogs. The bow window in the living room looks out over fields and meadows that could rival anyone's idea of the most beautiful place in the world. It is so beautiful, in fact, that Nanney admitted she rarely wants to leave it, even for a vacation. A rack of yarn stood in front of the window, brightly beautiful against the mostly green scene outside the glass.

Nanney went on to tell us about her sheep breeding program, illustrating the characteristics of different types of fiber with bits and pieces of yarn and fleece she has collected over the years. Her first sheep were hardy mixed-breed animals from North Haven Island, Maine. Their fleece was adequate, but had limited lanolin content and did not have all the qualities Nanney wanted in her fiber. Wanting to add some resilience and a lot more softness to her fleeces, Nanney crossed the island sheep with Australian Merinos. The result was a wonderful flock of hardy, small, easy-to-handle sheep with superior fleeces: "Sort of like the Shetland sheep of Maine!" After a few years Nanney then introduced some Border Leicester to give her fleeces more length and luster. Showing us various samples, Nanney explained that luster is how the fiber "catches the light." The yarn she produces now has "memory with integrity"—it is easy to work with, but holds its shape when knit into a garment.

Dumping a huge skein of chunky-spun, chocolate brown yarn in my lap, Nanney remarked, "This is what I call boyfriend yarn." I must have looked at her blankly because she went on to explain, "You know—girls want to knit a sweater for their boyfriend but want it to be done in a reasonable amount of time." I got it, and laughed. "The sweater is usually the kiss of death, though," added Nanney, and I laughed even more.

Nanney's experience with sheep comes from working on large sheep farms, one in New Zealand and several in New England. She loved the lifestyle and decided that it was what she wanted for herself and sons. "The economics need to make sense for me, though. It can't just be a fancy hobby." Besides selling about seven hundred pounds of yarn a year from her flock of 125 sheep, she also makes and sells an organic sausage, seasoning it with herbs she grows herself. Just hearing Nanney describe the work on the farm, let alone all the dyeing, was enough to make me tired. She wears a small air cast just below her right elbow; overuse of that arm has led to tendinitis.

Rather than adding salt and other mordants, Nanney uses sea water for dyeing, hauling it from the coast, about thirty minutes away, in five-gallon buckets. It is understandable why she is so careful to reuse the water from each dye bath as much as possible. Her yarn is dyed in two-pound lots, which when wet weigh considerably more. All that lifting and hauling is done solely with Nanney's right arm. With a broad smile and the ever present twinkle in her eye, she quips, "You know, I don't have a bunch of shepherds working for me!"

Next we headed out to Nanney's open-air "studio" to see her unusual dyeing process. Nanney capped off the foundation of her former farmhouse, which burned to the ground seven and a half years ago, creating a platform with plywood and black roll roofing. Several cold frames are lined up there, as well as an old claw foot bathtub, a drying rack, one big barrel of sea water and another of fresh, and many large pails. The bathtub is plumbed into the old septic system and is used for disposal of used water from the dye baths. Showing us the cold frames, Nanney explained that the same frames are used in her vegetable garden before and after the dyeing season. Her specialized dyeing method starts with cold water. The wet wool is packed into black plastic bags that are put into the cold frames to be solar heated.

Nanney demonstrated with some skeins of yarn she'd decided to re-dye because they were "ugly." She threw one skein into a pail already filled with water from an exhausted

NANNEY'S OUTDOOR DYEING STUDIO. KENNETH STRICK.

dye bath that still had some color left in it, then added powdered dye. As she swirled the skeins around to mix the dye, she told me she used to do all this without wearing gloves! "My hands were a different color every day of the week," she laughed. (After her doctor warned of the hazards, she started wearing rubber gloves, and is careful to hold her breath when sprinkling the dye.) When the color of the re-dyed wool was to her liking, she lifted the whole batch out of the pail and put it in a black plastic bag. (I could see why she developed tendinitis.) Pouring some of the dye bath into the bag with the yarn, she then hefted the bag into a cold frame. With warm temperatures and bright sunlight, a batch needs only one day of "cooking," but other times it can take three or four days.

Nanney uses no precise formulas or schedules; everything depends on the amount of water and dye, and the temperature of the day. There is no such thing as a disaster; if the yarn color is not right after a certain time, it can always be overdyed. When the color is deemed OK by Nanney's standards, she lifts the yarn out of the bag and hangs it on the drying rack with a pail underneath to catch the drips. After the yarn is rinsed in fresh water and put through the spin cycle of the washing machine several times, it goes back on the rack for the final drying.

It boggled me to see how nonchalantly Nanney sprinkled, poured, mixed, and dunked. It reminded me of how I loved to play at the kitchen sink as a child, mixing and pouring soapy water back and forth between glasses and pans. My mother used to call it "mishing and gishing." When I related this to Nanney, she put her hands on her hips and said with a laugh, "Candace, this is mishing and gishing to the *max*!"

Out of the corner of my eye I'd been watching Ben and Amos, Nanney's two sons, flying through the air as they bounced on their new trampoline. Their obvious fun captured my attention, and I asked if I could take a turn. One year (and four surgeries) earlier, I had badly injured my leg and ankle in an accident, yet I knew I had to try this. What a feeling of total abandonment and freedom! The boys joined in my giggling, then we all urged Ken to try it too. These two friendly and outgoing boys (the "Sons" of Nanney's business name) share their mother's love of life.

I arrived back on the ground to find Nanney preparing an undyed skein. She first soaked it in fresh water mixed with a little dishwashing detergent. When it was wet enough, she added vinegar to the water, then started putting in the dye powder. After it sat for awhile, she poured the sea water into the bag and set it in the cold frame. (Another method she sometimes uses is to put the wet hank into a black plastic bag and then sprinkle the dye powder directly on the yarn. For another effect, she will pour the vinegar directly on the yarn in a striped pattern.)

It all depends on what Nanney wants that day. She works intuitively, building on years of practice. She can duplicate a skein closely, but never exactly—but then she doesn't want to. New England weather can affect the results differently each day, but Nanney respects and enjoys this element of chance. "The effect will always be dependent on Mother Nature herself. I aspire to work *with* her rather than control her." Each dye lot is a limited edition; each skein a one-of-a-kind

NANNEY KENNEDY WITH A FEW OF HER HAND-DYED COLORS. CANDACE STRICK.

masterpiece. Nanney draws her inspiration from many sources: a walk in the woods, the ocean at sunset, an unusual rock, a bit of seaweed. A boat ride on the lake produces an idea for one skein, a fall leaf, another. "It's all about translating a moment into colors on yarn," she explained, "and for the inspired knitter, it provides the material to create your own moment."

"In this world of mall mentality, there is just no soul in anything anymore," Nanney lamented. After spending the afternoon with her, and watching her work and talk about what she loves, I now know exactly where Nanney's soul resides.

Rockport Gansey

A textured design with little open eyelets next to each shell, lacy cables, and a star design on the yoke make this sweater fun and interesting to knit. This sweater is worked in the round up to the armholes, then worked back and forth. The sleeves are knit in the round from the cuff to the shoulder, then set into the body. (Pictured on page 19. The sweater on the left is in Meadowcroft's Olive yarn.)

YARN
Meadowcroft Farm hand-dyed yarn (3.5 oz/200 yd skeins), 7–7–8 skeins Olive.

NEEDLES
#5 and #7 circular (24-inch), #5 and #7 circular (16-inch), #7 double-pointed. *(See page 10 for equivalent metric and Canadian needle sizes.)*

GAUGE
18 sts and 26 rows = 4 inches worked over yoke pattern.

FINISHED SIZES (IN INCHES)
Small	41.5
Medium	45
Large	48

(For information on converting measurements and skein weights to metric equivalents, see page 6.)

ABBREVIATIONS
C6F—Cable 6 front. Slip 3 sts to a cable needle and hold in front of work, K3 sts, then knit the 3 sts from the cable needle.

C6B—Cable 6 back. Slip next 3 sts to cable needle and hold in back of work, knit next 3 sts, then knit the 3 sts from cable needle.

PSSO—Pass slipped stitch over.

YO—Yarn over.

Patterns

Note for size Medium: Due to the pattern repeats, the Medium sweater has a 7-st chevron design panel at each side "seam" that begins in the ribbing and continues up to the armhole break. The size Medium directions given below include the sts for the chevron panel. At the beginning of the rnd, the chevron design will be worked on the first 4 sts, the next 91 sts will be worked in pattern, the last 3 sts before and the 4 sts following the next marker will be worked in chevron design, the next 91 sts will be worked in pattern, the last 3 sts will be worked in chevron design. *(It is easier to follow the pattern if you place a second marker halfway (98 sts) into the round. This will divide your work into front and back.)*

Seven-Stitch Rib, sizes Small and Large
Rnd 1: *K1, P1, K3, P1, K1*; repeat between *s.
Rnd 2: *K1, P5, K1*; repeat between *s.
Repeat these two rnds for pattern.

Seven-Stitch Rib, size Medium
Rnd 1: *P1, K3, [K1, P1, K3, P1, K1] 13 times, K3*; repeat between *s.
Rnd 2: *K1, P1, K2, [K1, P5, K1] 13 times, K2, P1*; repeat between *s.
Rnd 3: *K2, P1, K1, [K1, P1, K3, P1, K1] 13 times, K1, P1, K1*; repeat between *s.
Rnd 4: *K3, P1, [K1, P5, K1] 13 times, P1, K2*; repeat between *s.
Repeat these 4 rnds for pattern, ending ribbing with a completed rnd 4.

Little Shell pattern, sizes Small and Large
Rnds 1, 2, and 3: Knit.
Rnd 4: *K1, bring yarn to the front and around needle, P1, P3 together, P1, yarn over needle, K1*; repeat between *s.

Little Shell pattern plus Chevron, size Medium
Rnd 1: *P1, K3, K91, K3*; repeat between *s.
Rnd 2: *K1, P1, K2, K91, K2, P1*; repeat between *s.
Rnd 3: *K2, P1, K1, K91, K1, P1, K1*; repeat between *s.
Rnd 4: K3, P1, work the 7-st repeat of rnd 4 for sizes Small and Large 13 times, P1, K2*; repeat between *s.

Side Pattern I
Row 1 (right side): Knit.
Row 2: *K1, P1*; repeat between *s 8 times for size Large, 6 times for Medium. *For size Small, *P1, K1* ; repeat between *s 4 times, end P1.

Side Pattern II
Row 1 (right side): Knit.
Row 2: *P1, K1*; repeat between *s 8 times for size Large, 6 times for Medium. *For size Small, *P1, K1*; repeat between *s 4 times, end P1.

Lace Cable I
Row 1: K4, K2 together, YO, K2.
Row 2 and all even-numbered rows: Purl.
Row 3: K3, k2 together, YO, K3.
Row 5: K2, K2 together, YO, K4.
Row 7: K1, K2 together, YO, K5.
Row 9: K2 together, YO, C6F.
Row 10: Purl.
Repeat these 10 rows.

Lace Cable II
Row 1: K2, YO, slip 1, K1, PSSO, K4.
Row 2 and all even numbered rows: Purl.
Row 3: K3, YO, slip 1, K1, PSSO, K3.

Row 5: K4, YO, slip 1, K1, PSSO, K2.
Row 7: K5, YO, slip 1, K1, PSSO, K1.
Row 9: C6B, YO, slip 1, K1, PSSO.
Row 10: Purl.
Repeat these 10 rows.

Garter Stitch: When working in the round, knit 1 rnd, purl 1 rnd. When working back and forth, knit every row.

BODY: With #5 circular needle (24-inch) cast on 182–196–210 sts. Join and place a marker. Work in Seven-Stitch Rib for your size for 2.5–2.5–3 inches, ending with a completed rnd 4 for size medium. Change to #7 needle.

Work the 4 rnds of Little Shell pattern for your size for 10–11–12 inches, ending with a completed rnd 1. Next rnd: Knit 91–98–105 sts, place a marker, knit remaining 91–98–105 sts to original marker. (If you have followed the advice in the note about size Medium, this step is already taken care of.)

Work rnds 1 through 20 of CHART A, working the 91–98–105 sts across the front, then beginning again at right side of chart for the 91–98–105 sts of back.

Rnd 21: Divide for armholes: work to 3–4–3 sts before second marker, cast off next 6–7–6 sts, work to 3–4–3 sts before original marker, cast off next 6–7–6 sts.

Places sts for back on a holder.

FRONT: Work back and forth on the circular needle. Remember to read right-side (odd-numbered) rows from *right to left* and wrong-side (even numbered) rows from *left to right*.

Row 1: Work the first 16–12–9 sts in Side Pattern I, work row 1 of CHART B, work remaining 16–12–9 sts in Side Pattern II.

Row 2: Work row 2 of Side Pattern and row 2 of chart.

Continue working the 2 rows of Side Pattern, following Chart B for center panel up through row 44.

Shape front neck: On row 45, work 31–34–38 sts, place the next 23 sts on a holder for front neck. Leave remaining 31–34–38 sts on a spare needle. Work each side separately.

Left Front: Work one row. Starting on row 47, decrease 1 st at neck edge every other row 6 times. Work remaining 6 rows of chart, working last 2 rows of Side Pattern as knit. Place remaining 25–28–32 sts on holder for shoulder.

Right Front: Attach yarn. Work rows 45 and 46. Work remainder same as left front.

BACK: With right side facing, attach the yarn. Place the sts back on the circular needle and work as for front, disregarding front neck shaping. Work through row 60

Row 61: Work 25–28–32 sts, place middle 35 sts on a holder for back neck, leave remaining 25–28–32 sts on a spare needle. Working each side separately, complete remaining 2 rows of chart, working Side Pattern as knit. Place 25–28–32 sts on holders for shoulders.

JOIN SHOULDERS: Using the knitted seam method (page 11), join shoulders by holding work wrong side to wrong side.

NECK: With #5 circular (16-inch), and starting at right shoulder seam, pick up and knit 2 sts down right back, knit the 35 sts from back neck holder, pick up and knit 2 sts up left back to shoulder seam, pick up and knit 14 sts down left front, knit the 23 sts from front neck holder, pick up and knit 15 sts up right front neck to shoulder seam. Place a marker. (91 sts.) Work in the following rib pattern for 1.5 inches.

Rnd 1: K3, P1, K1, [K1, P1, K3, P1, K1] 12 times, K1, P1.
Rnd 2: P4, K1, [K1, P5, K1] 12 times, K1, P1.
Repeat these 2 rnds for pattern. Bind off loosely in knit.

SLEEVES: With #5 double-pointed needles cast on 44 sts, marking off the last stitch as the underarm stitch. For cuff, work in the following rib pattern for 2.5–2.5–3 inches.

Rnd 1: K2, P1, K1, [K1, P1, K3, P1, K1] 5 times, K1, P1, K2, knit underarm stitch.
Rnd 2: P3, K1, [K1, P5, K1] 5 times, K1, P3, knit underarm stitch.
Repeat these 2 rnds for rib pattern.

Change to #7 needles and commence Little Shell pattern and increases for sleeve:

Rnds 1 and 2: Knit.

Rnd 3: Increase in first stitch of rnd, knit to one stitch before underarm stitch, increase in this stitch, knit underarm stitch (46 sts).

Rnd 4: Yarn over needle, P3 together, P1, yarn over needle, K1, [K1, bring yarn to the front around needle, P1, P3 together, P1, yarn over needle, K1] 5 times, K1, bring yarn to the front around needle, P1, P3 together, P1, yarn over needle, knit underarm stitch.

Repeat these 4 rnds 9–8–8 times more, working the 2 extra sts into the Little Shell pattern on the increase rnd.

Then work increases on rnd 3 of *every other* repeat of the 4-rnd pattern 3–3–6 times.

Next, work increases on every *third* repeat of the 4-rnd pattern 1–1–0 time. (19–19–21 shells made; 72–72–74 sts.)

Note: For every P3 together you do, you must make up those two extra stitches by doing yarn overs. For example, if the rnd begins with a P3 together, you must remember to first bring the yarn forward and over the needle.

(When you have enough stitches, switch to the 16-inch circular needle for easier knitting.)

Knit 2 rnds, increasing 1 st at beginning and end of second rnd *for sizes S and M only.* (74 sts.)

Work the 21 rnds of CHART C.

Next rnd: Knit to the last 5 sts before the end of the round; cast off these 5 sts (this includes the underarm stitch). (69 sts.)

Next rnd: Cast of the first 4 sts of the round, work to end of rnd in K1, P1.

Working *back and forth* in the following 2-row pattern, bind off 4 sts at the beginning of the next 12 rows:

Row 1 (wrong side): Purl.
Row 2 (right side): *K1, P1*; repeat between *s.
Bind off remaining 17 sts.

FINISHING: Matching top of sleeve cap to shoulder seam, and underarm stitch of sleeve to side "seam" of sweater, sew sleeves to body of sweater. Weave in any loose ends. Steam lightly.

MEASUREMENTS IN INCHES

A. 41.5–45–48
B. 2.5–2.5–3
C. 10–11–12
D. 10–10–10
E. 17–17–18.5
F. 2.5–2.5–3

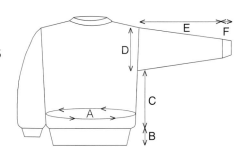

KEY FOR CHARTS

I	Knit
–	Purl
☉	Knit on wrong side; purl on right side
	Stockinette stitch

NUMBERS IN CHART B REFER TO ROW NUMBERS OF LACE CABLE PATTERN.

CHART A: **LOWER BODY**

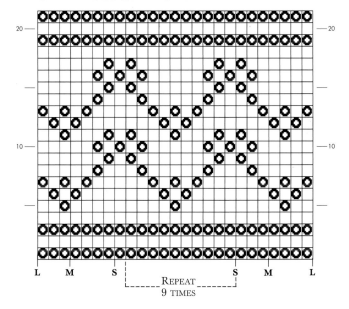

L   M   S   ⌐–––––––––––––¬   S   M   L
REPEAT
9 TIMES

CHART C: **SLEEVE**

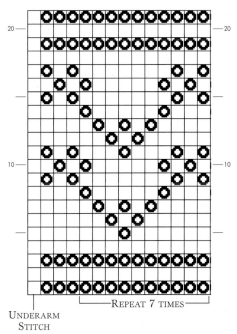

UNDERARM
STITCH

REPEAT 7 TIMES

CHART B: **UPPER BODY**

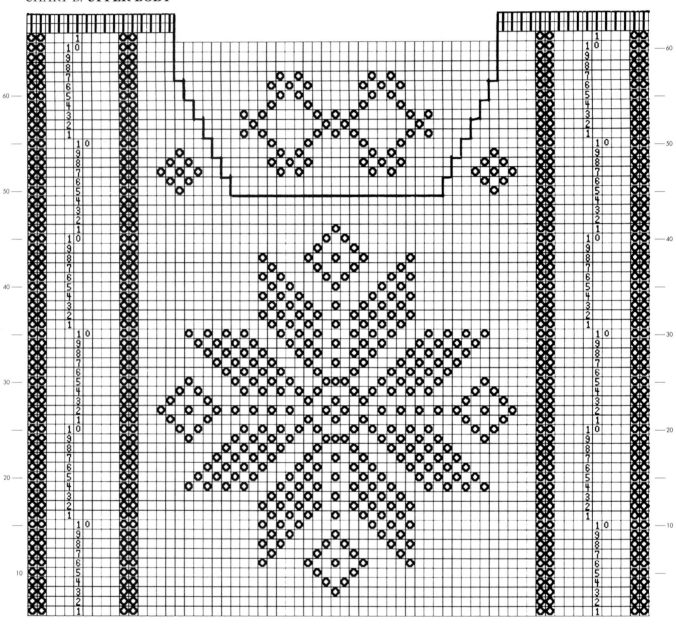

LACE CABLE II   LACE CABLE I

Camden Gansey

Make this gansey in any color. Knit in the round up to the arm-holes, it is then worked back and forth on the yoke pattern. The sleeves are worked from the shoulders to the cuff. There are no seams to sew. It's a perfect combination of interesting and easy! (Pictured on page 16.)

YARN

Meadowcroft Farm Seacolors Yarn (3.5 oz/200 yd skein), 7-7-8 skeins Blue.

NEEDLES

#5 and #7 circular (24-inch and 16-inch), #7 single-pointed, #5 and #7 double-pointed. *(See page 10 for equivalent metric and Canadian needle sizes.)*

GAUGE

17 sts and 27 rnds = 4 inches worked in stockinette stitch on #7 needles; 18 sts and 33 rows = 4 inches worked in yoke pattern on #7 needles

FINISHED SIZES (IN INCHES)

Small   42.5
Medium   45.5
Large   49.5

(For information on converting measurements and skein weights to metric equivalents, see page 6.)

ABBREVIATIONS

SSK—Slip 2 stitches, one at a time, from left needle to right needle. Insert left needle into the fronts of these 2 sts and knit them together.

Patterns

Stockinette Stitch: When working in the round, knit every rnd. When working back and forth, knit the right-side rows and purl the wrong-side rows.

Texture Pattern: The symbols on the chart are worked as purl stitches when working in the round. When working back and forth, they are worked as purl stitches on the right side, and knit stitches on the wrong side. (Explained in charts key.)

BODY: With #5 circular needle cast on 160-175-192 sts. Join and place a marker, which will be referred to as first marker. Work in K2, P2 ribbing for 1.5-2-2.5 inches, increasing 22-19-18 sts evenly spaced on the last rnd. (182-194-210 sts.) Purl the next 2 rnds, dividing the work in half by placing a marker (which will be referred to as second marker) after 91-97-105 sts. Change to #7 circular needle.

Following rnd 1 of CHART A and *beginning at the right-hand side of the chart at your size indication, work the 91-97-105 sts of the chart for the front, ending at your size indication at the left-hand side of the chart.* Repeat between *s for the back. Work rnd 2 of chart.

Repeat rnds 1 and 2 of Chart A until entire piece measures 16-17-18 inches.

Note: Only size Large will have a complete pattern repeat under the arms. On sizes Small and Medium, the panel of stockinette stitch under each arm will be slightly wider than those across the rest of the body. Each time you work around to a marker, remember to begin again at the point indicated on the right side of the chart.

Work rnds 3 through 8 of Chart A.

DIVIDE FOR ARMHOLES: Following rnd 9 of Chart A, work to 3 sts before second marker. Cast off the next 6 sts. Work to 3 sts before first marker, cast off the next 6 sts.

Do not break yarn. Leave the remaining stitch on the needle. (85-91-99 sts *each* for front and back.)

FRONT: Work now progresses back and forth. Use a single-pointed #7 needle to work the stitches off the circular needle, or use the circular needle and put the stitches for the back on a holder. Slip the first stitch that was left on the needle from the underarm cast off. Work rows 10 through 12 from Chart A 16-16-14 times on the 85-91-99 sts of the front.

Shape Front Neck: Following row 19-19-13 of chart, work 33-36-38 sts, place the middle 19-19-23 sts on a holder for front neck, attach another ball of yarn and work the remaining 33-36-38 sts. Working both sides at once, work row 20-20-14. Beginning on row 21-21-15, decrease 1 st at neck edge every other row 6-6-4 times, every third row 0-0-2 times, and every fourth row 2-2-3 times. Work 6 rows even. Place remaining 25-28-29 sts for each shoulder on a holder.

BACK: Work as for front, disregarding front neck shaping and repeating rows 10 through 12 from CHART A 25 times.

Shape Back Neck: Following row 43 of CHART A, work 25-28-29 sts, place middle 35-35-41 sts on a holder for back neck, attach another ball of yarn and work remaining 25-28-29 sts. Working both sides at once, work 2 more rows. Place remaining 25-28-29 sts for each shoulder on a holder.

JOIN SHOULDERS: Use the knitted seam method to join the shoulders with a flat, invisible seam (page 11).

NECK: With #5 circular needle (16-inch) and beginning at right-back shoulder, pick up and knit 4 sts down the right back, knit the 35–35–41 sts from back-neck holder, pick up and knit 4 sts up the left front to the shoulder seam, pick up and knit 15–15–20 sts down left front, knit the 19–19–23 from front-neck holder, pick up and knit 15–15–20 sts up right front to shoulder seam. Place a marker. (92–92–112 sts.) Purl 2 rnds. Work in K2, P2 ribbing for 1 inch. Purl 1 rnd. Bind off in purl.

SLEEVES: With #7 circular needle (16-inch) and beginning at underarm, pick up and knit 47 sts to shoulder, pick up and knit another 46 sts to underarm, place a marker, pick up and knit 1 stitch, place a marker. (94 sts.)

The stitch between the markers is the underarm st and is always worked in knit. All decreasing is done on either side of this stitch as follows: K2 together at beginning of rnd, work to 2 stitches before marker, SSK, work underarm stitch in knit.

Work rnds 1 through 6 of CHART B.

The rest of the sleeve pattern is done by repeating rnds 7 and 8. Decreasing is worked within the established pattern.

Round 7: Decrease 1 st at beginning and end of the rnd,

then every fourth rnd 6 times (80 sts), then every seventh rnd 10 times. (60 sts.) Work 0–7–14 rnds even. Change to #5 double-pointed needles. For the remainder of the sleeve, work the underarm stitch in pattern.

Purl 1 rnd, decreasing 20–20–16 sts evenly spaced. (40–40–44 sts.) Purl 1 rnd. Work in K2, P2 ribbing for 1.5–2–2.5 inches. Purl 1 rnd. Bind off in purl.

FINISHING: Weave in any loose ends. Steam gently.

MEASUREMENTS IN INCHES

A. 42.5–45.5–49.5
B. 1.5–2–2.5
C. 14.5–15–15.5
D. 10
E. 16–16–17
F. 1.5–2–2.5

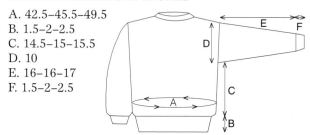

KEY FOR CHARTS

✗	Purl in the round; when working back and forth, purl on right side, knit on wrong side.
☐	Stockinette Stitch

CHART B: SLEEVE

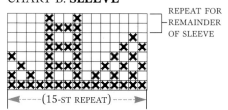

REPEAT FOR REMAINDER OF SLEEVE

←-----(15-ST REPEAT)-----→

CHART A: BODY

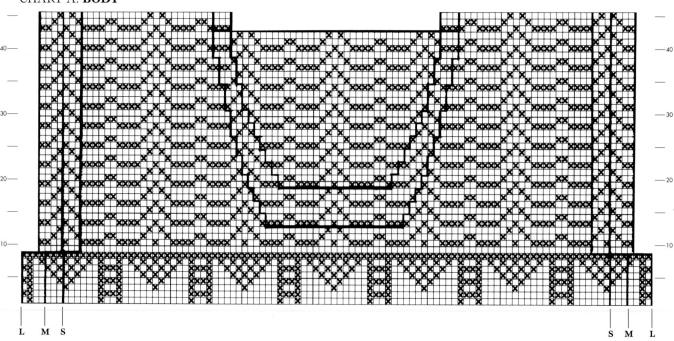

Meadowcroft Gansey

This hard-working Maine gansey has little cables made by working right and left twists. It is worked in the round up the armholes, and the sleeves are picked up around the shoulders and worked down to the cuff. (Pictured on page 12.)

YARN

Meadowcroft Seacolors yarn (100gm/200yd skein), 7-7-8 skeins Warm Cranberry.

NEEDLES

#6 and #8 circular (24-inch *and* 16-inch), #8 single-pointed, #6 and #8 double-pointed. *(See page 10 for equivalent metric and Canadian needle sizes.)*

GAUGE

16 sts and 24 rows = 4 inches worked in stockinette stitch on #8 needles.

FINISHED SIZES (IN INCHES)

Small   44.5
Medium   47.5
Large   51.5

(For information on converting measurements and skein weights to metric equivalents, see page 6.)

ABBREVIATIONS

SSK—(Slip, Slip, Knit.) Slip 2 stitches, one at a time, from left needle to right needle. Insert left needle into the fronts of these 2 sts and knit them together.

RT—(Right twist.) Knit 2 stitches together then knit the first again. Slip both sts from needle together.

LT—(Left twist.) Skip 1 st and knit through the back loop of the second st; knit both stitches through the back loops and slip them from the needle together.

M1—(Make 1 stitch.) Lift the horizontal thread between the stitches onto the left-hand needle and knit it (or purl it) through the back loop.

Patterns

Stockinette Stitch: When working in the round, knit every round; when working back and forth, knit the right side, purl the wrong side.

BODY: With #6 circular needle cast on 168-176-196 sts. Join and place a marker, which will be referred to as first marker.

Work ribbing for your size as follows:

Small: Rnd 1: *K2, P2, RT, LT, [(P2, K2) 2 times, P2, RT, LT] 5 times, P2 , K2, P2*, place a marker (referred to as second marker); repeat between *s.

Medium: Rnd 1: *(K2, P2) 2 times, RT, LT, [(P2, K2) 2 times, P2, RT, LT] 5 times, P2, K2, P2*, place a marker (referred to as second marker); repeat between *s.

Large: Rnd 1: *LT, [(P2, K2) 2 times, P2, RT, LT] 6 times, (P2, K2) 2 times, P2, RT*, place a marker (referred to as second marker); repeat between *s.

Rnds 2 and 3 (all sizes): Work in established pattern, but working K4 over every RT, LT.

Repeat these 3 rnds 4-5-6 times, then work rnds 1 and 2.

Keeping in pattern as for rnd 3, work the increase rnd for your size as follows:

Small: *Increase 1 st in each of next 2 sts, (P2, K4, P2, K2, P2, M1, K2) 5 times, P2, K4, P2, K2, P2*; repeat between *s. (182 sts.)

Medium: *K2, P2, M1, K2, M1, (P2, K4, P2, K2, P2, M1, K2) 5 times, P2, K4, P2, K2, M1, P2*; repeat between *s. (194 sts, 18 increases made.)

Large: *K2, P2, K2, P2, M1, K2, (P2, K4, P2, K2, P2, M1, K2) 5 times, P2, K4, P2, K2, P2, M1, K2, P2, K2*; repeat between *s. (210 sts.)

Change to #8 needle and commence pattern as follows:

Rnd 1: *(LT, P2 for Large only), K4-8-7, P2, RT, LT, P2, (K7, P2, RT, LT, P2) 5 times, K4-8-7, (P2, RT for Large only)*; repeat between *s.

Rnds 2 and 3: *(K2, P2 for Large only), K4-8-7, P2, K4, P2, (K7, P2, K4, P2) 5 times, K4-8-7, (P2, K2 for Large only)*; repeat between *s.

Repeat these 3 rnds until *entire* piece measures 14.5-15.5-16.5 inches, ending with a completed rnd 2.

(Purl 1 rnd, knit 1 rnd) 2 times, then work rnds 1 through 11 from CHART A.

DIVIDE FOR ARMHOLES: Following chart for rnd 12, work to 3 sts before second marker. Cast off the next 6 sts. Work to 3 sts before first marker, cast off the next 6 sts.

Do not break yarn. Leave the remaining stitch on the needle. (85-91-99 sts *each* for front and back.)

FRONT: Work now progresses back and forth on single-pointed needles. Use a single-pointed #8 needle to work the stitches off the circular needle, slipping the first stitch that was left on the needle from the underarm cast-off. Leave the stitches for the back on the circular needle or put on a holder.

Repeat rnds 13 through 24 of Chart A three times.

Shape Front Neck: Following row 13, work 34-37-39 sts, place the middle 17-17-21 sts on a holder for front neck, attach another ball of yarn and work the remaining 34-37-39 sts. Working both sides at once and beginning on row 14, decrease 1 st at neck edge every row 3 times, every other row 3 times, and every third row 2-2-3 times. Work 2 rows even. Place the remaining 26–29–30 sts for each shoulder on a holder.

BACK: Work as for Front, disregarding front neck shaping and repeating rows 13 through 24 four times.

For sizes Small and Medium, work rows 25 through 28; *for size Large,* work rows 25 through 31.

Back Neck Shaping: Following row 29–29–32 of Chart A, work 26–29–30 sts, place middle 33–33–39 sts on a holder for back neck, attach another ball of yarn and work remaining 26–29–30 sts. Working both sides at once, work 2 more rows. Place the remaining sts for each shoulder on a holder.

JOIN SHOULDERS: Use the knitted seam method described on page 11.

NECK: With #6 circular needle (16-inch) and beginning at right back shoulder, pick up and knit 4 sts down the right back; knit the 33–33–39 sts from back neck holder as K16–16–19, K2 together, K16–16–19; pick up and knit 4 sts up the left front to the shoulder seam; pick up and knit 17–17–20 sts down left front; knit the 17–17–21 sts from front neck holder as K8–8–10, K2 together, K7–7–9; pick up and knit 17–17–20 sts up right front to shoulder seam. Place a marker. (90–90–102 sts.)

Purl 1 rnd; knit 1 rnd; purl 1 rnd.

Work the following 3 rnds 3 times, then work rnd 1 again. Bind off loosely in pattern.

Rnds 1 and 2: *P2, K4*; repeat between *s.

Rnd 3: *P2, RT, LT*; repeat between *s.

SLEEVES: With #8 circular needle (16-inch) and beginning at middle underarm, pick up and knit 40–40–42 sts to shoulder, pick up and knit another 39–39–41 sts to underarm, place a marker, pick up and knit 1 stitch, place a marker. (80–80–84 sts.)

The stitch between the markers is the underarm stitch and is always worked in knit. All decreasing is done on either side of this stitch as follows: K2 together at beginning of rnd, work to 2 stitches before marker, SSK, work underarm stitch in knit.

(Purl 1 rnd, knit 1 rnd) 2 times.

To read Chart B (sleeve chart): Work begins at the right-hand side of chart at first vertical decrease line. Work the stitches from the line to left side of the chart, then work the full 15-st repeat until the stitches in the rnd are used up. *Decreases are shown only for the beginning of the rnd. Do not forget to do them at end of rnd also.*

Following CHART B, work rnd 1. Beginning on rnd 2, de-

crease 1 st at beginning of rnd, and 1 st at end of rnd every sixth rnd 9–9–10 times. (62–62–64 sts.) Work 1–1–4 rnds even. Decreasing is worked within the established pattern. Change to double-pointed needles when necessary.

(K1 rnd, P1 rnd) 2 times.

Rnd 1 (Decrease rnd; establish pattern): K2 together, K2–2–4, *P2, K4, P2, K7*; repeat between *s until 2 sts before marker, SSK, knit underarm st.

Rnd 2: K3–3–5, *P2, LT, RT, P2, K7*; repeat between *s to underarm st.

Rnd 3: K3–3–5, *P2, K4, P2, K7*; repeat between *s to underarm st.

Work in this established pattern, working decreases every sixth row 5–5–4 more times. The decrease rnd will begin with 1 st less of the established pattern each time it is repeated. (50–50–54 sts.)

Work 0–0–5 rnds even in pattern.

Establish ribbing: Decrease rnd: (P2 for L only), (K4, P2, K3, K2 tog,, K2, P2) 3 times, K4, (P2 for L only), knit underarm st. (47–47–49 sts.)

Change to #6 double-pointed needles.

Work the following 3 rnds 5–6–7 times.

Rnd 1: (P2 for L only), (LT, RT, P2, K2, P2, K2, P2) 3 times, LT, RT, (P2 for L only), knit underarm st.

Rnds 2 and 3: (P2 for L only), (K4, P2, K2, P2, K2, P2) 3 times, K4, (P2 for L only), knit underarm st.

Bind off loosely in pattern.

FINISHING: Weave in any loose ends. Steam gently, stretching out stockinette pattern between cable twists on lower section of body and sleeve. Try to not press directly on the cable twists, as this will flatten them out.

MEASUREMENTS IN INCHES

A. 44.5–47.5–51.5
B. 2–2.75–3
C. 14.5–15–15.5
D. 10
E. 16–16–18
F. 2–2.75–3

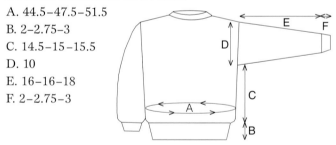

KEY FOR CHARTS

Purl on right side; knit on wrong side.

Stockinette stitch

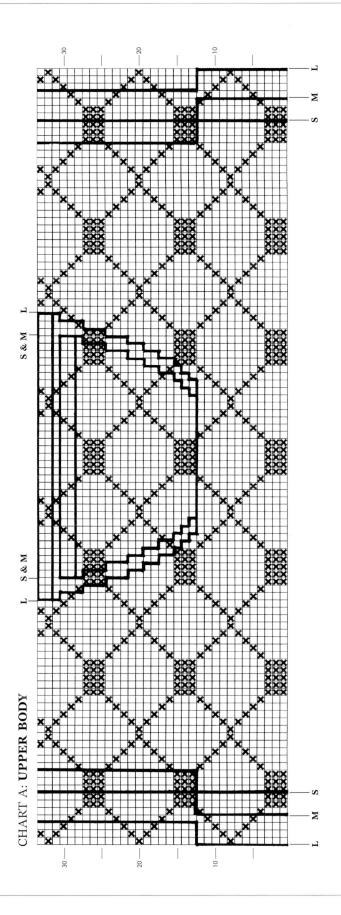

CHART A: **UPPER BODY**

CHART B: **UPPER SLEEVE**

Sizes S & M

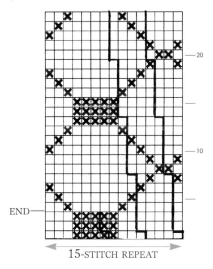

15-STITCH REPEAT

Size L

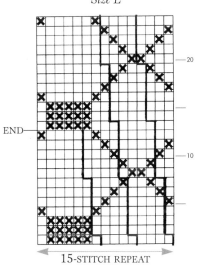

15-STITCH REPEAT

ALICE FIELD

Foxhill Farm

LEE • MASSACHUSETTS

The swirling flakes of a snow squall engulfed us a few miles before our exit as Ken and I drove up to Massachusetts on the Friday following Thanksgiving. By the time we pulled into the driveway of Foxhill Farm things had calmed down a bit, and the last large flakes were falling gently onto the backs of the grazing sheep. Alice Field opened the wire gate across the driveway so we might drive in. Sensibly dressed for the day's weather in a snowmobile jumpsuit, woolen hat, and boots, she was already well into her daily chores, and informed us that she must finish before we started our interview. Not a problem! We parked next to Alice's truck, which has a license plate on the front that reads "Ewe Haul." Laughing at the pun, we followed Alice into one of the barns.

When I had called Alice to set up this interview, she matter-of-factly told me that she was "just a farmer," and wasn't sure what she was supposed to talk about. I told her that I would ask questions if she got tongue tied. But she needn't have worried; from our first greeting to our last good-bye, not a second passed when she was not conveying her love of her sheep, her fiber, and her way of life.

The tidy barn we stepped into was the first proof that she was, indeed, a farmer. Watering the angora rabbits was the last of Alice's chores before she could relax with us. The fluffy guys were content and well cared for, sporting incredible variations of colors. I have always wanted an angora rabbit, and when I mentioned to Alice that I was particularly infatuated with the most colorful one and wanted to take him home, she said, "That can be arranged!"

The next stop was little Benny's pen. Benny, a brown ram was put in sick bay a few days ago. The hay was fresh and clean, and Benny seemed to be feeling much better. All of Alice's animals have names, and many of the sheep recognize when they are being spoken to. One of Alice's main concerns is that her sheep feel perfectly comfortable around people. She often keeps a radio playing for them so they will be used to human voices.

The crowning glory of the barn was the back section, where seven perfect Cormo ewes, each wearing a different colored jacket, were munching hay, their beautiful little faces gazing up as we stroked their foreheads. Cormos are Alice

Field's latest love, and she is working to establish the breed in New England. The Cormo breed's background is one-quarter Lincoln, one quarter Australian Merino, and one half superfine Saxon Merino. Until now, they have been bred and raised mostly in the western United States. Alice drove her Ewe Haul all the way to Montana to buy those seven, making a total of eighteen at the Foxhill Farm. Their wool is fine and soft, making it a handspinner's dream. In fact, spinners love it so much that they buy every ounce Alice has to sell. The jackets the sheep wear protect the wool from farm-yard debris and dirt, keeping it clean so it will require less washing after the shearing.

We moved into another barn, this one just as neat as the first. Here the Romneys were eating hay from Alice's new improved bins. The wire mesh over the feeders allows them to eat freely but cuts down on waste and prevents hay from getting stuck in their fleece. Pointing out her favorite ewe, Emma, Alice told us about her wonderful Romneys. They are a good "people" breed; easy to work with, not flighty, not too big, producing long, lustrous fleeces and mild-flavored meat. She sells many of her lambs to children for 4-H projects, and keeps track of them over the years.

The bred ewes were due to be sheared in December. Shivering, with my gloveless hands jammed in the pockets of my thin jacket, I registered surprise. Alice assured me that the ewes would not be cold, since this shearing would not take off as much wool as a regular one. The ewes were due to lamb soon after shearing, and this shearing would help to keep the mother's fleeces clean: "The first thing a lamb does is jump all over its mother, making her fleece all dirty!"

THE CORMO RAM'S FLEECE, JUST BEFORE SHEARING TIME. ALICE FIELD.

The total number of sheep inhabiting the thirty-plus acres of Foxhill Farm is roughly one hundred. Besides the fiber-producing sheep, goats, and the rabbits, Alice has a horse, four dogs, and seven cats. "In order to make a sheep farm work, you have to have certain numbers just for the genetic base. I consider myself a serious breeder." Before going into the house, we stopped by a fenced-in meadow to meet Mario Cormo (aptly named by Alice's husband), the resident ram who's job is to increase the Cormo flock. As we walked back, I asked Alice if she eats her sheep. "Not my own," she explained, "but I do eat lamb."

Alice's kitten, Scout, greeted us as we entered the house, and proceeded to follow us everywhere. She dove under bags of wool, dragged roving out for our inspection, and rolled in our laps, begging to play. If the stereotype of cats loving to play with balls of yarn is correct, then Scout must be in heaven at Foxhill Farm.

We entered the "wool room," and the fun began! The first thing Alice showed us was a natural colored fleece she was going to spin "in the grease" and uncarded. Alice's fleece is a myriad of different colors, and to comb it all together, she said, would destroy the gorgeous color sequence. We plunged our hands into this wonder, admiring the crimp, it's incredible softness, and the array of color. Without even thinking, I blurted out, "Could I buy it?" At that moment, all I wanted to do was take that glorious fleece to my spinning wheel. This one was Alice's, but she promised me the next fleece from the same sheep. "As soon as the fleece come off the animal at shearing, I immediately know what I want to do with it," Alice explained. "This is just so much fun!"

The next treat was a carton of angora, all carded and dyed, packed in little clear plastic boxes. The colors were breathtaking, and opening the boxes to feel the fiber was the best part of the day: clouds of fluff so soft they were almost weightless. I asked about the dyeing method, and how the colors could be so beautiful. Alice replied, "You just have to have the nerve to throw the dye in!" Dyeing angora can be tricky, though. If the dye bath gets too hot, the fiber gets brittle. It must be processed enough, however, to keep the dye colorfast. Alice's first attempts with dyeing, years ago, were with natural dyes. "I picked every plant on the farm and experimented with colors," she recalled. "It proved to me that if I wanted to do this on a serious basis, I needed to use commercial dyes."

A walk-in closet revealed yarn piled to the ceiling. A brimming basket of hanks held all of Alice's samples, both for color and for fiber composition. Each one was a masterpiece of handspinning and dyeing. Just to make sure she wasn't being ignored, Scout jumped into the basket for a roll. Not a single scrap of fiber is ever wasted in Alice's business. One half of all the wool grown is sold to handspinners, either as a fleece or as roving. Some parts of the fleece are made into slippers or mittens. Single skeins from experimental batches are knit into mittens or sold as kits.

When the skeins come back from being commercially spun, Alice dyes them into her masterpieces. Alice usually opens windows for ventilation when she dyes, and since the temperature hovered around freezing on the day Ken and I visited, she described how she dyes her yarn, rather than showing us. She uses two large stainless steel pots, and does all the work in her kitchen: "I aspire to have a stove outside—someday." The pre-soaked skeins are put into the pots, and the dyes are poured over them, having first been mixed with water. Certain basic formulas must be followed—for example, a certain amount of dye has to be used in order to ob-

tain good results—but the rest is "mostly thinking about what you want. As the temperature comes up, there is a certain amount of natural motion in the dye pot, and this affects the colors and their concentration." As soon as the yarn looks like what she wants, Alice takes it out of the pot. If she were to leave it any longer, any dye that is still left would eventually settle somewhere, ruining the initial effect. The skeins are rinsed in very hot water and then spun damp-dry in the washing machine. A dye lot consists of eight skeins to a pot. By measuring carefully, Alice is able to do two of the same dye lot at once, for a total of sixteen "*almost* identical" skeins.

Picking up Scout and dropping her gently off the kitchen table, Alice talked about how much she loves everything about her life. Throughout our interview, she used the word *fun* many times, as much to describe working with the fiber as taking care of the animals. As a shepherd of over one hun-

MIKE FIELD AND CAPONE—FOXHILL FARM'S MAREMMA SHEEP GUARD DOG— IN THE BARNYARD WITH THE YEARLING ROMNEYS. ALICE FIELD.

dred sheep, Alice is solely responsible for all the farm operations, from cleaning out stalls to lambing, from veterinary care to spinning.

"I wouldn't enjoy the fiber nearly as much if I didn't have the animals. Hauling the hay and shoveling the manure is all part of the yarn, " she observed. "I love it on every level. It's about more than money; it's about the quality of life. Once I got into this, I never looked back. I could never give up doing this. It's just so much fun!"

The snow had stopped falling, and Alice had to start packing the "Ewe-Haul" with her glorious paraphernalia for a show she was doing that afternoon. Ken and I said our good-byes and drove off. During the trip home, I had plenty of time to ponder Alice's description of herself as "just a farmer." Unpretentious and gentle, sheep are at the core of her existence. Without them, there can be no fiber. Without fiber, there can be no fun. To Alice Field, the fun starts right from the beginning.

Turkish Rose

Boxy, bulky, beautiful; it's Turkish curls and zigzags with a touch of beads. No ribbing makes it quick; I-Cord makes the finish. Knit it in a weekend—almost! (Pictured on page 17.)

YARN

Foxhill Farm Bulky 100% wool (4 oz/145 yd skeins), 7-7-8 skeins of Natural Gray

NEEDLES

#10 circular (24- or 32-inch and 16-inch), #10 single-pointed, #10 double-pointed. *(See page 10 for equivalent metric and Canadian needle sizes.)*

NOTIONS

(optional): Sew an assortment of beads into the center of each little diamond down the front of the sweater.

GAUGE

13.5 sts and 20 rows = 4 inches worked over pattern on #10 needle.

FINISHED SIZES (IN INCHES)

Small	40
Medium	44
Large	48

(For information on converting measurements and skein weights to metric equivalents, see page 6.)

Patterns

Stockinette Stitch: When working in the round, knit every round; when working back and forth, knit the right side, purl the wrong side. See chart for texture pattern.

BODY: Cast on 134-150-162 sts. Join and place a marker (referred to as first marker). Knit 1 rnd, placing a marker (referred to as second marker) after 67-75-81 sts.

Beginning on rnd 1-1-27 of CHART A, for sizes S and M, work the 36 rnds of the chart 1 time, then rnds 1 through 35. For size L, work rnds 27 through 36, work the 36 rnds of the chart 1 time, then rnds 1 through 35.

Divide for Armholes: For all sizes, on rnd 36, work to 2 sts before the second marker, bind off the next 4 sts, work to 2 sts before the first marker, bind off the next 4 sts (63-71-77 sts each for front and back). Work now progresses back and forth. (You may leave the stitches of the back on the circular needle, using single-pointed needles to work the front, or you may put the stitches of the back on a holder and use the circular needle to knit back and forth on the front.)

FRONT: Change to CHART B, working rows 1 through 29.

Shape Front Neck: Row 30 (wrong side). Work 27-30-33 sts, work middle 9-11-11 sts and place on a holder for front neck, work remaining 27-30-33 sts. Work each side separately.

Left Front: Work row 31 (right side).

Row 32: Cast off 2 sts at neck edge, then 1 st at neck edge every other row 5 times. (21-23-26 sts.) Work 2 rows even. Place remaining 21-23-26 sts on holder for shoulder.

Right Front: Work as for left front, but beginning shaping on row 31. Work 3 rows even after shaping is completed.

BACK: Work rows 1 through 39 from CHART B.

Shape Back Neck: Row 40 (wrong side). Work 23-26-29 sts, work middle 17-19-19 sts and place on holder for back neck, work remaining 23-26-29 sts. Work each side separately.

Right Side: Beginning on next row (41), decrease 1 st at neck edge every row 3 times. Place remaining 21-23-26 sts on holder for shoulder.

Left Side: Work as for right side.

Note: Back is worked one row *less* than front.

JOIN SHOULDERS: Holding right sides together, join shoulder using the knitted seam method (see page 11).

I-CORD TRIM FOR NECK: Work applied I-Cord around neck. This technique involves knitting a 3-stitch I-cord on double-pointed needles and simultaneously attaching it to the neck of the sweater. Before you can start actually knitting the I-cord, you must first pick up and knit live stitches around the neckline.

Starting at the right back shoulder and using a #10 circular needle (any length), pick up and knit 6 sts down the right back, knit the 17-19-19 live sts from the back neck holder, pick up and knit 6 sts up the left back, pick up and knit 15 sts down the left front, knit the 9-11-11 sts from the front neck holder, and pick up and knit 15 sts up the right front. Leave these stitches on the circular needle for now; they will be worked, one at a time, into the I-cord, which you will now start making with double-pointed needles

Making the I-Cord: Using double-pointed needles and a new skein of yarn, cast on 3 sts. Slip the sts to the right end of one needle and K2, slip 1. Beginning at the right shoulder with the right side of the sweater facing you, knit one stitch from the circular needle and pass the slipped st over it. *Slip the 3 sts to the right end of the needle, knit 2, slip 1, pick up and knit 1 st from the circular needle, pass the slipped stitch over.* Repeat between *s.

When the last stitch has been worked, break the yarn and sew the live sts into the beginning of the I-Cord.

SLEEVES: Work applied I-Cord around sleeve opening in the same manner as the neck edging. You will need to pick up and knit 72 sts around the sleeve opening (36 sts from underarm to shoulder seam, 36 sts from shoulder seam to underarm).

Work applied I-Cord around these 72 sts. Join as for neck.

Unrolling the I-Cord slightly, pick up and knit from the top of the I-Cord—36 sts from underarm to shoulder seam, and 36 sts from shoulder seam to underarm, placing a marker before and after the last st. (72 sts.) This last stitch is the underarm stitch. All decreasing is done on either side of this stitch as follows: K2 together at beginning of rnd, work to 2 sts before marked off underarm st, SSK, knit underarm st.

Work rnds 1 through 4 of sleeve chart. Beginning on next rnd, decrease 1 st at beginning and end of every fourth rnd 19–19–20 times. (34–34–32 sts.) Work 3–3–9 rounds even, ending on rnd 80–80–90. Knit 1 rnd, decreasing 9–9–0 sts evenly spaced. (25–25–32 sts.) Work applied I-Cord around the bottom of the sleeve, using the live sts on the needle.

FINISHING: Work applied I-Cord around the bottom of the sweater, picking up and knitting 134–150–162 sts to use.

MEASUREMENTS IN INCHES

A. 40–44–48
B. 14–14–16
C. 9.5
D. 17–17–18.5

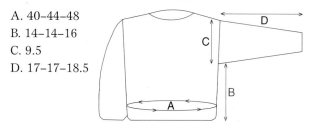

KEY FOR CHARTS

◆ Purl on right side; knit on wrong side.

Right side: knit through back of loop.
Wrong side: purl through back of loop.

All other sts (plain squares) are worked in stockinette stitch: K on right side, P on wrong side.

CHART A: **LOWER BODY**

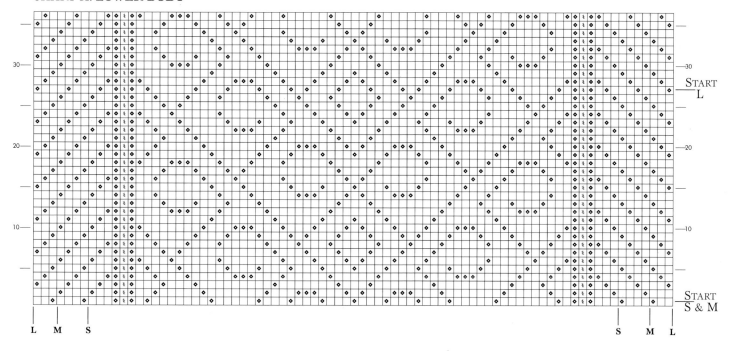

CHART B: **UPPER BODY**

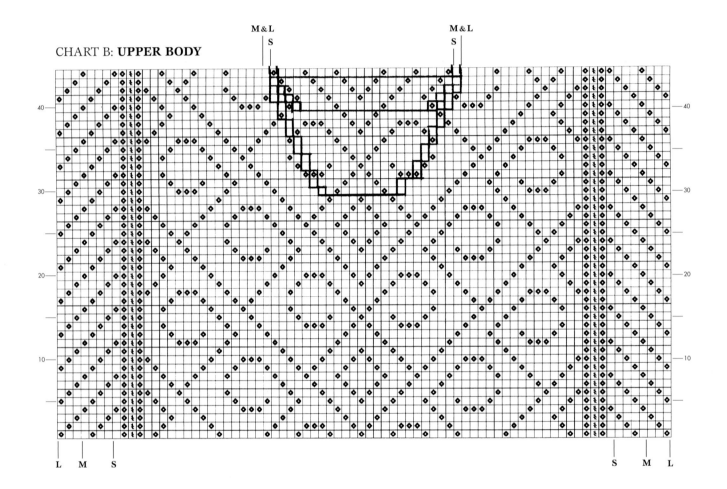

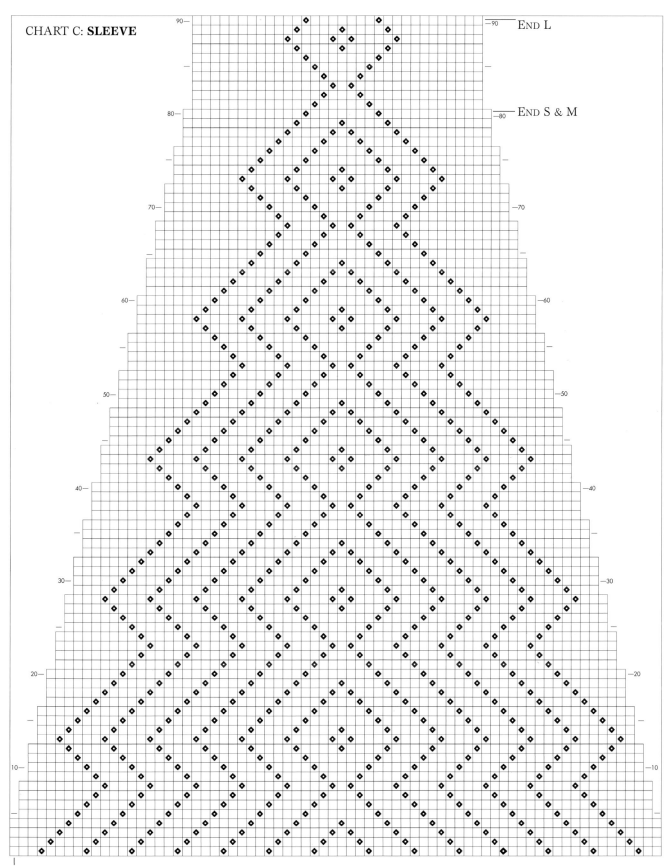

CHART C: **SLEEVE**

END L

END S & M

Foxhill Farm Trellis Jacket

This jacket is designed to fit snugly and come to just the waist-line. Applied I-Cord trim is worked all the way around and into button loops for the closures. (Pictured on page 18.)

YARN

Foxhill Farm Yarn (50% wool, 50% mohair; 4 oz/145 yd skeins)

COLOR	SMALL	MED.	LARGE
A. Light Variegated	3	4	4
B. Dark Variegated	3	4	4

NEEDLES

#5 and #7 single-pointed, #5 double pointed. *(See page 10 for equivalent metric and Canadian needle sizes.)*

GAUGE

18 sts and 25 rows = 4 inches worked over Trellis pattern on #7 needles.

18 sts and 28 rows = 4 inches worked over stockinette stitch on #7 needles.

FINISHED SIZES (IN INCHES)

Small	38.5
Medium	41
Large	43.5

(For information on converting measurements and skein weights to metric equivalents, see page 6.)

ABBREVIATIONS

PUL = pull up loop: Insert point of right-hand needle under the 2 strands of Color B, then knit the next st, at the same time slipping the 2 strands over to the back of the work.

wyif—with yarn in front.

wyib—with yarn in back.

WS—wrong side.

RS—right side.

Patterns

Trellis Stitch: Two-color pattern, multiple of 6 sts plus 5. See instructions below.

Stockinette Stitch: Knit one row, purl one row.

TRELLIS STITCH

Note: In order for the seam to lie flat and have less bulk, 2 edge stitches are worked in stockinette stitch on either side of the trellis pattern. The edge stitch directions are written out only in rows 1 and 2 below. Thereafter, they are understood to be worked on either side of the trellis pattern.

Row 1: (RS) Using COLOR B, knit the 2 edge sts, P4, *wyif slip 3 sts purlwise, P3*; repeat between *s to last stitch before marker, P1, knit the 2 edge sts.

Row 2: Purl the 2 edge sts, K4, *wyib slip 3 sts purlwise, K3*; repeat between *s to last st before marker, K1, purl the 2 edge sts.

(Hereafter, all directions are written for trellis stitch only. Continue to work 2 edge sts on either side of trellis pattern.)

Row 3: Change to COLOR A, knit.

Row 4: Purl.

Row 5: Change to COLOR B, K5, *PUL, K5*; repeat between *s.

Row 6: Purl.

Row 7: Change to COLOR A, P1, *wyif slip 3 sts purlwise, P3*; repeat between *s to last 4 sts, slip 3 sts purlwise, K1.

Row 8: K1, *wyib slip 2 sts purlwise, K3*; repeat between *s to last 4 sts, slip 3 sts purlwise, K1.

Row 9: Change to COLOR B, knit.

Row 10: Purl.

Row 11: Change to COLOR A, K2, *PUL, K5*; repeat between *s to last 3 sts, PUL, K2.

Row 12: Purl.

Repeat these 12 rows for trellis pattern.

Note: When working decreasing for shaping in Trellis pattern, do not work the slip stitches near the ends of rows 1, 2, 7, or 8 unless you will have enough stitches left in successive rows to work the PUL. Instead, just work the slip stitches in stockinette stitch. If the slip stitches *are* worked without there being enough stitches left to work the PUL, there will be funny loops on the right side of the fabric.

BACK: Using COLOR B and #5 needles, cast on 93–99–105 sts. Knit 2 edge sts, place a marker, knit to last 2 sts, place a marker, knit 2 edge sts.

Purl 1 row.

Change to #7 needles and work Trellis pattern until piece measures 9–10–10.5 inches.

Armhole Shaping: Bind off 5 sts at the beginning of the next 2 rows. (83–89–95 sts.)

Keeping the 2 edge sts on either side of pattern and beginning on next row (WS), decrease 1 st at each armhole edge every other row 9 times. (65–71–77 sts.)

Work even in Trellis pattern until armhole measures 9–9.5–9.5 inches.

Bind off 10–11–12 sts at the beginning of the next 2 rows, then 10–12–13 sts at the beginning of the next 2 rows. Slip remaining 25–25–27 sts onto a holder for back neck.

LEFT FRONT: Using COLOR B and #5 needles, cast on 45–51–57 sts. Knit 2 edge sts, place a marker, knit to last 2 sts, place a marker, knit 2 edge sts.

Purl 1 row.

Change to #7 needles and work in Trellis pattern until piece measures 9–10–10.5 inches, ending with a completed WS row.

Armhole Shaping: (RS) Bind off 5 sts at the beginning of the row. Work one row, working the 2 edge sts now after the bind-off section. Beginning on the next row, decrease 1 st at armhole edge every other row 9 times, working the decreases *after* the 2 edge sts.

Work even on 31–37–43 sts until piece measures 6.5–7.5–8 inches, ending with a completed RS row.

Shape Neck: (WS) Work 8–10–12 sts and place on holder for front neck. Beginning on the next row, decrease 1 st at neck edge every other row 3–4–6 times. Work even on 20–23–25 sts until piece measures exact length as back to shoulder shaping, ending on a completed WS row. Bind off 10–11–12 sts at the beginning of the next row. Work one row. Bind off remaining 10–12–13 sts.

RIGHT FRONT: Work as for left front, but reversing all shaping.

SLEEVES: Sleeves are worked in reverse stockinette stitch as 2 rows of COLOR A, 2 rows of COLOR B.

With #5 needles and COLOR A, cast on 48–48–52 sts. Knit 1 row, purl 1 row.

Change to #7 needles and COLOR B. Work in stockinette stitch, changing color every 2 rows and increasing 1 st each side every 8 rows 13–13–14 times. (74–74–80 sts.)

Work 1 row.

Shape Sleeve Cap: Bind off 5 sts at the beginning of the next 2 rows.

Decrease 1 st each side very other row 9 times. Work even on 46–46–52 sts until sleeve cap measures 7–7.5–7.5 inches.

At the beginning and end of the next 3 rows, work 3 sts together (P3 together on purl rows; for knit rows work slip 1 st, k2 together, pass slipped stitch over)

Next row: Bind off as follows: *(K2 together) 2 times, pass first st over second st*; repeat between *s.

FINISHING: Sew shoulder and side seams. Sew underarm sleeve seam so the wrong side of the stockinette pattern is on the outside of the sleeve. Set sleeves into armholes, matching the center of the sleeve cap to the shoulder seam.

APPLIED I-CORD TRIM: The trim is worked in COLOR B around the entire body of the sweater. This technique involves knitting a 3-stitch I-cord on double-pointed needles and simultaneously attaching it around the edge of the sweater. Before you can start actually knitting the I-cord, you must first use the circular needle to pick up and knit live stitches around the edge. *Note: You do not need to pick up and knit all the sts right at the start; you can do a few inches at a time as you proceed around with the applied I-Cord.*

Place 5 pins, evenly spaced, along the edge of the right front as markers for the button loops.

Picking up stitches: With #7 circular needle and COLOR B and beginning at the left shoulder, pick up and knit sts along the edge of the sweater. As you work across the shoulders and the lower edge, you will pick up and knit into each cast-on or cast-off st. When working down the straight edges of the fronts, you will pick up the *second* st from the edge, picking up 3 sts for every 4 along those edges. (This is an approximate number. You will have to adjust as you go in order to make sure the edges will lie flat.)

Making the I-Cord: With #7 double-pointed needles and a separate skein of COLOR B, cast on 3 sts. Knit 3. Slip the sts to the right end of the needle and knit 3. Slip the sts to the right end of the needle and K2, slip 1.

Beginning at the left shoulder with the right side of the sweater facing you, knit one stitch from the circular needle and pass the slipped st over it. *Slip the 3 sts to the right end of the double-pointed needle, knit 2, slip 1, knit 1 st from the circular needle, pass the slipped stitch over.* Repeat between *s, using the stitches from the circular needle (making more when necessary and using the stitches from holders as you come to them).

When turning corners, work 2 rows of knit 3 (without slipping a stitch), then continue as before.

Button Loops: Work the I-Cord to the first pin on the right front edge. Work rows of K3 until the I-Cord is the desired length for a button loop. Work K2, slip 1, then continue with using the picked-up stitches. Repeat for all 5 button loops.

To Finish I-Cord: When the last stitch has been worked, work one row of K3. Break the yarn and sew the live sts into the beginning of the I-Cord. Sew the tail from the beginning of the I-Cord into the shoulder seam to lie flat.

I-Cord for Sleeve Trim: Work I-Cord as above, beginning and ending at the sleeve seam, and picking up and knitting 1 st for each cast-on st on lower sleeve edge.

FINISHING: Steam all seams lightly. Sew on buttons opposite button loops.

MEASUREMENTS IN INCHES

A. 19.25–20.5–21.75
B. 9–10–10.5
C. 9–9.5–9.5
D. 17.5–17.5–18.5

ELLEN MINARD

Ellen's Half-Pint Farm

NORWICH · VERMONT

On the way home from a summer vacation in Quebec City, I stopped in Norwich, Vermont, to interview Ellen Minard—a spinner, dyer, knitter, and farmer. It is quite understandable how Vermont got its nickname of the Green Mountain State; everything from the border of Canada to Massachusetts was lush and green—scene after scene of breathtaking rural beauty. It was easy to romanticize about living a perfect life on a farm here.

Half-Pint Farm sits atop a small hill overlooking a pond, with green rolling hills in the distance. The small, tidy barn is home to Ellen's motley crew of fiber animals—a llama, an alpaca, and a cashmere goat; four sheep (a Dorset, a Rambouillet, and two Romneys), two Angora goats, and an Angora rabbit. Other animals residing at Half-Pint Farm include an Arabian horse, assorted chickens, two dogs, and several cats. Half-Pint Farm's four acres are supplemented by another four acres of fenced pasture on the neighbor's land.

Ellen is petite, soft-spoken, and filled with love for her animals and everyone else's. When she and her husband, Keith Pelton, moved to this land several years ago, her one goal was to have the barn totally finished before they moved. The house could wait for the finishing touches, but the barn was the first priority. In fact, Ellen's love of animals was instrumental in the evolution of her business. Her goal was to make just enough money from spinning and selling hand-dyed yarn to pay for the animals' hay and grain.

The whole concept of the farm began rather abruptly for Ellen and Keith when someone dropped off two goats on their front lawn. Keith built a lean-to on the end of the house for them, but after listening to the goats butt their heads against the house all night, they decided to trade them for some sheep. Fourteen years later, they still have one of those original sheep, Bridget. Although that ewe is now blind and infirm, Ellen loves her too much to even think of getting rid of her. They bred the ewes to a neighbor's ram, and soon had a flock of six. Ellen talks about how much fun it was to have the lambs around, but since neither she nor Keith had the heart to take them to the slaughterhouse, and the barn was only so big, they could not breed the sheep again.

The sheep's fleeces were the incentive for Ellen to start spinning, and she now has a large clientele of people who want custom, hand-spun yarn. She buys fiber from a wholesaler to supplement the yield from her own small flock.

I first met Ellen at the New Boston Wool Festival, where I was drawn to her booth like a magnet by the gorgeous display of hand-dyed skeins of yarn in bright, bold colors. Almost every fiber had equal representation, from wool to silk to alpaca, and each fiber took the dyes and colors somewhat differently. I was anxious to see Ellen's method of dyeing, and as promised, on the day we visited, her kitchen was all set up for dyeing a skein of bouclé in her color called Purple Majesty. The one-pound skein of wool was soaking in a sinkful of water. (The yarn must be wet in order for the fibers to open up and better accept the dye.) A large canning kettle was sitting atop the stove, and the countertop was covered with a large towel that had obviously already seen a lot of dyeing.

Ellen donned a pink sweatshirt covered with dye stains, then a pair of rubber gloves. She showed me the face mask she wears when she mixes the powdered dye with water. Someday she would like a separate dye studio, but for now she has to make do with the kitchen, being very careful to keep anything connected with food preparation out of her way. For her demonstration Ellen had pre-mixed the four colors she was going to use. When I asked her about for-

ELLEN'S YARNS GLOW WITH JEWEL-LIKE COLORS. ELLEN MINARD.

mulas, she replied, "I never measure anything. You don't have to be perfect with this."

She squeezed all the water out of the skein and laid it on a large piece of plastic wrap atop the towel. (Too much water left in the skein will make the dye too runny, and colors will blend together too much. Ellen sometimes puts the skein through the spin cycle of the washing machine to remove excess water.) Picking up the first bottle she poured dye on one part of the skein, kneading with her fingers to distribute the color through the fibers, lifting and turning to make sure no areas were missed. The same color might go on to three different parts of the skein. After pouring the second color, she kneads some more.

Where two colors meet, a third color appears, born from the blending of the two. However, if dye is poured on too heavily, the individual colors will run together and make "mud," so when necessary, Ellen will mop up the excess that has puddled on the plastic wrap. Ellen is extra careful at these intersections, making sure the two colors are well blended. Turning the skein over, she showed me where a color has spread irregularly down the back side. This is good, because when the yarn is knit, the colors will be less likely to build up, creating a splotchy look in the finished knitting. Sometimes Ellen will even make the sections of color asymmetrical to make sure that no blotchy or stripey patterns will result when the yarn is knit. Once the skein is colored to her liking, it is all wrapped up in the plastic, then put on the steaming rack in the kettle and steamed for thirty minutes. After it cools down, Ellen rinses it in the sink until the water runs clear, spins it dry in the washer, and hangs it up to dry. She can usually dye one skein in about five minutes, but the rainbow skeins take longer because they include yellow. The other colors cannot be allowed to run into the yellow sections, so she must take extra care.

While the sample skein was steaming, we sat at the kitchen table and Ellen talked about her work, her life, and her family. Her mother was the inspiration for Ellen's fiber business. She taught knitting and was a designer for a New York City shop. She also wrote all the pattern instructions for designs using Ellen's yarn. "Mom always had about twenty-five sweaters going all the time. There were baskets of knitting all over the house!" Ellen recalled. When her mom first taught her to knit, Ellen had no interest. A few years later, however, she felt the urge to try again and has been knitting ever since.

After taking a class on color theory, Ellen tried her hand at two-color knitting, and "hated it!" This lead her to develop her own skeins dyed with multiple colors. Wanting brighter colors than what was available in either commercially dyed or hand-dyed yarns, she created her special line of colors. (For one of the sweater designs in this book, I asked Ellen to custom dye a solid color for me. Since it was not part of her regular line, it had no name. Once the sweater was finished I asked her to choose a name for the color. After looking at and caressing the sweater for a moment, she said, "Dusty Miller. It was Mom's favorite flower.")

In her "other life," Ellen is a dental hygienist, working ten hours a day, three days a week. This leaves four full days for her to pursue her love of color and dyeing. Before a big show, she starts dyeing at seven a.m., working almost around

SHEEP AND LLAMAS SHARE A BRIGHT, EARLY SPRING DAY BY THE FARM POND. ELLEN MINARD.

the clock. She's careful to stop a few hours before bedtime, however, because the odor of the dye lingers in the house and makes sleeping unpleasant. Ellen and Keith travel to about ten shows a year. Most of them are in New England, but some are as far away as Ohio and Maryland, and they are contemplating going to a show in California. The economic reality that "time is money" is always a factor, but Ellen loves her yarn too much to let it interfere often. "For the hours you put in, the pay is not good," she confided, but in the next breath she declared that she would love to do this full time when she and Keith retire! They travel as a team; Keith drives the van and sets up the booth, and they both stand, side-by-side, selling Ellen's wondrous creations.

Ellen mentioned "the room upstairs." (It seems that all people who love and collect yarn have such a room in their houses.) After her mother's death, Ellen and Keith moved out all the yarn from her mother's house into this upstairs room. When she told me, "You can open the door, but you can't get any further into the room," I thought she might be exaggerating, but she was right! Bags and boxes of yarn fill it from floor to ceiling. Someday it will all get sorted out: some of the sweaters in progress will get finished, and a lot of the yarn will be donated to charity.

In contrast, the room across the hall, which Ellen calls

her shop, is orderly and tidy—a walk-in paradise of color. The back window, overlooking the pond, flooded the room with the last of the afternoon sunlight. I could see the alpaca and the llama grazing peacefully by the pond. Hanks and hanks of Ellen's beautiful creations hung from hooks, wallpapering the room with rainbows of color. I looked at a hank of roving, fluffs of fiber in bands of blues and pinks, and knew an instant desire to feel it slipping between my fingers and flowing onto the bobbin of the spinning wheel. Nearby sat Ellen's wheel, the bobbin filled with the softest alpaca imaginable, impeccably spun. It was a custom order for a woman who planned to knit an afghan from it. "I spend a lot of time in this room," Ellen said. There was no need to explain this to me.

Before I departed, we went to the barn to visit the animals.

DUCKS WAIT THEIR TURN BEHIND THE SHEEP WHEN IT'S TIME TO HEAD INTO THE BARN ON A SNOWY AFTERNOON. ELLEN MINARD.

It was feeding time, and they were more than happy to see us. The llama was friendly but wouldn't allow me to touch him. The angora goats were bolder, and started to nibble my writing tablet! Ellen told me their names and all their individual habits. This is Ellen's turf. Her every movement is for her animals, and her love for them is more than apparent. Bridget, the blind ewe, is kept separate from the others. Ellen spoke lovingly to her, letting Bridget know her whereabouts from her voice. "Good girl, Bridget," she crooned, bending over to pet her. Filling Bridget's bowl with grain, Ellen cut up an apple and placed it on top as a special treat. I was moved to tears by her kindness, wondering why everyone in the world can't be more like this, and I spent the ride home daydreaming of colorful hanks and the perfect little Vermont farm.

Madeira Lace Shawl

There are only a few pattern rows to keep track of on this lace shawl. The magic of it is that it begins with only three stitches, working into an Isosceles right triangle that is turned ninety degrees to wear. (Pictured on page 20.)

YARN
Ellen's Half-Pint Farm Alpaca (83 yds/oz), one 10-oz hank Rain Forest.

NEEDLES
#8 circular (32-inch to accommodate the number of stitches), crochet hook US size 1 or B (2.25 mm). *(See page 10 for equivalent metric and Canadian needle sizes.)*

FINISHED DIMENSIONS
Approximate size after blocking: 71 x 58 x 58 inches. *(For information on converting measurements and skein weights to metric equivalents, see page 6.)*

GAUGE
A 20-stitch by 16-row swatch of the lace pattern should measure about 4.75 inches wide by 2 inches long.

ABBREVIATIONS
YO—Yarn over.
M1—Make one stitch by lifting the horizontal thread between the stitches and placing it on the right-hand needle and purling into the back of it.
PSSO—Pass slipped stitch over.
K2 tog—Knit 2 stitches together.

Patterns

LACE PATTERN
Row 1: K2, *YO, slip 1, K2 tog, PSSO, YO, K1*; repeat between *s until 1 st before marker. Knit the last st before marker, slip marker, K2.
Rows 2, 4, 6, and 8: P2, slip marker, M1, purl to end.
Row 3: K2, *K1, YO, slip 1, K2 tog, PSSO, YO*; repeat between *s until 2 sts. before marker. Knit the 2 sts. before marker, slip marker, K2.
Row 5: K1, K2 tog, *YO, K1, YO, slip 1, K2 tog, PSSO*; repeat between *s until 2 sts before marker, YO, K2, slip marker, K2.
Row 7: K2, K2 tog, *YO, K1, YO, slip 1, K2 tog, PSSO*; repeat between *s until 2 sts before marker, YO, K2, slip marker, K2.

SHAWL
Cast on 3 sts. Knit 3 sts.
Purl 2, place a marker, M1, P1.

Knit the next row.
Row 1: P2, M1, purl to end of row.
Row 2: Knit.
Repeat these 2 rows until there are 8 sts.
Work the 8 rows of Lace pattern until there are 168 sts. End with a purl row.
Knit 1 row.
Bind off *loosely* in purl.

CROCHET EDGING
In these instructions edge A is the straight side that was at the beginning of the needle on right-side rows. Edge B is the increase side that was at the end of right-side rows and beginning of wrong-side rows. Edge C is the bind-off edge. The shawl is worn with edge B across the shoulders.

Row 1: With right side facing and beginning at end of edge A where the original cast-on sts were, single crochet 324 times along the edge. This is about 1 single crochet in each stitch. When you get to the corner of edges A and C, do 3 single crochets in the same stitch. Along edge C, single crochet 324 times. This is 2 single crochets in every stitch except for 12 stitches in which you do only 1 single crochet. Try to space these 12 stitches evenly along the side. (*Note:* This not brain surgery. If you do not have exactly 324 single crochets, it is not crucial. The main point is to pick up the same number of stitches along both edges, making sure the edges stay flat.)
You are now at the corner of edges C and B. *Note: You will not need to crochet across edge B, as it is already a nice finished line.*
Row 2: Working back across edge C, *Chain 5, skip 4 stitches, make shell by doing [3 double crochets in one stitch, chain 2, 3 double crochets] all in same stitch*. Repeat between *s to end of side, placing last shell 4 sts from the corner. (You may have to do some fudging if it does not work our perfectly.) Chain 5, work last shell in corner, chain 5. Continue making shells along edge A, working the corner shell as above. Work along edge B, working last shell in corner. Slip st to base of chain 5.
Row 3: Continuing onto edge C, *Chain 10, slip st in top of chain 5, (chain 4, slip st in same space) 2 times*. Repeat between *s around all 3 sides. End chain 3, slip st to base of chain 10.

FINISHING: Wash shawl in tepid water and mild soap. Roll in towel to remove all excess moisture. Fold in half so that sides A and C are together. Pin out. Let dry thoroughly.

Child's Jester Sweater

I-cord dangling from jester triangles, and a bright rainbow of color will make everyone smile when a youngster wears this playful sweater. (Pictured on page 21).

YARN

Ellen's Half-Pint Farm Hand-Dyed Falkland Wool (84 yd/oz)

COLOR	OUNCES
Rainbow	5.5–5.5–5.5–6–6
Light Gray	4–4.5–5–5.5–6

NEEDLES

#4 double-pointed, #4 circular (32-inch and 16-inch), #4 and #6 single-pointed. *(See page 10 for equivalent metric and Canadian needle sizes.)*

GAUGE

24.5 sts and 48 rows = 4 inches worked over Slip Stitch pattern on #6 needles.

FINISHED SIZES (IN INCHES)

2 years	27
4 years	30
6 years	32
8 years	34
10 years	36

(For information on converting measurements and skein weights to metric equivalents, see page 6.)

Patterns

Slip Stitch: (multiple of 3 sts plus 2.)

Note: On all right-side rows (odd-numbered) slip stitches as if to purl with yarn in the back. On all wrong-side rows (even-numbered) slip stitches as if to purl with the yarn in the front. In other words, *the yarn is always on the wrong side of your work when you are slipping stitches.*

Row 1: (right side) Using Light Gray, K3, slip 1, *K2, slip 1*; repeat between *s, end K1.

Row 2: Using Light Gray, K1, *slip 1, K2*; repeat between *s, end K1.

Rows 3 and 4: Using Rainbow, K2, *slip 1, K2*; repeat between *s.

Row 5: Using Light Gray, work row 2.

Row 6: Using Light Gray, work row 1.

Rows 7 and 8: Using Rainbow, work rows 1 and 2.

Rows 9 and 10: Using Light Gray, work rows 3 and 4.

Rows 11 and 12: Using Rainbow, work rows 5 and 6.

Repeat these 12 rows for pattern.

Edging Triangles

With #4 double-pointed needles and Rainbow, cast on 3 sts.

Work in I-cord as follows: *Knit 3 sts. Without turning the work, slip all 3 sts to the right end of the needle.* (The yarn will be coming from the last st on the needle.) Repeat between *s until I-cord measures 2.5 inches. Turn work, K3.

Row 1: (right side) YO, K3.

Row 2: YO, K4.

Row 3: YO, K5.

Row 4: YO, K6.

Continue in this pattern, working 1 more stitch each row, until you have worked YO, K10.

Next row: Knit 11. One triangle complete.

Break yarn, place finished triangle onto a #4 single-pointed needle with right side facing. Thread yarn onto a tapestry needle and bury end of yarn into I-cord; tie the I-cord into a knot.

Repeat until you have the desired number of triangles.

FRONT

Edging: Make 7–8–8–9–9 edging triangles. With right side facing and all the triangles lined up on the single-pointed needle, attach yarn and knit 1 row across all sts of triangles, fastening in the ends of yarn as you work across the row. (77–88–88–99–99 sts.)

Knit across the next row (wrong side), working the following for your size:

Size 2: Cast on 3 sts at beginning of row. (80 sts.)

Size 4: Cast on 2 sts at beginning of row. (90 sts.)

Size 6: Cast on 3 sts at beginning of row, increase 4 sts evenly spaced over row. (95 sts.)

Size 8: Cast on 2 sts at beginning of row, inc 1 st over row. (101 sts.)

Size 10: Cast on 3 sts at beginning of row, inc 5 sts evenly spaced over row. (107 sts.)

Next row: (right side) Knit across row, casting on 3–2–3–2–3 sts at beginning of row. (83–92–98–104–110 sts.)

Knit one row.

Body: Change to #6 needle. Repeat the 12 rows of Slip Stitch pattern for 4.5–6.5–8–9–9.5 inches, ending with a completed wrong-side row.

Armhole Shaping: Bind off 4–4–5–5–5 sts at beginning of next 2 rows. (75–84–88–94–100 sts.) Continue in pattern until piece measures 4.5–5–5–5.5–6 inches from armhole.

Shape Front Neck: Work 29–31–33–36–38 sts, place middle 17–22–22–22–24 sts onto a holder for front neck, attach another ball of yarn and work remaining 29–31–33–36–38 sts. Working both sides at once, work 1 row. Beginning on next row, decrease 1 st at each neck edge every other row 6–6–6–7–7 times.

Work even until shoulders measure 2–2–2.25–2.5–2.5 inches from neck, ending with a completed right-side row in Rainbow. Place remaining 23–25–27–29–31 sts onto holders for shoulders.

BACK: Work as for front, disregarding front neck shaping, until piece measures .75 inch less than completed front piece, ending with a completed wrong-side row.

Shape Back Neck: Work 27–29–31–33–35 sts, place middle 21–26–26–28–30 sts onto a holder for back neck, attach another ball of yarn and work remaining 27–29–31–33–35 sts. Work 1 row. Beginning on next row, decrease 1 st at each side of neck every other row 4 times.

Work until back measures the same as front, ending with a completed right-side row in Rainbow. Place remaining 23–25–27–29–31 sts onto holders for shoulders.

JOIN SHOULDERS: Holding right sides together, join shoulders using the knitted seam method. See page 11.

SLEEVES: With #4 needles and Rainbow, cast on 38 sts. Work in K1, P1 ribbing for 1.5–1.5–2–2–2 inches, increasing 6 sts evenly spaced on last row. (44 sts.) Knit 1 row. Change to #6 needles.

The remainder of the sleeve is worked in Slip Stitch pattern. *Note:* As you increase, work the extra stitches into pattern by working between *s.

Work sleeve shaping as follows: Increase 1 st each side of sleeve every 3–4–4–4–4 rows 17–19–22–27–29 times. (78–82–88–98–102 sts.) Work even until Slip Stitch pattern measures 5.5–7–8–9.5–10 inches, ending with a completed wrong-side row. At the beginning of the next 2 rows cast off 4–4–5–5–5 sts. (70–74–78–88–92 sts.)

Sleeve Cap: Bind off 2 sts at the beginning of the next 12 rows. Bind off remaining 46–50–54–64–68 sts.

NECK: With #4 double-pointed needles and Rainbow, starting at the right back shoulder, pick up and knit 6–9–9–8–7 sts down right back, knit the 21–26–26–28–30 sts from back neck holder, pick up and knit 6–9–9–8–7 sts up left back, pick up and knit 13–11–11–11–15 sts down left front, knit the 17–22–22–22–24 sts from front neck holder, pick up and knit 14–11–11–11–16 sts up right front. Place a marker. (77–88–88–88–99 sts.)

Knit one round.

On a separate #4 needle make 7–8–8–8–9 triangles for edging, placing each completed one on the 32-inch #4 circular needle. Knit across all triangles, fastening in ends. Turn work. Purl 1 row.

Holding the needle with the triangles on top of the neck needle (wrong side of triangles to right side of neck), knit the sts together using the 16-inch #4 circular needle.

Knit another 7 rnds.

Bind off loosely in knit.

FINISHING: Sew sleeves to sweater, matching center of sleeve cap to shoulder seam. Sew sleeve seams; sew side seams of sweater.

MEASUREMENTS IN INCHES

A. 13.5–15–16–17–18
B. 4.5–6.5–8–9–9.5
C. 6.5–7–7.25–8–8.5
D. 7.5–9.5–11–12.5–13
E. 1.5–1.5–2–2–2

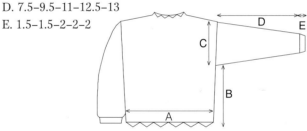

Ellen's Alpaca Sweater

The simplicity of this pattern is enhanced by the luxurious fiber and color of this glorious alpaca. You will never want it to end! (Pictured on page 22.)

YARN

Ellen's Half-Pint Farm Hand Dyed Alpaca (560 yd/7 oz), 2-2-3-3 skeins Dusty Miller

NEEDLES

#3 and #6 circular (24-inch and 16-inch), #6 single-pointed, #3 and #6 double pointed. *(See page 10 for equivalent metric and Canadian needle sizes.)*

GAUGE

23 sts and 30 rows = 4 inches worked in stockinette stitch on #6 needles.

FINISHED SIZES (IN INCHES)

Petite	35
Small	38.5
Medium	42.5
Large	46

(For information on converting measurements and skein weights to metric equivalents, see page 6.)

ABBREVIATIONS

C4F—Cable 4 front. Slip 2 sts to cable needle and hold in front of work, knit 2 sts, then knit the 2 sts from the cable needle.

C4B—Cable 4 back. Slip 2 sts to cable needle and hold in back of work, knit 2 sts, then knit the 2 sts from the cable needle.

Patterns

Two-Row Rib: Rnd 1: *K1, P1*; repeat between *s to end of rnd. Rnd 2: Knit.

Stockinette Stitch: When working in the round, knit every row; when working back and forth, knit one row, purl one row.

BODY: With #3 circular needle (24-inch) cast on 180-202-218-236 sts. Join and place a marker. All rounds begin and end at marker.

Work Two-Row Ribbing for 2.5-2.5-3-3 inches, ending with a completed row 1.

Next row: Knit, increasing 20-22-26-28 sts evenly spaced. (200-224-244-264 sts.)

Change to #6 needle and work in stockinette stitch for 13-13.75-14-14.5 inches.

Next row: Work 100-112-122-132 sts, place a marker, work remaining 100-112-122-132 sts.

DIVIDE FOR ARMHOLES: Work to 2 sts before marker, cast off next 4 sts, work to 2 sts before original marker, cast off next 3 sts, break yarn and pull through remaining st.

Work continues on #6 single-pointed needles. (96-108-118-128 sts each for front and back.)

FRONT: With wrong side facing, attach yarn and knit one row, working the stitches from the circular needle onto a single-pointed needle. Leave remaining sts for back on the circular needle.

Next row: purl.

Begin Yoke Pattern: Starting on the next row (wrong side). Work the 8 rows of CHART A 7 times, then work the first 0-0-4-4 rows again. (56-56-60-60 rows.)

Front Neck Shaping: Change to CHART B. Following row 1, work 36-42-46-50 sts, work middle 24-24-26-28 sts and place on a holder for front neck, work remaining 36-42-46-50 sts. Working both sides at once and beginning on next row, decrease 1 st at each neck edge every row 3-3-5-5 times, work 1 row, then decrease 1 st at each neck edge on next and every other row 5-5-7-7 times.

Work 5-5-3-3 rows even. Place 28-34-34-38 sts on holders for shoulders.

BACK: Work as for front, but repeating the 8 rows of CHART A 8-8-9-9 times, then working the first 7 rows again.

Shape Back Neck: Following Chart A, row 8, work 31-37-37-41 sts, work middle 34-34-44-46 sts and place on holder for back neck, work remaining 31-37-37-41 sts. Switching to CHART B, row 17-17-21-21, and working both sides at once, decrease 1 st at each neck edge on next 3 rows.

Place the remaining 28-34-34-38 sts on holders for the shoulders.

JOIN SHOULDERS: Holding right sides together, join shoulders using the knitted seam method (page 11).

NECK: With #3 circular needle (16-inch), starting at the right shoulder, pick up and knit 4 sts down right back; knit the 34-34-44-46 sts from back neck holder, decreasing 2 sts over the 12-st cable; pick up and knit 4 sts up left back; pick up and knit 18-18-23-23 sts down left front; knit the 24-24-26-28 sts from front neck holder, decreasing 2 sts over the 12-st cable ; pick up and knit 18-18-23-23 sts up right front. Place a marker. (98-98-120-124 sts.)

Purl 2 rnds.

Beginning with a row 2, work in Two-Row Rib for 1–1–1.5–1.5 inches.

Purl 1 rnd.

Bind off loosely in rib.

SLEEVES: With #6 circular needle (16-inch) or double-pointed needles, starting at middle of underarm cast-off, pick up and knit 48–48–57–57 sts to shoulder seam, pick up and knit 49–49–58–58 sts to underarm, marking off the last st. (97–97–115–115 sts.) This last stitch is the underarm stitch and is always worked in knit. All decreasing will be done on either side of this stitch as follows: knit 2 together at beginning of rnd, work to 2 sts before underarm st, SSK, knit underarm st.

Purl 2 rnds.

Work 9 rnds of Two-Row Rib, decreasing 1 st at beginning and end of rnds 4 and 7.

Purl 2 rnds, decreasing 1 st at beginning and end of second rnd.

Working in stockinette stitch, decrease one st at beginning and end of every seventh rnd 14–15–15–16 times.

Work 3–0–3–0 rnds even. (101–105–108–112 rnds of stockinette stitch; 63–61–79–77 sts.)

Next rnd: Knit, decreasing 31–23–37–33 sts evenly spaced. (32–38–42–44 sts.)

Change to #3 double-pointed needles and work 2.5–2.5–3–3 inches of Two-Row Rib. Bind off loosely in rib.

MEASUREMENTS IN INCHES

A. 35–38.5–42.5–46
B. 2.5–2.5–3–3
C. 13–13.75–14–14.5
D. 9.5–9.5–10.5–10.5
E. 15–15.5–16–16.5
F. 2.5–2.5–3–3

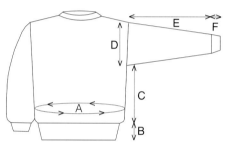

KEY FOR CHARTS

⊙	Purl on right side; knit on wrong side
🔲🔲🔺🔺	Cable 4 front
🔲🔲🔻🔻	Cable 4 back
☐	Stockinette stitch

CHART A: **BODY**

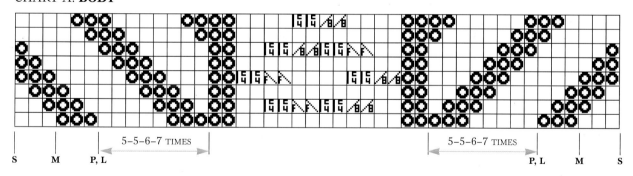

5–5–6–7 TIMES   5–5–6–7 TIMES

S   M   P, L   P, L   M   S

CHART B – **NECKLINE** *Sizes P and S*

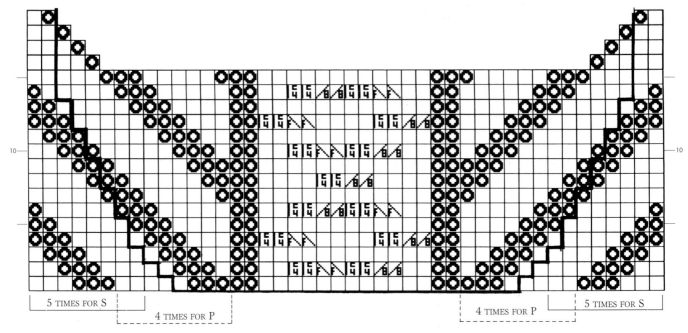

5 TIMES FOR S

4 TIMES FOR P

4 TIMES FOR P

5 TIMES FOR S

CHART B – **NECKLINE** *Sizes M and L*

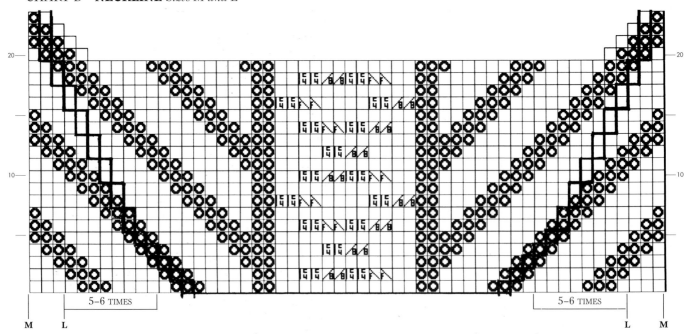

5–6 TIMES

5–6 TIMES

M L

L M

Silk and Jewels

There is no greater luxury than a yarn of blended silk and Merino. Combine it with the sumptuous colors of this yarn, and you will want to knit forever. (Pictured on page 23.)

YARN

Ellen's Half-Pint Farm Hand Dyed Silk and Merino (124 yds/oz)

COLOR	OUNCES
A. Stormy Skies	3–3.5–4–4.5
B. Deep Ocean Waters	3–3.5–4–4.5
C. Summer Sunset	3–3.5–4–4.5
D. Natural White	5.5–5.5–6–6.5

NEEDLES

#4 and #6 single-pointed, #4 circular (16-inch and 32-inch), #4 double-pointed. *(See page 10 for equivalent metric and Canadian needle sizes.)*

GAUGE

27 sts and 64 rows = 4 inches worked in Slip Stitch pattern on #6 needles.
23 sts and 46 rows = 4 inches worked in sleeve pattern on #6 needles.

FINISHED SIZES (IN INCHES)

Petite	38
Small	40
Medium	42
Large	44

(For information on converting measurements and skein weights to metric equivalents, see page 6.)

Patterns

Shell Edging: (See photo detail.) With #4 single-pointed needles and COLOR A, cast on 13 sts.

Purl 1 row. Turn.

Pass the second st over the first, pass the next st over the first, continue in this manner until all the stitches have been passed over the first. (1 st remaining on needle.)

Without turning work, pick up and knit 2 sts along the

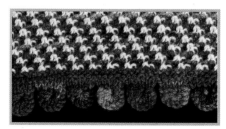

SHELL EDGING DETAIL.

LYNN KARLIN.

upper right edge of the shell, knit the st on the needle, pick up and knit 2 sts along the upper left edge top of the shell. (5 sts.) The right side of the shell is facing you.

Turn work (wrong side) and purl these 5 sts.

Break the yarn. Transfer the finished shell, with right side facing you, to an empty #4 needle. Weave the cast-on tail of yarn into the back side of the shell.

Slip Stitch Pattern (for front and back)

Multiple of 3 sts plus 2. On all right-side rows (odd-numbered) slip stitches as if to purl with yarn in the back (on the wrong side). On all wrong-side rows (even-numbered) slip stitches as if to purl with the yarn in the front. In other words, *the yarn is always on the wrong side of your work when you are slipping stitches.*

Work *two rows each* of pattern in the following color sequence: *A, D, B, D, C, D*; repeat between *s.

Row 1: (right side) K3, slip 1, *K2, slip 1*; repeat between *s, end K1.

Row 2: K1, *slip 1, K2*; repeat between *s, end K1.

Rows 3 and 4: K2, *slip 1, K2*; repeat between *s.

Row 5: Work row 2.

Row 6: Work row 1.

Repeat these 6 rows for pattern.

Sleeve Pattern

Rows 1 and 2: With Color A, knit.

Rows 3 and 4: With Color B, knit.

Rows 5 and 6: With Color C, knit.

Row 7: With Color D, knit.

Row 8: With Color D, purl.

Repeat these 8 rows for pattern.

BACK

Shell Edging: Make 23–25–27–29 shells in the color sequence *A, C, B, C*; repeat between *s. *Do not break yarn from last shell.*

With the completed shells lined up, right sides facing, knit across the row using the yarn from the last completed shell. Fasten off the individual ends of the shells as you work across the row. (115–125–135–145 sts.)

Next row: (wrong side) Knit.

Next row: (right side) Cast on 3 sts at beginning of row, knit, increasing 10–6–2–1 st(s) evenly spaced across row.

Next row: Cast on 3 sts at beginning of row, knit across the row. (131–137–143–152 sts.)

Shell edging completed.

Body: Change to #6 needles and commence Slip Stitch pattern. Work in pattern until piece measures 9–9.5–10–10 inches, not counting shell edging.

Armhole Shaping: Bind off 5–6–6–7 sts at the beginning of next 2 rows. Decrease 1 st each side every other row 6–8–9–10 times, then every row 3 times. (103–103–107–112 sts.)

Work even until armhole measures 7–7.5–7.5–8 inches, ending with a completed wrong-side row.

Back Neck: Work 35–35–35–37 sts, place middle 33–33–37–38 sts on a holder for back neck. Work each side separately.

Right Shoulder: Beginning on next row, decrease 1 st at neck edge every other row 7 times. (28–28–28–30 sts.) Work even until armhole measures 8–8.5–8.5–9 inches. Bind off 9–9–9–10 sts from shoulder edge 2 times, then 10 sts once.

Left Shoulder: With RS facing, attach yarn at neck edge and work one row. Follow shaping as for right shoulder.

FRONT: Work as for back until armhole measures 5 inches, ending with a completed wrong-side row.

Front Neck: Work 36–36–37–39 sts, place middle 31–31–33–34 sts on a holder for front neck. Work each side separately.

Left Front Shoulder: Beginning on next row, decrease 1 st at neck edge every fourth row 8–8–9–9 times. Work even until front measures exactly the same as back to shoulder bind-off same as for back.

Right Front Shoulder: With right side facing, attach yarn at neck edge and work 1 row. Shape as for left front shoulder.

SHOULDER SEAMS: Sew seams with a tapestry needle.

NECK: With #4 double-pointed needles and COLOR A, and starting at right back shoulder seam, pick up and knit 14–14–14–16 sts down right back, knit the 33–33–37–38 sts from back neck holder, pick up and knit 13–13–14–16 sts up left back to shoulder seam, pick up and knit 30–32–31–33 sts down left front, knit the 31–31–33–34 sts from front neck holder, pick up and knit 29–32–31–33 sts up right front. Place a marker. (150–155–160–170 sts.)

Knit 3 rounds. Break yarn.

Shell Edging: Make 30–31–32–34 shells as for body and sleeves. Do not break yarn from last shell. Join the shells by knitting across the row, fastening off the individual ends of the shells. Using the #4 circular needle (32-inch), knit one row.

Holding the shells on top of the sweater neck, wrong side of shells to right side of sweater, knit the 2 sets of stitches together using the #4 circular 16-inch needle.

Work in K1, P1 ribbing, decreasing 14–15–16–18 sts evenly spaced. (136–140–144–152 sts.) Work 4 more rows of ribbing (2 rows each of the other 2 variegated colors).

Bind off firmly in ribbing pattern.

SLEEVES: Make 8–8–9–9 shells; joining on the needle as for back. (40–40–45–45 sts.)

Knit 1 row.

Work the next two rows as knit, casting on 3 sts at the beginning of each row. (46–46–51–51 sts.)

Change to #6 needles and commence Sleeve pattern.

Work 8–7–8–7 rows.

Beginning on the next row, increase 1 st each side every 9–8–9–8 rows 19–22–20–22 times. (84–90–91–95 sts.)

Work 1–0–0–8 rows even.

At the beginning of the next 2 rows, bind off 5–6–6–7 sts.

At the beginning of the next 10 rows, bind off 2 sts.

Decrease 1 st each side every other row 10 times, then every eighth row 2 times.

Work 0–2–4–6 rows even.

At the beginning *and* the end of the next 4 rows, work 3 sts together.

Bind off remaining sts as follows: K2 together twice, *pass second st over first, K2 together*; repeat between *s across row. Fasten off last stitch.

FINISHING: Sew side seams of body and sleeve seams. Set in sleeves, matching center of sleeve cap to shoulder seam. Weave in all loose ends; steam lightly.

MEASUREMENTS IN INCHES

A. 38–40–42–44

B. 1

C. 9–9.5–10–10

D. 8–8.5–8.5–9

E. 16–16.5–16.75–17

F. 1

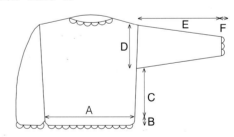

LINDA MACMILLAN

Oak Grove Yarns

PUTNEY · VERMONT

On a beautiful spring day in April, my husband and I drove to Putney, Vermont, to meet Linda Mac-Millan and watch her dye yarn. I had discovered Linda through a post I put out over the Internet with the Knitlist. Several people wrote to tell me that she was "the" person in Vermont to contact about hand-dyed yarns. In response to my contact, she sent me samples of her yarn. The people on the Knitlist obviously knew what they were talking about; Linda's yarns are breathtaking. I was delighted when she agreed to let me write about her. I knew only one thing about her process: She dyed her variegated yarn using a method she called layering. Having no idea what that meant, I was totally unprepared for what I was going to see and learn that afternoon.

The small studio was crammed with yarn in every form—hanks, balls, undyed, dyed, wet, dry—occupying every nook and cranny of the room. A knitting machine sat in the middle of the floor flanked by a television, a computer, and a desk. On a typical workday, Linda goes back and forth between projects on the stove and on the knitting machine, all while watching old movies on TV. Along the wall of windows was a waist-high counter with scatterings of powdered dye. Jars of liquid dye were lined up along with books, pictures, and more yarn. The far corner of the room was taken up by a four-burner gas stove, a double enamel sink, an old washing machine, a low table covered with pots and utensils, and several carts filled with beakers of dye.

I had come to learn and write about Linda's method of dyeing. Because two different batches were already underway, and each was at a different stage in the process, I started to learn right away. I was able to witness the whole procedure in half the amount of time it normally takes to dye a batch of yarn.

Without missing a beat, Linda wielded simmering water, tongs, acetic acid, dye, and hanks of yarn. Two large stainless-steel pans—the shallow, long trays used on restaurant steam tables—bubbled on the stovetop. Each of the pans, which had plastic lids, occupied two burners.

While Linda tended the baths and poked the simmering yarn with a long-handled stick (a wok utensil she has used for seven years), she mentioned some of the pitfalls of being a yarn dyer. She laughingly admitted to sucking dye through a pipette right into her mouth on one occasion. She wears sandals without socks because she once spilled boiling water on her feet while clad in shoes and socks. The socks soaked up the boiling water and kept the heat in, and she had to wrestle off the shoes *and* the wet socks before she could plunge her feet into cold water.

LINDA'S LAYERING METHOD OF DYEING PRODUCES WONDERFULLY VARIEGATED YARNS. CANDACE STRICK.

Linda's shop occupies the ground floor of a converted goat barn. Her dyeing studio is on the second floor, accessible from an outside staircase to a deck. Linda greeted us on the deck and ushered us in. We were met with the aroma of acetic acid wafting from two large pans bubbling on the stove. To the right of the door under the eaves were fifty-four skeins of newly dyed yarn, ranging from one ounce to eight ounces, hanging to dry. This visual treat was enough for me at the moment, and I had to stop right there to touch the yarn and admire the richness of the colors.

While waiting for the timer to signal the next procedure in the dyeing process, Linda explained the types of fibers she uses: "My colors are a constant effort to maximize the beauty and softness of the fibers. As a hand spinner, I understand the dynamics of how the yarn is made."

Before she phased out her flocks of sheep and goats, she used her own wool and mohair. The fleece she uses now comes from all over the country. Angora rabbits are the only animals she still tends. Each of her forty rabbits is clipped four times a year, yielding about seven ounces of fiber from each clip. The hair goes into her Angora Blend (27 percent angora and 73 percent Merino wool). This line of yarn is dyed mostly in dark colors or left natural.

Her mohair-Cormo blend is a luscious combination of solid and variegated colors. (Cormo refers to a Merino-Corriedale cross. The Corriedale breed, originally developed in Tasmania, produces a long, lustrous fiber; Merino sheep's wool is known for its fineness and softness.) Linda buys the Cormo fleece from a farm in Montana. She explained that blending similar fiber lengths produces a superior yarn. Thus, the Cormo is blended with mohair; the angora rabbit fiber is blended with Merino. Both of these yarns are spun in Putney, Vermont, at Green Mountain Spinnery.

The day I visited, Linda was dyeing kid mohair, an English-spun yarn of 80 percent kid mohair, 20 percent wool, with tiny loops made during the spinning process. She also carries a heavier bouclé made from silk and mohair, and other assorted hand-spun yarns, all hand dyed.

Eighteen skeins of yarn simmered in each pan on the stove. Three skeins of yarn had been pulled through each of six notebook binder rings, then all six rings threaded onto a dowel. Resting the dowel on the sides of the pan allows a portion of the yarn to be suspended above the bath if Linda so chooses. The skeins were positioned lengthwise in the pans. Acetic acid is used as a mordant to "fix" the dye, so that when the skeins are laundered, the colors will not wash out. The amount of

LARGE COMMERCIAL STEAM TRAYS MAKE USEFUL VATS FOR DYEING. CANDACE STRICK.

acid also determines how each color will "take." Linda explained more about this but asked that I not divulge one of her trade secrets.

Four colors were used to dye each skein, and they were poured at different times across the width of certain portions of the skeins. I saw how the colors, instead of blending into a muddy combination in the dye pan, stayed separate but blended just enough at the interfaces to make a masterpiece.

The process began with small amounts of dye. As the water got hotter, Linda added more and more dye—sometimes diluted with water, sometimes in concentrated

form. Dye tends to sink, but some colors sink more than others. If the dye sinks too fast and spreads too far, it will ruin the adjacent colors. By maintaining just the right amount of water in the pan, and the temperature just below boiling, Linda is able to keep the dyes where she wants them. She was constantly adding water, removing water, adding acid and checking the pH balance with a strip of litmus paper, and monitoring the temperature while at the same time poking and lifting the skeins to see the underneath portions. She then lifted the dowel holding the skeins and turned over the whole batch, so the part that was on the bottom of the pan was now on top, and the whole process was begun again.

Taped to the wall above the stove are Linda's dye formulas. Her timer is sometimes set for a specific number of minutes; other times she can just look at the skeins and know when the color is right. The dyes are exhausted when the water is clear. This means that the skeins have taken in all the color. When the skeins are finished to her satisfaction, she next rinses them in a soapy solution, puts them in the washing machine on the spin cycle, then rinses them in clear water and spins them again in the washer. Then she hangs them on a dowel to dry.

"Every dye lot is unique," Linda explained as she worked. "It depends on what kind of mood I'm in." I asked her if she ever makes mistakes, and also what happens to the yarn when she does. "I've always been able to sell my yarns. Some of my worst screw-ups are someone else's treasure," she confided.

Linda also talked about her life and her aspirations. With a master's degree in business, she worked for many years for a large corporation as a bookkeeper. Her hobbies then included raising sheep and knitting. Frustrated with inexpensive commercial yarns but unable to afford the most expensive ones, she began spinning her own. When the corporation she worked for moved, her choice was to move with them or quit. She decided to open a shop featuring handcrafted Vermont and New Hampshire yarns.

In 1988, her shop offered a course on hand dyeing. After taking the course herself and learning the fundamentals of dyeing, she still was not satisfied with her results. She envisioned variegated colors, and at the time there was nothing of that sort on the market. So she experimented first with three colors, then started adding more. Explaining how five colors gets too complicated and difficult to keep separate, Linda showed me a color wheel and illustrated how she uses 'split complements.' Imagine the color wheel with a Y drawn in the middle. The colors at

LINDA'S BRIGHT, WELL-ORGANIZED STUDIO IS ON THE SECOND FLOOR ABOVE HER SHOP. CANDACE STRICK.

the end of each leg of the Y are almost always harmonious. Using three or four colors for dyeing actually creates six or seven colors in the finished skein due to the blending of adjacent colors.

After a year of experimenting, Linda had her formulas. "I never realized how creative I was until I started working with colors," she said. "Everybody I met was knitting for someone else. I wanted to make beautiful yarns to make knitters want to knit for *themselves*."

Linda took me downstairs to her shop. Hanging on dowels and in cubbies were her finished masterpieces, in skeins and in garments. Her shop is appropriately named The Passionate Palette. The silks shimmered, the angora begged to be stroked, the colors seduced me. I marveled, touched, and dreamed of the glorious garments I was going to knit. I knew right away that any design I created would play second fiddle to Linda's yarn. All I could do was give it a shape.

Ken and I drove back home to Connecticut awed by Linda's skill. A master chemist, artfully manipulating simmering skeins, mordants, and dubious-smelling dyes, Linda MacMillan is a woman possessed and passionately in love with color and her art.

Jade Cabled Pullover

Twisting and weaving around each other, the crosses and cables of this pullover will mesmerize you as you knit it. The color is pure richness. (Pictured on page 25.)

YARN

Oak Grove Cormo Blend Yarn (1.5 oz/100 yd skeins), 16 skeins Jade.

NEEDLES

#5 and #7 single-pointed; #5 circular (16 inch) *or* #5 double-pointed. *(See page 10 for equivalent metric and Canadian needle sizes.)*

GAUGE

20 sts and 31 rows = 4 inches worked over Side Panel pattern on #7 needles.

FINISHED SIZE

Medium, 42 inches.

(For information on converting measurements and skein weights to metric equivalents, see page 6.)

ABBREVIATIONS

M1 (make one)—Increase one stitch by lifting the horizontal thread between the two stitches; knit into the back of this loop.

inc—Increase 1 stitch by knitting into the row below the stitch, then knitting the stitch.

RT (right twist)—Knit 2 together, then knit first stitch, slip both stitches from needle.

LT (left twist)—Skip first stitch, knit into back of second stitch, knit both stitches together through the back and slip both from needle.

C4F (cable 4 front)—Slip 2 stitches to cable needle and hold in front of work, knit 2, then knit the 2 stitches from the cable needle.

C4B (cable 4 back)—Slip 2 stitches to cable needle and hold in back of work, knit 2, then knit the 2 stitches from the cable needle.

LCp (left cross, purl)—Slip 2 stitches to cable needle and hold in front of work, purl 1, then knit the 2 stitches from the cable needle.

LCk (left cross, knit)—Slip 2 stitches to cable needle and hold in front of work, knit 1, then knit the 2 stitches from the cable needle.

RCp (right cross, purl)—Slip 1 stitch to cable needle and hold in back of work, knit 2 stitches, then purl the stitch from the cable needle.

RCk (right cross, knit)—Slip 1 stitch to cable needle and hold in back of work, knit 2 stitches, then knit the stitch from the cable needle.

Seed (Seed Stitch)—Knit the purl stitches and purl the knit stitches.

FRONT

Ribbing: With #5 needles, cast on 110 sts.

Row 1 (right side): (P2, K2) 5 times, P2, RT, (P2, K2) 15 times, P2, LT, P2, (K2, P2) 5 times.

Row 2 (wrong side): (K2, P2) 27 times, K2.

Repeat these 2 rows for 2 inches, ending with a completed row 2.

Next row (increase): P2, K2, P2, increase 1 st in each of the next 4 K2s of the ribbing, work through the RT, (P2, K2) 7 times, P1, M1, P1, increase 1 st in each of the next 2 sts, P1, M1, P1, (K2, P2) 7 times, work LT, P2, increase 1 st in each of the next 4 K2s of the ribbing, P2, K2, P2. (122 sts.)

Body: Change to #7 needles. The body of the sweater consists of a wide center panel with the charted cable design flanked by textured side panels.

Side Panels will be worked as follows:

Row 1: Purl.
Row 2: Knit.
Row 3: Purl.
Row 4A: K4, (P1, K3) 5 times.
Row 4B: (K3, P1) 5 times, K4.
Row 5: Purl.
Row 6: Knit.
Row 7: Purl.
Row 8A: K2, P1, (K3, P1) 5 times, K1.
Row 8B: K1, (P1, K3) 5 times, P1, K2.

Repeat these 8 rows for pattern.

(WS) Work Row 1 of Side Panel pattern over 24 sts, reading chart from left to right. Follow set-up row from CHART A over the next 24 sts. Work row 1 of Side Panel pattern over the remaining 24 sts.

Continue working the first 24 sts in Side Panel pattern in row sequence, working the A portion on rows 4 and 8; work the middle 74 sts in row sequence following the chart; work the last 24 sts in Side Panel pattern, working the B portion on rows 4 and 8.

Work the 68 rows of CHART A one time, then rows 1 through 44.

Shape Armholes: Cast off 3 sts at the beginning of rows 45 and 46. Work through row 68, keeping continuity of pattern in the side panels, then work rows 1 through 24.

Shape Neck: (Row 25) Work 45 sts, place middle 26 sts on a holder for neck, attach another ball of yarn, work remaining 45 sts. (Work both sides at the same time from this point on.) Work 1 row. Beginning on next row, decrease 1 st at each neck edge every other row 7 times. Work 1 row. Place 38 sts for each shoulder on holders.

BACK: Work as for front, disregarding front neck shaping and working through row 34.

Row 35: Work 40 sts, place middle 36 sts on a holder for neck, attach another ball of yarn and work remaining 40 sts. (Work both sides at the same time from this point on.) Work 1 row. Beginning on next row, decrease 1 st at each neck edge every other row 2 times. Work 1 row. Place 38 sts for each shoulder on holders.

JOIN SHOULDERS: With right sides together, join shoulders using the knitted seam method (page 11).

NECK: Using #5 circular needle (16-inch) or #5 double-pointed needles, beginning at right back shoulder, pick up and knit 5 sts down right back; knit the sts from back neck holder as follows: K14, K2 tog, (K1, K2 tog) twice, K14 (3 sts decreased); pick up and knit 5 sts up left back to shoulder seam; pick up and knit 11 st down left front; knit the sts from front neck holder as follows: K8, place a marker, K2, work the next 6 sts in established Seed Stitch pattern, K2, place a marker, K8; pick up and knit 12 sts up right front, place a marker. (92 sts.)

Row 1: (P2, K2) 14 times, P2, RT, P2, LCp, work 4 sts in established Seed Stitch, RCp, P2, LT, (P2, K2) 4 times.

You will work the following rows in established ribbing, working the RT and LT as K2s on the even-numbered rows, and as twists on the odd-numbered rows. The 10 sts between the markers are worked as follows:

Row 2: P1, K2, Seed 4, K2, P1.
Row 3: P1, LCp, Seed 2, RCp, P1.
Row 4: P2, K2, Seed 2, K2, P2.
Row 5: P2, LCp, RCp, P2.
Row 6: P3, K4, P3.
Row 7: P2, C4B, P3.
Row 8: P3, K4, P3.

Bind off loosely in knit, decreasing 2 sts over the top of the 4-st cable in center front.

SLEEVES: With #5 needles, cast on 46 sts. Work ribbing as follows:

Row 1 (right side): (K2, P2) 3 times, RT, P2, (K2, P2) 4 times, LT, (P2, K2) 3 times.

Row 2 (wrong side): (P2, K2) 11 times, P2.

Repeat these 2 rows for 2 inches, ending with a completed row 1.

Next row (increase): Increase 7 sts evenly spaced in the next 10 sts, P2, RT, (M1, increase 1 st in next st) 2 times, K2, (M1, inc 1 st in next st) 2 times, K2, P2, K2 (M1, inc 1 st in next st) 2 times, K2, (M1, inc 1 st in next st) 2 times, LT, P2, inc 7 sts evenly spaced in next 10 sts. (76 sts.)

Change to #7 needles. The sleeves, like the body, consist of a center cabled design with textured side panels on either side.

Side Panels for Sleeves will be worked as follows:
Rows 1 and 5: Purl.
Rows 2 and 6: Knit.
Rows 3 and 7: Purl.
Row 4A: K1, (P1, K3) 4 times.
Row 4B: (K3, P1) 4 times, K1.
Row 8A: (K3, P1) 4 times, K1.
Row 8B: K1, (P1, K3) 4 times.
Repeat these 8 rows for pattern.

Beginning with a wrong-side row, establish sleeve pattern: Work row 1 of Side Panel, reading chart from left to right, work the set-up row from CHART B over the next 42 sts, work row 1 of Side Panel.

Establish sleeve pattern by working the first and last 17 sts in Side Pattern and following Chart B for the middle 42 sts. Increase 1 st each side every ninth row 12 times. Work the extra stitches into the established side pattern. (100 sts.) Work the 68 rows of Chart B one time, then work rows 1 through 41 again.

At the beginning of rows 42 and 43, bind off 3 sts. Decrease 1 st at the beginning of the next 8 rows. Bind off remaining 86 sts, decreasing 2 sts over the top of the center cable.

FINISHING: Sew sleeves to body, matching the center cable to shoulder seams. Sew sleeve and body seams. Weave in any loose ends. Steam sweater lightly, but do not press cables!!!

MEASUREMENTS IN INCHES

A. 21
B. 2
C. 17
D. 9.5
E. 18
F. 2

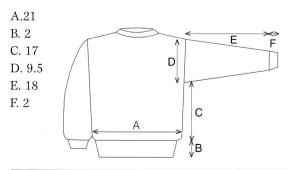

KEY FOR CHARTS

I	Knit on right side; purl on wrong side.
−	Purl on right side; knit on wrong side.
R T	RT
L T	LT
Ⅎ	Knit into back on right side; purl on wrong side.
	C4F
	C4B
	LCp
	LCk
	RCp
	RCk
I I	A row of RC or LC that requires no cabling. Knit on right side; purl on wrong side.

CHART A:
**BODY CABLE
DESIGN**

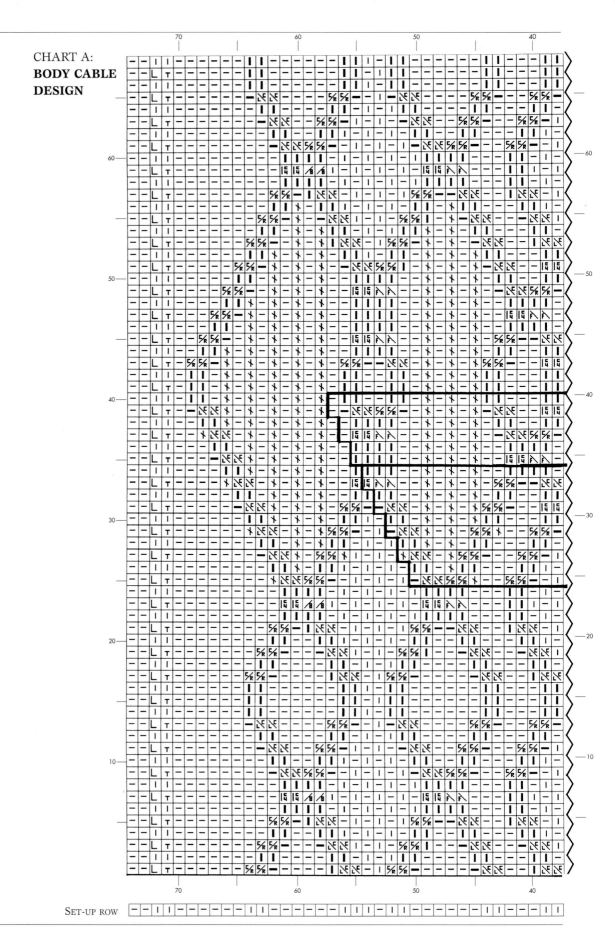

SET-UP ROW

SET-UP ROW

CHART B:
**SLEEVE CABLE
DESIGN**

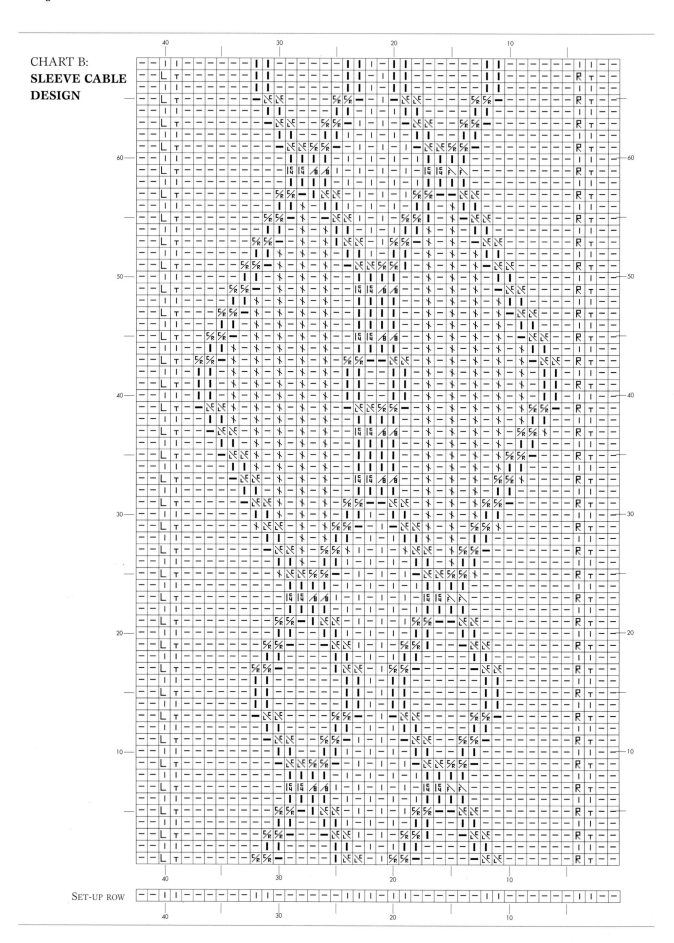

SET-UP ROW

Oak Grove Tesselation

Bands of interlocking designs blend together in a sequence of beautiful color. The Fair Isle method is used in this sweater (two colors per row), and although it may appear complicated, it is quite easy to knit. (Pictured on page 16.)

YARN

Oak Grove Yarn Cormo blend—60% mohair, 40% wool (1.5 oz/100 yd skeins)

COLOR	PETITE	SMALL	MEDIUM	LARGE
A. Wine	3	4	4	4
B. Greyblue	3	4	4	4
C. Palace	3	4	4	4
D. Lavender	3	3	4	4
E. Teal	3	3	3	4
F. Grape	3	3	3	4

NEEDLES

#3, #4, and #7 circular (24-inch and 16-inch), #3, #4, and #7 double-pointed. *(See page 10 for equivalent metric and Canadian needle sizes.)*

GAUGE

20.5 sts and 24 rows = 4 inches worked over pattern on #7 needle.

FINISHED SIZES (IN INCHES)

Petite	41
Small	44
Medium	46.5
Large	49

(For information on converting measurements and skein weights to metric equivalents, see page 6.)

ABBREVIATIONS

wyib—With yarn in back.

SSK—Slip 2 sts, one at time, to right-hand needle. Knit these 2 sts together through the fronts, and slip both from needle together.

Pattern

Slip Stitch Rib

Rnd 1: With COLOR B, *slip 1 st purlwise, K1*; repeat between *s.

Rnd 2: *Wyib slip 1 st purlwise, P1*; repeat between *s.

Rnds 3 and 4: With COLOR C, knit.

Rnds 5 and 6: Repeat rnds 1 and 2, using COLOR D.

Rnds 7 and 8: Repeat rnds 3 and 4, using COLOR E.

Rnds 9 and 10: Repeat rnds 1 and 2, using COLOR F.

BODY: With #3 circular needle (24-inch) and COLOR A cast on 105–112–119–126 sts, place a marker (referred to as second marker), cast on another 105–112–119–126 sts, place a marker (referred to as first marker). Join the round, making sure stitches are not twisted. (210–224–238–252 sts.)

Rnds 1 and 2: *K1, P1*; repeat between *s.

Rnds 3 and 4: Knit.

Change to #4 needle and work the 10 rnds of Slip Stitch Rib Pattern.

Change to #7 needle and begin CHART A for your size, working the 7-st repeat 30–32–34–36 times around the body. For sizes P, S, and M, begin on rnd 15–1–1, work through rnd 42, then work rnds 1 through 41. For size L, begin on rnd 29, work through rnd 42, work the 42 rnds of the chart, then rnds 1 through 41. (69–83–83–97 rnds total.)

Divide for armholes: On rnd 42, work to 3–4–3–4 sts before second marker, cast off the next 6–7–6–7 sts, work to 3–4–3–4 sts before first marker, cast off the next 6–7–6–7 sts. Work now progresses back and forth on 99–105–113–119 sts for the front. Place remaining sts on a holder for back. *REMEMBER: When working back and forth, right-side rows are read from right to left on chart; wrong side rows from left to right.*

FRONT: Following CHART B for your size, work the 42 rows on 99–105–113–119 sts.

Shape Front Neck: Following row 1 of CHART C, work 41–44–46–49 sts, place the middle 17–17–21–21 sts on a holder for front neck. Work each side separately from here on.

·Left side: Beginning on row 2, decrease 1 st at neck edge every other row 7 times, then every 3rd row 2–2–4–4 times. Work 1–1–2–2 row(s) even. Place 32–35–35–38 sts on a holder for shoulder.

Right side: Attach yarn and work row 1 of chart. Work as for left side.

BACK: Work the 42 rows of CHART B for your size, then repeat rows 1 through 16 for Petite and Small; rows 1 through 23 for Medium and Large.

Shape Back Neck: Switch to CHART C, row 17–17–24–24. Work 37–40–40–43 sts, place middle 25–25–33–33 sts on holder. Work each side separately.

Right side: Decrease 1 st at neck edge every row 5 times. Place 32–35–35–38 sts on holder for shoulder.

Left side: Attach yarn and work row 17–17–24–24, then work as for right side.

JOIN SHOULDERS: Use the knitted-seam method (page 11) to join the shoulders with a smooth seam over an uninterrupted pattern. Place each set of shoulder stitches on a #7 double-pointed needle and work with Color D.

NECK: With #4 circular needle (16-inch) and COLOR E, starting at the right back shoulder seam, pick up and knit 8 sts down right back, knit the 25–25–33–33 sts from back neck holder, pick up and knit 8 sts up left back to shoulder seam, pick up and knit 21–21–28–28 sts down left front, knit the 17–17–21–21 sts from front neck holder, pick up and knit 21–21–28–28 sts up right front to shoulder seam. Place a marker. (100–100–126–126 sts.)

Knit 1 row.

Work Slip Stitch Rib Pattern, working 2 rows each of the following colors: F, C, D, A, B.

Change to #3 needle (16-inch) and knit one rnd in COLOR A.

Next 2 rnds: Still using Color A, *K1, P1*; repeat between *s.

Bind off very loosely in rib.

SLEEVES: With #7 needle (16-inch) and COLOR D, starting at center of bound-off underarm stitches, pick up and knit 53–53–60–60 sts to shoulder seam, pick up and knit another 53–53–60–60 sts to underarm, place a marker, pick up and knit 1 st, place a marker. (107–107–121–121 sts.)

The stitch between the markers is the underarm stitch. All decreasing is done on either side of this stitch as follows: K2 together at beginning of rnd, work to 2 sts before marker, SSK, knit the underarm stitch in COLOR B, D or F.

Following CHART D for your size, decrease 1 st at beginning and end of every fourth rnd 24–24–26–27 times. (59–59–69–67 sts.)

Work 2–2–1–1 rnd(s) even.

Change to #5 double-pointed needles. With COLOR E, knit 1 rnd, decreasing 23–21–27–23 sts evenly spaced. (36–38–42–44 sts.)

Work Slip Stitch Rib Pattern the same as for neck, using double-pointed needles.

FINISHING: Weave in any loose ends; steam lightly.

MEASUREMENTS IN INCHES

A. 41–44–46.5–49
B. 1.5
C. 11.5–14–14–16.5
D. 10.75–10.75–12–12
E. 16.5–16.5–17.5–18
F. 1.5

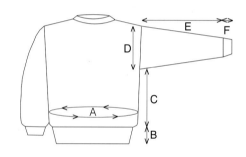
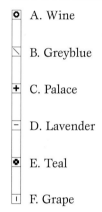

KEY FOR CHARTS

⊙	A. Wine
◣	B. Greyblue
⊞	C. Palace
⊟	D. Lavender
✦	E. Teal
⊺	F. Grape

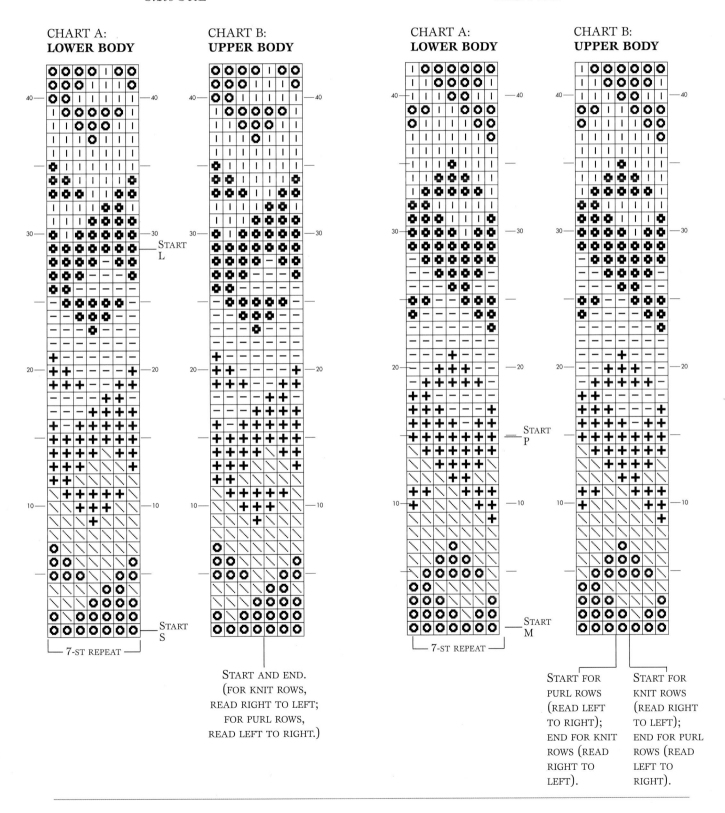

Sizes S&L

CHART A:
LOWER BODY

CHART B:
UPPER BODY

Sizes P&M

CHART A:
LOWER BODY

CHART B:
UPPER BODY

7-ST REPEAT

START
S

START
L

START AND END.
(FOR KNIT ROWS,
READ RIGHT TO LEFT;
FOR PURL ROWS,
READ LEFT TO RIGHT.)

START
M

START
P

START FOR
PURL ROWS
(READ LEFT
TO RIGHT);
END FOR KNIT
ROWS (READ
RIGHT TO
LEFT).

START FOR
KNIT ROWS
(READ RIGHT
TO LEFT);
END FOR PURL
ROWS (READ
LEFT TO
RIGHT).

CHART C: **NECK SHAPING** *left*

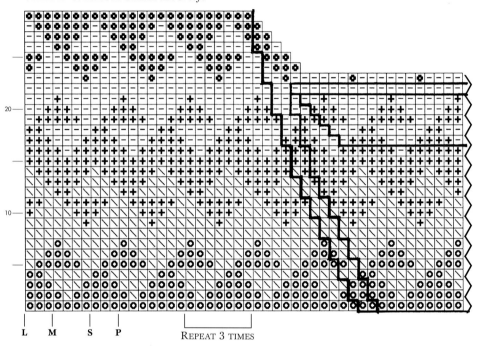

L M S P REPEAT 3 TIMES

CHART D: **SLEEVE** *Sizes P & S*

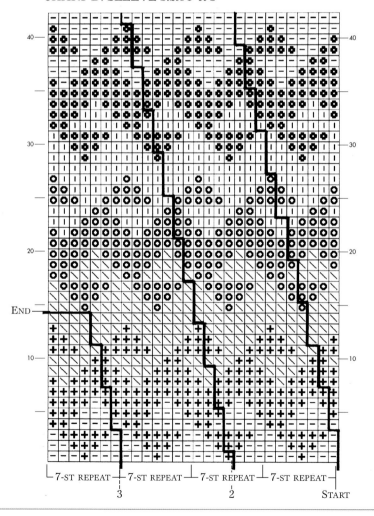

└ 7-ST REPEAT ┘ 7-ST REPEAT ┘ 7-ST REPEAT ┘ 7-ST REPEAT ┘

3   2   START

END

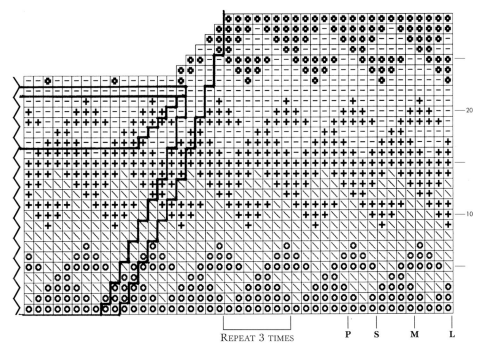

REPEAT 3 TIMES   P   S   M   L

CHART D: **SLEEVE** *Sizes M & L*

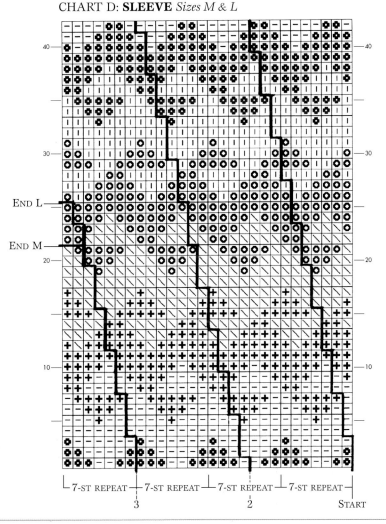

END L

END M

└─7-ST REPEAT─┴─7-ST REPEAT─┴─7-ST REPEAT─┴─7-ST REPEAT─┘
                    3   2   START

Lily Pond Pullover

My friend Lenore invariably loses or misplaces, at least three times, the directions to the sweater she is working on. For her most recent project we made many copies of the directions, and even put one in her safe deposit box! She asked me to include a design in this book that would be so simple that she would be able to finish it even if the directions were lost. Lenore, this one's for you! (Pictured in two colorways using Oak Grove yarns: Desert Nights with Navy Blue on page 12, Lily Pond with Palace on page 13.)

YARN

Oak Grove Yarn Angora blend—25% angora, 75% merino wool (50 gm/150 yd)

COLOR	SMALL	MED.	LARGE
A. Lily Pond	6	6	7
B. Palace	6	6	7

Alternate colorway: A. Desert Nights, B. Navy Blue.

NEEDLES

#5 and #7 circular (24-inch and 16-inch), #5 and #7 double-pointed. *(See page 10 for equivalent metric and Canadian needle sizes.)*

GAUGE

19.5 sts and 30 rows = 4 inches worked over pattern.

FINISHED SIZES (IN INCHES)

Small	38
Medium	42
Large	46

(For information on converting measurements and skein weights to metric equivalents, see page 6.)

ABBREVIATION

SSK—Slip two stitches, one at a time, to right-hand needle; knit both stitches together through the fronts, slip both from needle.

Pattern

In the round:

Rnds 1, 2, and 3: Working with COLOR A, *K1, P1*; repeat between *s.

Rnd 4: Change to COLOR B, knit.

Rnd 5: With Color B, purl.

Repeat these 5 rnds for pattern.

Back and forth:

Row 1 (right side): Working with COLOR A, *K1, P1* repeat between *s.

Rows 2 and 3: continuing with Color A, knit the knit sts, purl the purl sts.

Rows 4 and 5: Change to COLOR B, purl.

Row 6 (wrong side): With COLOR A, *P1, K1*; repeat between *s.

Rows 7 and 8: Same as rows 2 and 3.

Row 9 and 10: With COLOR B, knit.

Repeat these 10 rows for pattern.

Note: When you are working back and forth after the armhole break, your yarn will not always be at correct side for the next row. Because you are working back and forth using the circular needle, just start at the end with the correct color yarn. You just need to be careful to maintain the pattern, which consists of three rows of K1, P1 in Color A—the knits over the knits, the purls over the purls—followed by 2 rows of Color B which form a contrast ridge. The first row of the ridge is made by knitting on the right side or purling on the wrong side. The second row of the ridge is formed by doing the opposite action: purling if on the right side; knitting if on the wrong side.

BODY: With #5 circular needle (24-inch) and COLOR B cast on 166–184–200 sts. Join and place a marker. Work in K1, P1 ribbing for 2.5–2.5–3 inches.

Next rnd: Knit, increasing 18–20–22 sts evenly spaced. (184–204–222 sts.)

Change to #7 needle. Work in pattern (following directions for "in the round") until piece measures 15–16–17 inches, ending with a completed rnd 4.

Divide for Armholes: Following row 5 of pattern, work 91–101–110 sts, bind off the next 3 sts, work to 1 st before next marker, bind off 1 st in COLOR B, bind of the next 2 sts in COLOR A.

FRONT: Work now progresses back and forth on 89–99–108 sts. (See note above about working back and forth after armhole break.) Work in pattern for 53 rows.

Shape Neck: Work 36–40–43 sts, place middle 17–19–22 sts on a holder for front neck, attach another ball of yarn and work the remaining 36–40–43 sts. Working both sides at once, work 1 row. Decrease 1 st at each neck edge every other row 6 times, then every third row 2–3–4 times.

Work 1–3–5 row(s) even. Place 28–31–33 sts on holders for shoulders.

BACK: Work as for front, working 70–75–80 rows after armhole divide.

Shape Back Neck: Work 31–34–36 sts, place middle 27–31–36 sts on a holder for back neck, attach another ball of yarn, work remaining 31–34–36 sts. Working both sides at once, decrease 1 st at each neck edge 3 times. Work 1 row even. Place 28–31–33 sts on holders for shoulders.(You should end on a completed first row of COLOR B.)

JOIN SHOULDERS: Using the knitted-seam method (see page 11), the shoulders will be joined together with a ridge on the right side. Place each set of shoulder stitches on a #7 double-pointed needle, hold work wrong side to wrong side, and work with Color B.

NECK: Use COLOR B. With #5 circular needle (16-inch), and starting at right back shoulder seam, pick up and knit 5 sts down right back, knit the 27–31–36 sts from back neck holder, pick up and knit 5 sts up left back to shoulder seam, pick up and knit 14–17–19 sts down left front, knit the 17–19–22 sts from front neck holder, pick up and knit 14–17–19 sts up right front neck to shoulder seam. Place a marker. (82–94–106 sts.)

Purl one round.

Work in K1, P1 ribbing for 1.25–1.25–1.5 inches.

Knit 5 rnds. Bind off very loosely in knit.

SLEEVES: With #7 circular needle (16-inch) and COLOR B, starting at center underarm, pick up and knit 1 st, place a marker, pick up and knit 43–46–49 sts to shoulder seam, pick up and knit 43–46–49 sts to underarm, place a marker. (87–93–99 sts.)

The stitch between the markers is the underarm stitch and is always worked in *knit*. All decreasing is done on either side of this stitch as follows: K2 together at beginning of rnd, work to 2 sts before underarm stitch, SSK, knit underarm st.

Beginning on rnd 5 of pattern in the round, decrease 1 stitch at beginning and end of rnd every fifth rnd 17–18–19 times, then every tenth rnd 2 times. (Change to double-pointed needles when work becomes too tight for circular needle.)

Work even on 49–53–57 sts for 9 rnds, ending on a last pattern rnd of COLOR A.

Next rnd: With COLOR B, knit, decreasing 13–15–15 sts evenly spaced. (36–38–42 sts.)

Change to #5 double-pointed needles and work in K1, P1 ribbing for 2.5–2.5–3 inches. Bind off very loosely in knit.

FINISHING: Weave in any loose ends. Steam very lightly.

MEASUREMENTS IN INCHES

A. 38–42–46
B. 2.5–2.5–3
C. 12.5–13.5–14
D. 9–10–11
E. 15–16–17
F. 2.5–2.5–3

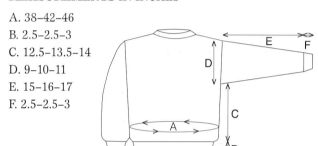

Bear Hill Farm

BOZRAH • CONNECTICUT

I came across Sonja Fuller's yarn while working on an altogether different book idea from this one. Contacting many yarn companies and responding to advertisements in knitting magazines, I sent out the usual form letter describing my book idea and requesting yarn samples. As soon as Sonja received my letter, she telephoned me. She was interested but didn't want to send me samples yet; she said I could not possibly appreciate the beauty of her yarn unless I saw it in person and knit up. The next day she was on my doorstep, laden with bags of yarn and sweaters. She was right; to fully appreciate her yarn, I had to have it before my eyes and in my hands. She told me that any color I wanted she could dye for me and any amount I needed she would deliver to me. I started knitting and designing with her yarn. I thought it was the best-kept secret in New England.

Although I had been to Sonja's home in the Thames Valley several times before my official visit to interview her for this book and watch the dye process, on this day especially I was struck by the beauty of the land. The approach to the house is up a steep hill; the view is of green fields dotted with grazing sheep, both black and white.

The first settlers arrived in the Thames Valley of Connecticut in 1659. They saw—overlooking the valley and the stream running through it—a steep, rocky hill, already clear of trees, that offered good grazing ground. By 1700, this land was jointly owned by the proprietors of Norwich, and sheep were sent to graze there. In 1786, the area was incorporated into a township named Bozrah, which means "sheepfold," and the hill became known as Bare Hill. Sometime during the 1800s, the name evolved into Bear Hill.

A flock of Corriedale sheep still grazes here, the animals' complacent wanderings enhancing the scene of New England tranquility. The 1728 saltbox of John Gager, at the lower end of the hill, now belongs to Sonja Pederson Fuller, descendent of John Gager and the owner of Bear Hill Farm. Ignoring the presence of power lines and the occasional car that climbs the steep road, one could easily be transported back to an eighteenth-century sheep farm.

Sonja shares her home with her ninety-two-year-old mother, her daughter and son-in-law, eleven cats, and two dogs. Spinning wheels sit in many corners; an antique clock skeiner is in another. Skeins of yarn dot the chairs and shelves. Knitted projects lie here and there. Pictures of sheep abound, from the calendar in the bathroom to the splendid pen and ink drawings on the walls. The house leans with age, and the patina of its wainscoting and wide-board floors is enriched every day by the life that goes on here. During the winter months, the mantel over the four-foot-wide fireplace in the keeping room is host to an enticing array of colorful skeins, hung to dry over the woodstove. The barn, with a simple sign proclaiming "Corriedale," is shared by the sheep, goats, and barn swallows. In the loft are stored boxes of yarn, dyed and undyed. The stockpile of skeins finds overflow storage in a trailer parked in the yard next to the barn.

Sonja Pederson Fuller unabashedly loves sheep and anything having to do with them. Her twenty-seven sheep and two angora goats produce the wool for the hand-dyed skeins of yarn that she sells at fairs all around New England. Their fleece is sent to Wisconsin to be carded and spun, then the wool is blended with 15 percent mohair and shipped back in one-pound cones. After Sonja winds it into four-ounce skeins on her antique clock skeiner, it is ready for the dye pot. From her four-burner gas stove and stone sink in the kitchen, where she does her dyeing, come the colors of New England. A few of Sonja's mouthwatering colors are Chocolate Cake, a sinfully deep brown-red; Pumpkin Pie, a creamy, smooth peachy beige; and Cinnamon, a blushing brown. The beauty of woods and meadows abound in such colors as Lichen, Black Forest, Lilac, Green Fields, and Hyacinth. Historical colors are represented by such choices as Antique Red, Cupboard Blue, and Old Gold. Although the colors echo the soft, glowing look of natural dyes, they actually are created with chemical dyes.

By utilizing both naturally colored and white wool, Sonja can produce two distinct colors from the same dye bath. For example, Chocolate Cake and Antique Red come from the

WASHED SKEINS CATCH THE GLOW OF AUTUMN SUNLIGHT. SONJA FULLER.

HEADING OUT TO GRAZE ANOTHER DAY IN THE
ROLLING PASTURES OF BEAR HILL FARM. SONJA FULLER.

same dye bath, but Chocolate Cake is dyed on skeins of natural dark gray wool, while Antique Red is dyed on skeins of natural white. This is the idea behind the wonderful line of colored ragg yarn that Sonja produces. Ragg yarn, usually a strand of natural dark and white plied together, takes on an exciting new dimension when Sonja dyes it into such colors as Rose, Hyacinth, Smoky Turquoise, and Salmon.

Sonja keeps records of every dyeing session. Sometimes a mistake becomes a welcome new color for her color card. Pumpkin Pie, intended to be Raffia, evolved from a mistake in measuring.

While visiting Sonja, I had the privilege of watching her dye eight skeins of yarn into a beautiful soft peach color that I had requested. We went out to the barn to retrieve the skeins, which had already been washed. Before they could be dyed, they had to soak in the sink for about ten minutes. Meanwhile, Sonja prepared the dye pot—a huge, square copper tub that covered all four burners of the gas stove. We filled it with water, fire-brigade style, with pans from the sink. When the water in the dye pot was at the proper level, Sonja turned all the burners on high.

While we worked, Sonja talked. "The first rule for beautiful dyeing is to start with good wool," she began, then excused herself to open the kitchen window, letting one cat in and another one out. Letting cats and dogs in and out continued throughout my visit.

To the pot of water on the stove Sonja added Glauber's salt, which is a setting agent. At that point, Sonja's mother, Frances, came into the kitchen to greet me and ask where my parrot was! Sonja sent her to fetch the vinegar. Frances came back with a gallon jug and opened it, then retired to the keeping room off the kitchen and kibitzed from there for the rest of the morning. Sonja measured the correct portion of vinegar and poured it into the pot. The next addition was a chemical called albegal set, which ensures an even color. While waiting for the water to come to temperature, Sonja mixed the dye.

Then she retrieved a battered cardboard box, which she called her "magic box," that contained powdered dyes and her books of records. Upon finding her formula, she measured out the required amounts of dye and put them into a cup of warm water. The color in the cup was red. She strained the mixture back and forth many times through a steel mesh strainer, then dumped it into the dye pot. The water in the pot was the color of blood. This is supposed to be peach? I thought to myself.

We gently placed the skeins of yarn into the dye pot, one at a time, and watched them sink into the crimson depths. We then waited for the water to reach 190 degrees Fahrenheit, just short of boiling, which took about forty-five minutes. The skeins had to be stirred frequently during the process to avoid becoming streaked. The stirring also equalized the temperature of the dye bath, because the hottest areas were directly over the burners.

Frances came back into the kitchen to fix us lunch but refused my offer to help. Ten minutes later she handed me a gorgeous egg salad sandwich on toast, then ushered me to the most comfortable seat by the huge fireplace in the keeping room. I asked her about her secret of longevity. In the long, long story of her life that ensued, I found the answer to my question: You must believe that you will live long, and you must stay away from doctors! Throughout lunch, Sonja or I got up to stir the dye pot every now and then.

I did not have time to stay until the skeins were taken out of the dye pot, but Sonja explained the process. Once the dye bath reaches the proper temperature, the heat is turned off and the skeins are left to sit in the water while it cools. The longer the skeins sit, the more dye they take up. When they are cool enough to handle, they are washed by hand in warm, soapy water, then put into the washing machine to spin out the water. They are hung up to dry—outside if it is nice, inside by the mantel if it is rainy.

I did get to go with Sonja to the barn to bottle-feed a lamb. While we were there she talked about her farm with love. "I wallow in a farm. When I have a farm, I have a *farm*! I'm not nearly as concerned over dirty shoes in my house as I am about a dirty barn." Since she was five years old, Sonja knew she wanted to be around sheep, but she had to wait a long time to realize her dream of owning a sheep farm. Turning their wool into a palette of gorgeous colors has been her goal over the past six years, and she has expanded her line from thirty to more than seventy colors. She looked around her farm, taking in the beauty. "I can't imagine my life without all of this, or the heartbreak should I ever lose it." She asked me if I had seen the movie *Out of Africa*. I had. "The poignancy of Meryl Streep's opening line in that movie sums it all up for me," Sonja said, and she quoted: "I once had a farm in Africa."

SONJA'S ANCESTOR, JOHN GAGER, BUILT THE HOUSE
AT BEAR HILL FARM IN 1728. SONJA FULLER.

Sonja's Song

I named this pattern after Sonja, whose mood is always one of happy singing! This cropped pullover is knit in the round up to the armholes. The front and back are then worked back and forth. Sleeves are worked by picking up stitches around the armholes and knitting down to the wrists. (Pictured on page 22.)

YARN

Bear Hill Farm Yarn—85% wool, 15% mohair (4 oz/280 yd skein), 1 skein each of the following colors:

    A. Forest Green
    B. Smoky Amethyst
    C. Dark Lichen
    D. Raspberry
    E. Medium Lichen
    F. Mauve
    G. Teal
    H. Sea Foam

(For alternate colorway, see directions on page 117.)

NEEDLES

#3 and #7 circular (24-inch), #7 single-pointed, #3 and #7 double-pointed. *(See page 10 for equivalent metric and Canadian needle sizes.)*

GAUGE

20.5 sts and 22.5 rows = 4 inches worked over stockinette stitch pattern.

FINISHED SIZES (IN INCHES)

Small	37.5
Medium	42
Large	47

(For information on converting measurements and skein weights to metric equivalents, see page 6.)

Patterns

Border

Row 1: *K3, P3*; repeat between *s.
Row 2: *P3, K3* repeat between *s.

Stockinette Stitch: When working in the round, knit every row; when working back and forth, knit on the right side, purl on the wrong side.

ABBREVIATION

SSK—slip 2 stitches, one at a time knitwise, from the left needle to the right needle, insert the left needle into the fronts of the slipped stitches and knit them together.

A Note on Working with Two Colors: To maintain a proper gauge, always carry yarn not used loosely across back of work, spreading stitches on the needle to their true width. Yarn carried too tightly will cause the work to pucker. Also, yarn carried more than 3 or 4 stitches must be woven under and over the color being worked with.

BODY: With #3 circular needle and COLOR A, cast on 192–216–240 sts. Work 2 rnds of Border pattern in each of the following colors: A, B, C, D, E, F, G, H.

Change to #7 needle and work CHART A. Beginning on rnd 7–1–19 of chart, work the 12-st repeat 16–18–20 times around the body of the sweater. Work through rnd 24, then work the entire 24 rnds of the chart once again. Work rnds 1 through 10 once more.

On rnd 11, work 96–108–120 sts, place a marker, work the remaining 96–108–120 sts to end of rnd. This divides your work into front and back.

Rnd 12: Bind off 4 sts at beginning of rnd, work to 3 sts before next marker, bind off next 7 sts, work to 3 sts before original marker, bind off 2 sts, break yarn and pull through last stitch. (89–101–113 sts *each* for front and back.)

Work now progresses back and forth on single-pointed needles.

FRONT: With right side facing, attach yarns at right edge of work. The first row is worked off the circular needle onto a single-pointed needle. The stitches of the back can be left on the circular needle as a holder.

Beginning with a knit row, work the 24 rows of CHART B. The chart is read as follows: *For sizes S and L,* work the first 2 sts at right side of chart, work the 12-st repeat 7–9 times, then work the last 3 sts at left edge of chart. (For purl rows, begin at left side of chart.) *For size M,* begin at the fifth stitch within the repeat, work to end of repeat, work entire 12-st repeat 7 times, then work the first 9 sts of the repeat. (For purl rows, begin at left side of chart.)

Change to CHART C. Work through row 11.

Shape Front Neck: On row 12, work the first 36–42–48 sts, work the middle 17 sts and place on a holder for front neck, work the remaining 36–42–48 sts. Work each side separately.

Left Side: Work row 13. Beginning on next row bind off 2 sts at neck edge every other row twice, then decrease 1 st at neck edge every other rnd 6–6–10 times. Work 2–2–0 rnds even. Place remaining 26–32–34 sts on holder for shoulder.

Right Side: Beginning on row 13, bind off 2 sts at neck edge every other row twice, then decrease 1 st at neck edge every other row 6–6–10 times. Work 3–3–1 row(s) even. Place remaining 26–32–34 sts on holder for shoulder.

BACK: Work as for front, disregarding front neck shaping and working through row 26–26–30 of CHART C.

Shape Back Neck: On row 27–27–31, work 29–35–37 sts, work middle 31–31–39 sts and place on holder for back neck, work remaining 29–35–37 sts. Work each side separately. Decrease 1 st at neck edge every row 3 times. Place remaining sets of 26–32–34 sts on holders for shoulders.

JOIN SHOULDERS: With right sides together, join shoulders using the knitted seam method (page 11).

NECK: Starting at right back shoulder seam with COLOR H and #3 double-pointed needles (or 16-inch circular), pick up and knit 5 sts down right back, knit the 31–31–39 sts from back neck holder, pick up and knit 5 sts up left back to shoulder seam, pick up and knit 18–18–25 sts down left front, knit the 17 sts from front neck holder, pick up and knit 18–18–23 sts up right front. Place a marker. (96–96–114 sts.)

Work 2 rnds each of Border pattern in the colors H, G, F, E, D, C, B, A.

Bind off loosely in knit using COLOR A.

SLEEVES: With COLOR F and #7 double-pointed needles (or 16-inch circular), starting at underarm, pick up and knit 43–43–48 sts to shoulder seam, pick up and knit 43–43–48 sts to underarm, place a marker, pick up and knit 1 more st, place a marker. (87–87–97 sts.)

The stitch between the markers is the underarm stitch and is always knit in background (lighter) color. All decreasing is done on either side of this stitch as follows: Knit 2 tog at beginning of rnd, work to 2 sts before marker, SSK, knit underarm stitch.

How to Follow Sleeve Chart: Work begins at the first stitch on the right side of Chart D. Work the stitch repeat as many times as it takes to complete the rnd for your size. When you have worked all 26 rnds of the chart, begin at the bottom at the next vertical line. *Note: Decreases are only shown at the beginning of the rnd; do not forget to do them at the end of the rnd also.*

Following CHART D, work decreases in every fifth rnd 16–18–18 times. (55–51–61 sts.)

Work 4–0–6 rnds even, ending with a completed rnd 12–18–24.

Change to #3 double-pointed needles and COLOR H. Knit 1 rnd, decreasing 7–3–7 sts. (48–48–54 sts)

Work 2 rnds of Border pattern in colors H, G, F, E, D, C, B, A.

Bind off loosely in knit using COLOR A.

FINISHING: Weave in any loose ends. Steam lightly.

DIRECTIONS FOR ALTERNATE COLORWAY

YARN

Bear Hill Farm Yarn—85% wool, 15% mohair (4 oz/280 yd skein). 2 skeins each of the following colors:
A. Chocolate Cake
B. Old Gold
C. Raffia
D. Antique Red

All the graphs are the same as for the original colorway, with the exception of the color key. Follow the color key on the *right*, below.

Because there are only 4 colors in this version, some of the symbols of the original colorway will stand for the same color in the alternate colorway. All directions are to be worked the same, except for the color changes noted below.

Body: Work the Border pattern in the following color sequence: A, B, C, D, A, B, C, D.

Neck: Pick up and knit the stitches using Color D. Work the Border pattern in the following color sequence: D, C, B, A, D, C, B, A.

Sleeves: Pick up stitches using Color B. Work the border pattern in the following color sequence: D, C, B, A, D, C, B, A.

MEASUREMENTS IN INCHES

A. 37.5–42–47
B. 2.75
C. 9.5–10.5–11.75
D. 9.5–9.5–10.5
E. 15–16–17
F. 2.75

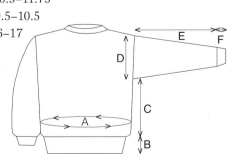

KEY FOR CHARTS   *Alternate Colorway Key*

Symbol	Key for Charts	Alternate Colorway Key
✪	A. Forest Green	A. Chocolate Cake
╱	B. Smoky Amethyst	B. Old Gold
▪	C. Dark Lichen	A. Chocolate Cake
⌣	D. Raspberry	C. Raffia
✛	E. Medium Lichen	D. Antique Red
✧	F. Mauve	B. Old Gold
◉	G. Teal	D. Antique Red
	H. Sea Foam	C. Raffia

CHART A: **LOWER BODY**

CHART B: **UPPER BODY**

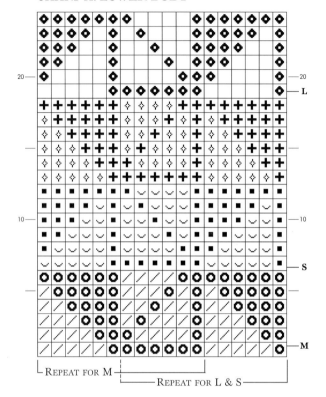

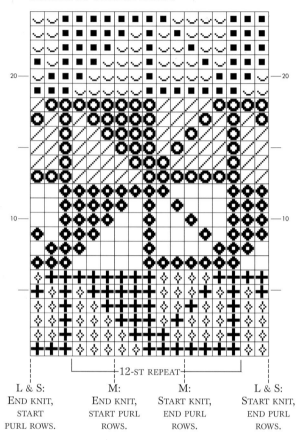

| L & S: END KNIT, START PURL ROWS. | M: END KNIT, START PURL ROWS. | M: START KNIT, END PURL ROWS. | L & S: START KNIT, END PURL ROWS. |

—12-ST REPEAT—

CHART C: **NECK SHAPING** *left*

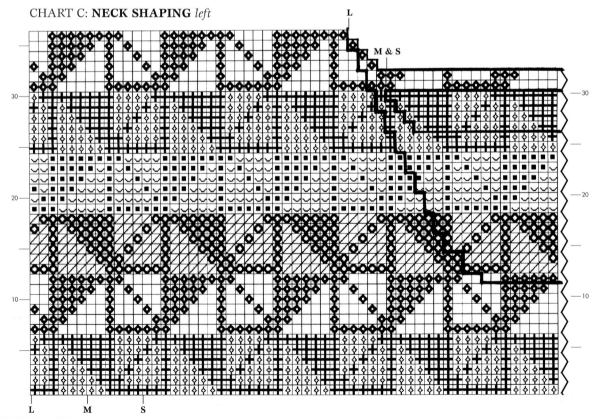

CHART D: **SLEEVE**

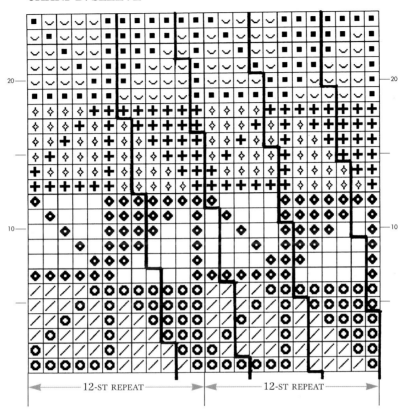

CHART C: **NECK SHAPING** *right*

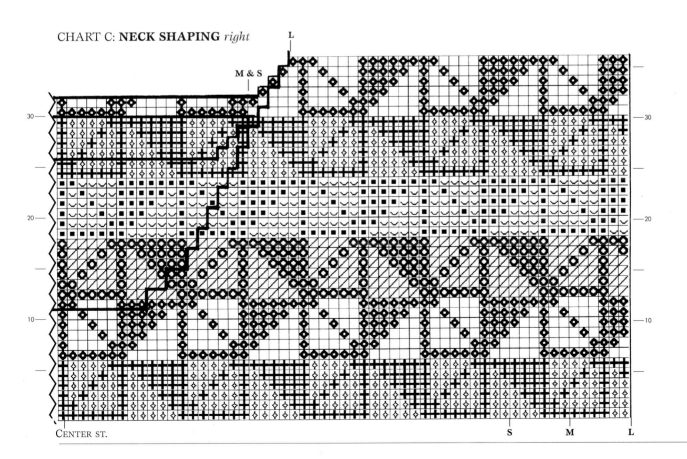

Sienna Tunic

Deeply textured, with little scallops for a bottom, this sweater is the color of the rich earth. (Pictured on page 24.)

YARN

Bear Hill Farm Yarn—85% wool, 15% mohair (280 yd/4 oz skein), 7 skeins Sun Tea.

NEEDLES

#5 and #7 single-pointed, #4 circular (16-inch) or #4 double-pointed. *(See page 10 for equivalent metric and Canadian needle sizes.)*

GAUGE

21.5 sts and 29 rows = 4 inches worked over Wickerwork pattern on #7 needles.

FINISHED SIZES (IN INCHES)

Small   41
Large   47

(For information on converting measurements and skein weights to metric equivalents, see page 6.)

ABBREVIATIONS

LT (left twist)—Skip first stitch, knit through back of second stitch then knit both stitches together through back.

RT (right twist)—Knit 2 together, then knit first stitch, slip both stitches from needle.

NOTE ON PATTERNS: This sweater has three different patterns, each having a different number of rows per repeat: **Triplet Cable** (16 rows), **Seed Wishbone Cable** (8 rows), and **Wickerwork** (12 rows). After 48 rows, all three patterns will once again begin at row 1 simultaneously. This has all been set up as a table of instructions to make your knitting enjoyable and easy to follow. *All special abbreviations are printed at the bottom of the table for easy reference.*

ADDITIONAL SLEEVE PATTERN: Seed Stitch

Row 1: *K1, P1*; repeat between *s.
Row 2: *P1, K1*; repeat between *s.

BACK

Scallop Cast-On: Using #5 needles, tie a loop on one needle. This is the first stitch, referred to below as "original loop." *Cast on 3 sts. Knit these 3 sts, purl the 3 sts, knit the 3 sts, purl the 3 sts. The 3 sts you have just worked are on the left-hand needle. Slip the second st over the first, then slip the third st over the first.* You have remaining the original loop, plus one stitch on top of one scallop. Repeat between the *s until you have 29–33 scallops.

(*Note:* instead of turning your work to purl the 3 sts, it is easier to knit them backward. This saves the task of frequent turning. See page 11.)

Next row: *Knit 1, pick up (through the back loop, single strand only) and knit 3 sts along the top of the scallop.* Repeat between *s for all scallops. Knit last st on needle. (117–133 sts.)

Body: Knit 4 rows. Change to #7 needles and establish patterns as follows:

(Wrong side) work row 1 of Wickerwork over the next 32–40 sts, P2, work row 1 of Seed Wishbone Cable over the next 12 sts, P2, work row 1 of Triplet Cable over the next 21 sts, P2, work row 1 of Seed Wishbone Cable over the next 12 sts, P2, work row 1 of Wickerwork over the next 32–40 sts.

Next row (right side—follow row 2 of all three patterns from table): Work Wickerwork over next 32–40 sts, LT, work Seed Wishbone Cable over next 12 sts, RT, work Triplet Cable over next 21 sts, LT, work Seed Wishbone Cable over next 12 sts, RT, work Wickerwork over next 32–40 sts.

Continue working the three patterns in numerical row sequence and working all established LTs and RTs on right-side rows, and as P2 on wrong-side rows.

Work the 48 rows of the table 3 times, then rows 1 through 37. Bind off in knit, decreasing 1 st in the middle of each wishbone cable.

FRONT: Work as for back, but after the 48 rows of the table have been repeated 3 times, work rows 1 through 22.

Shape Front Neck: Following row 23, work 53–61 sts, work middle 11 sts and place on holder for front neck, work remaining 53–61 sts.

Left Front: Work row 24. Beginning on next row (25) bind off 3 sts at neck edge every other row 2 times, bind off 2 sts once, then 1 st *every row* 6 times. Work even through row 37. Bind off remaining 39–47 sts.

Right Front: Work same as above, but beginning shaping on row 24.

SLEEVE #1: With #5 needles, cast on 48 sts. Establish ribbing pattern as follows:

Row 1 (wrong side): P2, (K2, P2) 4 times, work row 1 of Seed Wishbone Cable over next 12 sts, P2, (K2, P2) 4 times.

Row 2 (right side): K2, (P2, K2) 3 times, P2, LT, work row 2 of Seed Wishbone Cable over the next 12 sts, RT, (P2, K2) 4 times.

Working in established pattern and keeping Seed Wishbone Cable in numerical row sequence, work through row 19 of table.

Row 20: Knit the next 16 sts, increasing 8 sts within these sts, LT, work row 20 of Seed Wishbone Cable, RT, knit the next 16 sts, increasing 8 sts within these sts. (64 sts.)

Change to #7 needles and establish pattern as follows:

Row 21 (follow row 21 of pattern directions): Work the next 24 sts in Wickerwork, P2, work the next 12 sts in Seed Wishbone Cable, P2, work the next 24 sts in Wickerwork.

Continue in established pattern, working RTs and LTs on right-side rows, and as P2 on wrong-side rows. Work through row 23.

Row 24 (increase row): Increase 1 st at beginning and end of row, working these extra stitches and all subsequent increase stitches in Seed Stitch. Continue in pattern, working increases *(see increase note below)* every sixth row until there are 100 sts, ending on row 33 for size Small. *For size Large only*, work 6 more rows even, ending on row 39.

Increase Note: These increases are not worked at the very ends of the rows, as is normally the case. The increase on the right-hand side of the sleeve is done in the *first stitch* of Wickerwork, incorporating the extra stitch into the Seed Stitch pattern; the increase on the left-hand side of the sleeve is done in the *last stitch* of Wickerwork, incorporating the extra stitch into the Seed Stitch pattern. As the increasing progresses, your sleeve will take on a slightly rounded look at the top.

Row 34 (Small), 40 (Large): Cast off the first 41 sts, work to end of row.

Row 35 (Small), 41 (Large): Cast off the first 41 sts, work remaining sts.

Shoulder Strap: The Wishbone Cable pattern continues along the shoulder strap.

Row 36 (Small), 42 (Large): K1, LT, work Wishbone Cable over next 12 sts, RT, K1.

Row 37 (Small), 43 (Large): P3, work cable over next 12 sts, P3.

Continue shoulder strap in established pattern, working the first and last stitch in stockinette stitch (knit on right side, purl on wrong side), and working cable in numerical row sequence. Work until shoulder strap measures same length as front cast-off shoulder. Cast off stitches in knit, decreasing 1 st over center of cable.

SLEEVE #2: Work as for sleeve #1, but working RT for LT, and LT for RT.

FINISHING: Sew shoulder straps to sweater front and back, making sure the end of the strap is even with the neck edge of shoulder. Beginning at center of shoulder strap, measure 10.5 inches down sides of back and front and mark that distance. Sew sleeve tops to body, matching sides of sleeve to marks on body. Sew underarm seam and side seams.

NECK: With #5 circular needle (or #5 double-pointed) and starting at middle of right shoulder strap, pick up and knit 57 sts across back of sweater to middle of left shoulder strap, pick up and knit 23 sts over other half of left shoulder strap and down left front, knit 11 sts from front neck holder, pick up and knit 23 sts up right front and across remaining half of right shoulder strap. Place marker. (114 sts.)

Work in K2, P2 ribbing for 1.75 inches, decreasing 2 sts over center back on first round. (112 sts.)

Knit 7 rows. Bind off loosely in knit.

MEASUREMENTS IN INCHES

A. 20.5–23.5
B. .5
C. 16.75
D. 10.5
E. 15–16
F. 2.5
G. 7.5–8.5

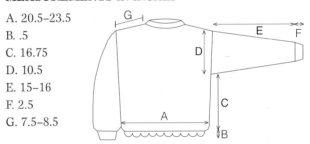

ROW INSTRUCTIONS FOR SIENNA TUNIC PATTERNS

ROW #	TRIPLET CABLE SEED (16-ROW REPEAT)	SEED WISHBONE CABLE (8-ROW REPEAT)	WICKERWORK (12-ROW REPEAT)
1	K7, P1, K1, P3, K1, P1, K7	K2, P1, K1, P3, K1, P2, K2	P1, *K2, P2*, K2, P1
2	P6, BC, K1b, FC, P6	P2, BC, FC, P2	*K1, P1, RT, LT, P1, K1*
3	K6, (P1, K1) 4X, P1, K6	K2, (P1, K1) 3X, P2, K2	*P1, K1, P1, K2, P1, K1, P1*
4	5, BC, K1, K1b, K1, FC, P5	P2, (K1, P1) 3X, K2, P2	*K1, RT, P2, LT, K1*
5	K5, P1, K1, (P1, K2) 2X, P1, K1, P1, K5	K2, (P1, K1) 3X, P2, K2	P2, *K4, P4*, K4, P2
6	P4, BC, K2, K1b, K2, FC, P4	P2, (K1, P1) 3X, K2, P2	Knit
7	K4, P1, K1, P2, K2, P1, K2, P2, K1, P1, K4	K2, (P1, K1) 3X, P2, K2	P1, *K2, P2*, K2, P2
8	P3, BC, (K1b, K2) 2X, K1b, FC, P3	P2, K1, P1, K3, P1, K2, P2	*LT, P1, K2, P1,RT*
9	K3, (P1, K1) 2X, (P1, K2) 2X, (P1, K1) 2X, P1, K3	K2, P1, K1, P3, K1, P2, K2	*K1, P1, K1, P2, K1, P1, K1*
10	P2, BC, K1, (K1b, K2) 2X, K1b, K1, FC, P2	P2, BC, FC, P2	*P1, LT, K2, RT, P1*
11	K2, P1, K1, (P1, K2) 4X, P1, K1, P1, K2	K2, (P1, K1) 3X, P2, K2	K2, *P4, K4*, P4, K2
12	P1, BC, (K2, K1b) 3X, K2, FC, P1	P2, (K1, P1) 3X, K2, P2	Knit
13	(K1, P1) 2X, K3, (P1, K2) 2X, P1, K3, (P1, K1) 2X	K2, (P1, K1) 3X, P2, K2	P1, *K2, P2*, K2, P1
14	(P1, K1b) 2X, K3, (MB, K2) 2X, MB, K3, (K1b, P1) 2X	P2, (K1, P1) 3X, K2, P2	*K1, P1, RT, LT, P1, K1*
15	(K1, P1) 2X, K3, (P1b, K2) 2X, P1b, K3, (P1, K1) 2X	K2, (P1, K1) 3X, P2, K2	*P1, K1, P1, K2, P1, K1, P2*

ROW #	TRIPLET CABLE SEED (16-ROW REPEAT)	SEED WISHBONE CABLE (8-ROW REPEAT)	WICKERWORK (12-ROW REPEAT)
16	(P1, K1b) 2X, P3, K1b, P1, K3b, P1, K1b, P3, (K1b, P1) 2X	P2, K1, P1, K3, P1, K2, P2	*K1, RT, P2, LT, K1*
17	K7, P1, K1, P3, K1, P1, K7	K2, P1, K1, P3, K1, P2, K2	P2, *K4, P4*, K4, P2
18	P6, BC, K1b, FC, P6	P2, BC, FC, P2	Knit
19	K6, (P1, K1) 4X, P1, K6	K2, (P1, K1) 3X, P2, K2	P1, *K2, P2*, K2, P1
20	P5, BC, K1, K1b, K1, FC, P5	P2, (K1, P1) 3X, K2, P2	*LT, P1, K2, P1, RT*
21	K5, P1, K1, (P1, K2) 2X, P1, K1, P1, K5	K2, (P1, K1) 3X, P2, K2	*K1, P1, K1, P2, K1, P1, K1*
22	P4, BC, K2, K1b, K2, FC, P4	P2, (K1, P1) 3X, K2, P2	*P1, LT, K2, RT, P1*
23	K4, P1, K1, P2, K2, P1, K2, P2, K1, P1, K4	K2, (P1, K1) 3X, P2, K2	K2, *P4, K4*, P4, K2, P2
24	P3, BC, (K1b, K2) 2X, K1b, FC, P3	P2, K1, P1, K3, P1, K2, P2	Knit
25	K3, (P1, K1) 2X, (P1, K2) 2X, (P1, K1) 2X, P1, K3	K2, P1, K1, P3, K1, P2, K2	P1, *K2, P2*, K2, P1
26	P2, BC, K1, (K1b, K2) 2X, K1b, K1, FC, P2	P2, BC, FC, P2	*K1, P1, RT, LT, P1, K1*
27	K2, P1, K1, (P1, K2) 4X, P1, K1, P1, K2	K2, (P1, K1) 3X, P2, K2	*P1, K1, P1, K2, P1, K1, P1*
28	P1, BC, (K2, K1b) 3X, K2, FC, P1	P2, (K1, P1) 3X, K2, P2	*K1, RT, P2, LT, K1*
29	(K1, P1) 2X, K3, (P1, K2) 2X, P1, K3, (P1, K1) 2X	K2, (P1, K1) 3X, P2, K2	P2, *K4, P4*, K4, P2
30	(P1, K1b) 2X, K3, (MB, K2) 2X, MB, K3, (K1b, P1) 2X	P2, (K1, P1) 3X, K2, P2	Knit
31	(K1, P1) 2X, K3, (P1b, K2) 2X, P1b, K3, (P1, K1) 2X	K2, (P1, K1) 3X, P2, K2	P1, *K2, P2*, K2, P2
32	(P1, K1b) 2X, P3, K1b, P1, K3b, P1, K1b, P3, (K1b, P1) 2X	P2, K1, P1, K3, P1, K2, P2	*LT, P1, K2, P1, RT*
33	K7, P1, K1, P3, K1, P1, K7	K2, P1, K1, P3, K1, P2, K2	*K1, P1, K1, P2, K1, P1, K1*
34	P6, BC, K1b, FC, P6	P2, BC, FC, P2	*P1, LT, K2, RT, P1*
35	K6, (P1, K1) 4X, P1, K6	K2, (P1, K1) 3X, P2, K2	K2, *P4, K4*, P4, K2
36	P5, BC, K1, K1b, K1, FC, P5	P2, (K1, P1) 3X, K2, P2	Knit
37	K5, P1, K1, (P1, K2) 2X, P1, K1, P1, K5	K2, (P1, K1) 3X, P2, K2	P1, *K2, P2*, K2, P1
38	P4, BC, K2, K1b, K2, FC, P4	P2, (K1, P1) 3X, K2, P2	*K1, P1, RT, LT, P1, K1*
39	K4, P1, K1, P2, K2, P1, K2, P2, K1, P1, K4	K2, (P1, K1) 3X, P2, K2	*P1, K1, P1, K2, P1, K1, P2*
40	P3, BC, (K1b, K2) 2X, K1b, FC, P3	P2, K1, P1, K3, P1, K2, P2	*K1, RT, P2, LT, K1*
41	K3, (P1, K1) 2X, (P1, K2) 2X, (P1, K1) 2X, P1, K3	K2, P1, K1, P3, K1, P2, K2	P2, *K4, P4*, K4, P2
42	P2, BC, K1, (K1b, K2) 2X, K1b, K1, FC, P2	P2, BC, FC, P2	Knit
43	K2, P1, K1, (P1, K2) 4X, P1, K1, P1, K2	K2, (P1, K1) 3X, P2, K2	P1, *K2, P2*, K2, P1
44	P1, BC, (K2, K1b) 3X, K2, FC, P1	P2, (K1, P1) 3X, K2, P2	*LT, P1, K2, P1, RT*
45	(K1, P1) 2X, K3, (P1, K2) 2X, P1, K3, (P1, K1) 2X	K2, (P1, K1) 3X, P2, K2	*K1, P1, K1, P2, K1, P1, K1*
46	(P1, K1b) 2X, K3, (MB, K2) 2X, MB, K3, (K1b, P1) 2X	P2, (K1, P1) 3X, K2, P2	*P1, LT, K2, RT, P1*
47	(K1, P1) 2X, K3, (P1b, K2) 2X, P1b, K3, (P1, K1) 2X	K2, (P1, K1) 3X, P2, K2	K2, *P4, K4*, K2, P2
48	(P1, K1b) 2X, P3, K1b, P1, K3b, P1, K1b, P3, (K1b, P1) 2X	P2, K1, P1, K3, P1, K2, P2	Knit

SPECIAL ABBREVIATIONS for Row Instructions Table
Note: FC and BC are worked differently on the Seed Wishbone Cable than on the Triplet Cable.

Wickerwork
RT (right twist)—Knit 2 together, then knit 1st stitch; slip both sts from needle.
LT (left twist)—Skip first st, knit into back of second st, knit both sts together through the back and slip both from needle.

Seed Wishbone Cable
BC (back cable)—Slip 3 sts to cable needle and hold in back, k1, then p1, k1, p1 from cable needle.
FC (front cable)—Slip 1 st to cable needle and hold in front, k1, p1, k1, then k1 from cable needle.

Triplet Cable
FC (front cable)—Slip 3 sts to cable needle and hold in front, k1, then k1b, p1, k1b from cable needle.
BC (back cable)—Slip 1 st to cable needle and hold in back, k1b, p1, k1b, then k1 from cable needle.
MB (make bobble)—(K1, yarn over, k1, yarn over, k1) in same st, turn and p5, turn and k3, k2 together, then pass the 3 knit sts one at a time over the k2 together st.

Peach Cropped Pullover

Cables and bobbles dance up this sweater, and the color will make you want to sing! (Pictured on page 20). The Amethyst Cardigan on page 126 is very similar but is longer.

YARN

Bear Hill Farm Yarn—85% wool, 15% mohair (4 oz/280 yd skein), 6-6-7 skeins Peach.

NEEDLES

#5 and #7 single-pointed, #5 circular (16-inch) or #5 double-pointed. *(See page 10 for equivalent metric and Canadian needle sizes.)*

GAUGE

18 sts and 28 rows = 4 inches worked over Moss Stitch on #7 needles.

FINISHED SIZES (IN INCHES)

Small	40
Medium	43
Large	46

(For information on converting measurements and skein weights to metric equivalents, see page 6.)

NOTE ON PATTERNS: This sweater has four different patterns in the center panel, each having a different number of rows per repeat: **Same Cable** (4 rows), **Moss Zigzag I and II** (20 rows), and **Bobble Cable** (12 rows). After 60 rows, all patterns will again begin at row 1 simultaneously. This has all been set up as a table of instructions to make your knitting enjoyable and easy. *All special abbreviations are printed at the bottom of the table for easy reference.*

ADDITIONAL PATTERN:

Moss Stitch

Row 1 (wrong side): *K1, P1*; repeat between *s, *or* *P1, K1*.

Row 2 (right side): Knit all knit sts, purl all purl sts.

Row 3: Purl all knit sts, knit all purl sts.

Row 4: Knit all knit sts, purl all purl sts.

Repeat rows 3 and 4 for pattern.

ABBREVIATIONS

M1 (make one)—Increase one stitch by lifting the horizontal thread between the two stitches; knit into the back of this loop.

Inc—Increase 1 st by knitting into the row below the stitch, then knitting the stitch

YO—Yarn over.

MB (make bobble)—Knit, YO, knit, YO, knit all in the same stitch. Turn and purl these 5 sts. Turn and knit 3 sts, then K2 together. Pass the three sts, one at a time, over the K2 stitch.

K1B and P1B—Knit (or purl) into back of stitch.

FRONT

Scallop Cast-On: Using #5 needles, tie a loop on one needle. This is the first stitch. *Cast on 3 sts. Knit these 3 sts, purl the 3 sts, knit the 3 sts, purl the 3 sts. (*Note:* instead of turning your work to purl the 3 sts, it is easier to knit them backward, saving the task of frequent turning. See page 11.)

The 3 sts you have just worked are on the left-hand needle. Slip the 2nd st over the first, then slip the 3rd st over the first.* You have remaining the original loop, plus one stitch on top of one scallop. Repeat between the *s until you have a total of 23-25-27 scallops.

Next row: *Knit 1, pick up (through the back loop, single strand only) and knit 3 sts along the top of the scallop.* Repeat for all scallops. Knit last st on needle. (93–101–109 sts.)

Bobble Border: Work as follows:

Row 1 (wrong side): Knit.

Row 2: K2, MB, (K3, MB) 22-24-26 times, K2.

Row 3: Knit.

Row 4 (increase row): Work every st as knit. K 27-31-35, increase 1 st in each of next 4 sts, K4, M1, K3, M1, K4, increase 1 st in each of next 3 sts, K1, increase 1 st in next st, K1, increase 1 st in each of next 3 sts, K4, M1, K3, M1, K4, increase 1 st in each of next 4 sts, K 27-31-35. (112–120–128 sts.)

Body: Change to #7 needles and establish patterns as follows, referring to the Row Instructions table on page 124.

(Wrong side) work row 1 of Moss Stitch (*K1, P1*) over the next 24-28-32 sts, P1b, work row 1 of Same Cable over the next 12 sts, P1b, work row 1 of Moss Zigzag II over the next 7 sts, P1b, work row 1 of Bobble Cable over the next 20 sts, P1b, work row 1 of Moss Zigzag I over the next 7 sts, P1b, work row 1 of Same Cable over the next 12 sts, P1b, work Moss Stitch (*P1, K1*) over the next 24-28-32 sts.

Next row (right side—follow row 2 of all four patterns from table): Work patterns over established number of stitches, working the P1b sts between cables as K1b.

Continue in established pattern, working the four patterns in numerical row sequence and working all established K1b sts on right-side rows as P1b on wrong-side rows.

Work the 60 rows of the table 2 times, then rows 1 through 7 for Small and Medium, and 1 through 17 for Large.

Shape Front Neck: Next row: Following row 8-8-18, work the first 47-51-54 sts, work the middle 18-18-20 sts and place on a holder for front neck, work the remaining 47-51-54 sts. Work each side separately from this point on.

Right Shoulder: Work 1 row. Beginning on next row (row 10-10-20), work bind-offs at neck edge every other row as follows: 3 sts once, 2 sts twice, 1 st 6 times. Work 3 rows even. Place 34–38–41 sts on holder for shoulder.

Left Shoulder: With wrong side facing, attach yarn at neck edge. Beginning on this row, (9–9–19), work shaping same as right shoulder. Work 4 rows even. Place shoulder sts on holder.

BACK: Work as for front, but after the 60 rows of the table have been repeated 2 times, work rows 1 through 23 for sizes Small and Medium, and 1 through 33 for size Large.

Shape Back Neck: Following row 24–24–34, work 39–43–46 sts, place middle 34–34–36 sts on holder for back neck. Work remaining 39–43–46 sts.

Right Shoulder: Decrease 1 st at neck edge on the next 5 rows. Place remaining 34–38–41 sts on holder.

Left Shoulder: With right side facing, attach yarn and work row 24–24–34. Beginning on next row, work shaping same as right shoulder.

SLEEVES: With #5 needles, cast on 50–50–54 sts. Work the following 2 rows of ribbing for 2.5 inches, ending with a completed row 2.

For sizes Small and Medium:
Row 1 (right side): (K2, P2) 12 times, end K2.
Row 2 (wrong side): (P2, K2) 12 times, end P2.
For size Large:
Row 1 (right side): P2, (K2, P2) 13 times.
Row 2 (wrong side): K2, (P2, K2) 13 times.
Work an increase row as follows:
For Small and Medium: (K2, P2, M1) 4–4–5 times, K2, P2, (increase in each of next 2 sts, P2) 3 times, (K2, P2, M1) 4–4–5 times, K2. (64–64–68 sts.)
For Large: Work as above but adding a P2 at beginning and end of row.

Change to #7 needles and establish pattern as follows:
Row 1 (wrong side): Work row 1 of Moss Stitch (*K1, P1*) over next 21–21–23 sts, P1b, work row 1 of Bobble Cable over next 20 sts, P1b, work Moss Stitch (*K1, P1*) over next 21–21–23 sts.

Continue in established pattern for 5 more rows, working the P1b stitches as K1b on right side rows, and following Bobble Cable in numerical row sequence.

Row 7 (increase row): Increase 1 st at beginning and 1 st at end of this row, then every seventh row 14–14–16 times, working all extra increase sts into the pattern of Moss Stitch. (92–92–100 sts.)

Work 9–9–0 rows even.

Shape Sleeve Cap: At the beginning of the next 8 rows, bind off 1 st. Bind off remaining 84–84–92 sts, decreasing 5 sts evenly spaced over the 16 stockinette sts of bobble cable as follows: (K1, K2 together) 5 times, K1.

JOIN SHOULDERS: With right sides together, join shoulders using the knitted seam method (page 11).

SEW SLEEVES: Measure down 9.5–9.5–10 inches from shoulder seam and mark edges of sweater front and back. Sew sleeve top to body of sweater between markers, matching the beginnings of the rounded edges of sleeve cap to markers. Sew sleeve seams and side body seams.

NECK: With #5 short circular needle and starting at right back shoulder, pick up and knit 7 sts down right back, knit the sts from the back neck holder as follows: K11–11–10, (K1, K2 tog) 4–4–5 times, K11, pick up and knit 7 sts up left back to shoulder seam, pick up and knit 22 sts down left front, knit the sts from the front holder as follows: K3–3–2, (K1, K2 tog) 4–4–5 times, K3, pick up and knit 22 sts up right front. (102–102–104 sts.)

Purl 2 rnds, decreasing 1 st at center front and 1 st at center back *for sizes Small and Medium only*. (100–100–104 sts.)

Work in K2, P2 ribbing for 6 rnds. Knit 4 rnds. Bind off loosely in knit.

FINISHING: Steam seams lightly. Do not press cables!!

MEASUREMENTS IN INCHES

A. 20–21.5–23
B. .75
C. 11–11–12
D. 9.5–9.5–10
E. 16.5–16.5–17
F. 2.5

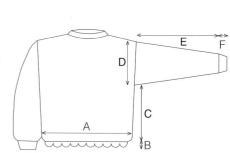

ROW INSTRUCTIONS FOR PEACH CROPPED PULLOVER PATTERNS
(ALSO USED FOR AMETHYST CARDIGAN)

Row #	SAME CABLE (4-ROW REPEAT)	MOSS ZIGZAG I (20-ROW REPEAT)	BOBBLE CABLE (12-ROW REPEAT)	MOSS ZIGZAG II (20-ROW REPEAT)
1	K2, P8, K2	K5, P2	K2, P16, K2	P2, K5
2	P2, 4BC, 4FC, P2	FC, P4	P2, K16, P2	P4, BC
3	K2, P8, K2	K all Ks, P all Ps	K2, P16, K2	K all Ks, P all Ps
4	P2, K8, P2	K1, FC, P3	P2, K16, P2	P3, BC, K1
5	K2, P8, K2	K all Ks, P all Ps	K2, P16, K2	K all Ks, P all Ps
6	P2, 4BC, 4FC, P2	P1, K1, FC, P2	P2, 8CF, K3, MB, K4, P2	P2, BC, K1, P1
7	K2, P8, K2	K all Ks, P all Ps	K2, P16, K2	K all Ks, P all Ps
8	P2, K8, P2	K1, P1, K1, FC, P1	P2, K16, P2	P1, BC, K1, P1, K1

Row #	SAME CABLE (4-ROW REPEAT)	MOSS ZIGZAG I (20-ROW REPEAT)	BOBBLE CABLE (12-ROW REPEAT)	MOSS ZIGZAG II (20-ROW REPEAT)
9	K2, P8, K2	K all Ks, P all Ps	K2, P16, K2	K all Ks, P all Ps
10	P2, 4BC, 4FC, P2	(P1, K1) 2X, FC	P2, K16, P2	BC, (K1, P1)2X
11	K2, P8, K2	K all Ks, P all Ps	K2, P16, K2	K all Ks, P all Ps
12	P2, K8, P2	(K1, P1) 2X, BC	P2, K4, MB, K3, 8CB, P2	FC, (P1, K1) 2X
13	K2, P8, K2	K all Ks, P all Ps	K2, P16, K2	K all Ks, P all Ps
14	P2, 4BC, 4FC, P2	P1, K1, P1, BC, P1	P2, K16, P2	P1, FC, P1, K1, P1
15	K2, P8, K2	K all Ks, P all Ps	K2, P16, K2	K all Ks, P all Ps
16	P2, K8, P2	K1, P1, BC, P2	P2, K16, P2	P2, FC, P1, K1
17	K2, P8, K2	K all Ks, P all Ps	K2, P16, K2	K all Ks, P all Ps
18	P2, 4BC, 4FC, P2	P1, BC, P3	P2, 8CF, K3, MB, K4, P2	P3, FC, P1
19	K2, P8, K2	K all Ks, P all Ps	K2, P16, K2	K all Ks, P all Ps
20	P2, K8, P2	BC, P4	P2, K16, P2	P4, FC
21	K2, P8, K2	K5, P2	K2, P16, K2	P2, K5
22	P2, 4BC, 4FC, P2	FC, P4	P2, K16, P2	P4, BC
23	K2, P8, K2	K all Ks, P all Ps	K2, P16, K2	K all Ks, P all Ps
24	P2, K8, P2	K1, FC, P3	P2, K4, MB, K3, 8CB, P2	P3, BC, K1
25	K2, P8, K2	K all Ks, P all Ps	K2, P16, K2	K all Ks, P all Ps
26	P2, 4BC, 4FC, P2	P1, K1, FC, P2	P2, K16, P2	P2, BC, K1, P1
27	K2, P8, K2	K all Ks, P all Ps	K2, P16, K2	K all Ks, P all Ps
28	P2, K8, P2	K1, P1, K1, FC, P1	P2, K16, P2	P1, BC, K1, P1, K1
29	K2, P8, K2	K all Ks, P all Ps	K2, P16, K2	K all Ks, P all Ps
30	P2, 4BC, 4FC, P2	(P1, K1) 2X, FC	P2, 8CF, K3, MB, K4, P2	BC, (K1, P1) 2X
31	K2, P8, K2	K all Ks, P all Ps	K2, P16, K2	K all Ks, P all Ps
32	P2, K8, P2	(K1, P1) 2X, BC	P2, K16, P2	FC, (P1, K1) 2X
33	K2, P8, K2	K all Ks, P all Ps	K2, P16, K2	K all Ks, P all Ps
34	P2, 4BC, 4FC, P2	P1, K1, P1, BC, P1	P2, K16, P2	P1, FC, P1, K1, P1
35	K2, P8, K2	K all Ks, P all Ps	K2, P16, K2	K all Ks, P all Ps
36	P2, K8, P2	K1, P1, BC, P2	P2, K4, MB, K3, 8CB, P2	P2, FC, P1, K1
37	K2, P8, K2	K all Ks, P all Ps	K2, P16, K2	K all Ks, P all Ps
38	P2, 4BC, 4FC, P2	P1, BC, P3	P2, K16, P2	P3, FC, P1
39	K2, P8, K2	K all Ks, P all Ps	K2, P16, K2	K all Ks, P all Ps
40	P2, K8, P2	BC, P4	P2, K16, P2	P4, FC
41	K2, P8, K2	K5, P2	K2, P16, K2	P2, K5
42	P2, 4BC, 4FC, P2	FC, P4	P2, 8CF, K3, MB, K4, P2	P4, BC
43	K2, P8, K2	K all Ks, P all Ps	K2, P16, K2	K all Ks, P all Ps
44	P2, K8, P2	K1, FC, P3	P2, K16, P2	P3, BC, K1
45	K2, P8, K2	K all Ks, P all Ps	K2, P16, K2	K all Ks, P all Ps
46	P2, 4BC, 4FC, P2	P1, K1, FC, P2	P2, K16, P2	P2, BC, K1, P1
47	K2, P8, K2	K all Ks, P all Ps	K2, P16, K2	K all Ks, P all Ps
48	P2, K8, P2	K1, P1, K1, FC, P1	P2, K4, MB, K3, 8CB, P2	P1, BC, K1, P1, K1
49	K2, P8, K2	K all Ks, P all Ps	K2, P16, K2	K all Ks, P all Ps
50	P2, 4BC, 4FC, P2	(P1, K1) 2X, FC	P2, K16, P2	BC, (K1, P1) 2X
51	K2, P8, K2	K all Ks, P all Ps	K2, P16, K2	K all Ks, P all Ps
52	P2, K8, P2	(K1, P1) 2X, BC	P2, K16, P2	FC, (P1, K1) 2X
53	K2, P8, K2	K all Ks, P all Ps	K2, P16, K2	K all Ks, P all Ps
54	P2, 4BC, 4FC, P2	P1, K1, P1, BC, P1	P2, 8CF, K3, MB, K4, P2	P1, FC, P1, K1, P1
55	K2, P8, K2	K all Ks, P all Ps	K2, P16, K2	K all Ks, P all Ps
56	P2, K8, P2	K1, P1, BC, P2	P2, K16, P2	P2, FC, P1, K1
57	K2, P8, K2	K all Ks, P all Ps	K2, P16, K2	K all Ks, P all Ps
58	P2, 4BC, 4FC, P2	P1, BC, P3	P2, K16, P2	P3, FC, P1.
59	K2, P8, K2	K all Ks, P all Ps	K2, P16, K2	K all Ks, P all Ps
60	P2, K8, P2	BC, P4	P2, K4, MB, K3, 8CB, P2	P4, FC

SPECIAL ABBREVIATIONS for Row Instructions Table

cn—Cable needle.

YO— Yarn over.

tog—Together.

4FC—Slip 2 sts to cable needle, hold in front, K2, K2 from cable needle.

4BC—Work as 4FC but hold sts in back.

FC (front cable)—Slip 2 sts to cable needle, hold in front, P1, then k2 from cable needle.

BC (back cable)—Slip 1 st to cable needle, hold in back, k2, then P1 from cable needle.

8CF—Slip 4 sts to cable needle, hold in front, K4, then K4 from cable needle.

8CB—Work as 8CF but hold sts in back.

MB (make bobble)—(K1, YO, K1, YO, K1) in same st, turn and P5, turn and K3, K2 together then pass

Amethyst Cardigan

The Amethyst cardigan is a close cousin to the Peach Cropped Pullover on page 123. In fact, the same row-by-row pattern instructions are used for both sweathers. (Pictured on page 20.)

YARN

Bear Hill Farm—85% wool, 15% mohair (4 oz/280 yd skeins), 6-6-7 skeins Amethyst

NEEDLES

#5 and #7 single-pointed, #5 circular (16-inch) or #5 double-pointed. *(See page 10 for equivalent metric and Canadian needle sizes.)*

GAUGE

18 sts and 28 rows = 4 inches worked over Moss Stitch on #7 needles.

FINISHED SIZES (IN INCHES)

Small	40
Medium	43
Large	46

(For information on converting measurements and skein weights to metric equivalents, see page 6.)

NOTE ON PATTERNS: This sweater has four different patterns in the center panel, each having a different number of rows per repeat: **Same Cable** (4 rows), **Moss Zigzag I and II** (20 rows), and **Bobble Cable** (12 rows). After 60 rows, all patterns will again begin at row 1 simultaneously. This has all been set up as a table of instructions (page 124) to make your knitting enjoyable and easy. *All special abbreviations are printed at the bottom of the table for easy reference.*

ADDITIONAL PATTERN
Moss Stitch

Row 1 (wrong side): *K1, P1*; repeat between *s, *or* *P1, K1*.
Row 2 (right side): Knit all knit sts, purl all purl sts.
Row 3: Purl all knit sts, knit all purl sts.
Row 4: Knit all knit sts, purl all purl sts.
Repeat rows 3 and 4 for pattern.

ABBREVIATIONS

<u>M1</u> (make one)—Increase one stitch by lifting the horizontal thread between the two stitches; knit into the back of this loop.

<u>Inc</u>—Increase 1 st by knitting into the row below the stitch, then knitting the stitch

<u>YO</u>—Yarn over.

<u>MB</u> (make bobble)—Knit, YO, knit, YO, knit all in the same stitch. Turn and purl these 5 sts. Turn and knit 3 sts, then K2 together. Pass the three sts, one at a time, over the K2 stitch.

<u>K1B</u> and <u>P1B</u>—Knit (or purl) into back of stitch.

LEFT FRONT

Scallop Cast-On: Using #5 needles, tie a loop on one needle. This is the first stitch. *Cast on 3 sts. Knit these 3 sts, purl the 3 sts, knit the 3 sts, purl the 3 sts. (*Note:* instead of turning your work to purl the 3 sts, it is easier to knit them backward, saving the task of frequent turning. See page 11.)

The 3 sts you have just worked are on the left-hand needle. Slip the 2nd st over the first, then slip the 3rd st over the first.* You have remaining the original loop, plus one stitch on top of one scallop. Repeat between the *s until you have a total of 11-12-13 scallops. (45-49-53 sts.)

Bobble Border. Work as follows:
Row 1 (wrong side): Knit.
Row 2: K2, MB, (K3, MB) 22-24-26 times, K2.
Row 3: Knit.
Row 4: (increase row; work all sts as knit) Knit 19-23-27, increase 1 st in each of next 4 sts, K3, increase 1 st in each of next 3 sts, K3, increase 1 st in each of next 9 sts, K4. (61-65-69 sts.)

Body: Change to #7 needle and establish pattern as follows, referring to the Row Instructions table on page 124:

Row 1 (wrong side): P2 (center front edge sts), P1b, work row 1 of Bobble Cable over next 20 sts, P1b, work row 1 of Moss Zigzag I over next 7 sts, P1b, work row 1 of Same Cable over next 12 sts, P1b, work row 1 of Moss Stitch (K1, P1) over next 16-20-24 sts.

Row 2: Work pattern as established, working the P1b sts as K1b on right side, and the first 2 sts at center front edge in stockinette stitch (K on right side, P on wrong side).

Work the 60 rows of the table 2 times, then rows 1 through 28 for sizes Small and Medium, and rows 1 through 38 for size Large.

Shape Neck: Following row 29-29-39, bind off 14-14-15 sts as follows: bind off 5 sts, (K2 tog, bind off 1 st, K1, bind off 1 st) 3 times. *For Large size only:* bind off 1 more st.

Work 1 row.

Beginning on next row, work bind-offs at neck edge every other row, as follows: 3 sts once; 2 sts twice; 1 st six times.

Work 2 rows even. Place 34-38-41 sts on holder.

RIGHT FRONT: Work as for left front up to increase row.

Work increase row as follows: K4, increase 1 st in each of next 9 sts, K3, increase 1 st in each of next 3 sts, K3, increase 1 st in each of next 4 sts, K19-23-27. (61-65-69 sts.)

Body: Change to #7 needles and establish pattern as follows, referring to the Row Instructions table on page 124:

Work row 1 of Moss Stitch (K1, P1) over next 16–20–24 sts, P1b, work row 1 of Same Cable over next 12 sts, P1b, work row 1 of Moss Zigzag II over next 7 sts, P1b, work row 1 of Bobble Cable over next 20 sts, P2 (center front edge sts).

Work the 60 rows of table 2 times, then rows 1 thorough 29 for sizes Small and Medium, and rows 1 through 39 for size Large.

Shape neck: (Row 30–30–40) Bind off same as left front neck, and work shaping same as left front; work 1 row even.

BACK: Work the 60 rows of the Row Instructions table twice, then work rows 1 through 43 for sizes Small and Medium, and rows 1 through 53 for size Large.

Shape neck beginning on row 44–44–54: work 39–43–46 sts, bind off middle 34–34–36 sts for back neck, decreasing 8 sts evenly spaced over the middle 16 sts of the bobble cable. Work remaining 39–43–46 sts.

Right Shoulder: Decrease 1 st at neck edge on the next 5 rows. Place remaining 34–38–41 sts on holder.

Left Shoulder: With right side facing, attach yarn and work row 24–24–34. Beginning on next row, work shaping same as right shoulder.

JOIN SHOULDERS: With right sides together, join shoulders using the knitted seam method (page 11).

NECK AND FRONT BANDS: Work Scallop Cast-On until there are 64–64–69 scallops. Work rows 1 through 3 of Bobble Border. Knit 1 row. Bind off *very loosely* in purl.

Fold scallop band in half lengthwise and mark center with a pin. Pin center of band to center of back neck edge. Beginning at lower right edge of cardigan, sew band to body. Generally, take up 3 threads on body to every 2 threads of band, then sew evenly around neck curve to center back. Sew other side beginning at lower left edge of cardigan. End at center back neck.

SLEEVES: With #5 needles, cast on 50–50–54 sts. Work the following 2 rows of ribbing for 2.5 inches, ending with a completed row 2.

For sizes Small and Medium:
Row 1 (right side): (K2, P2) 12 times, end K2.
Row 2 (wrong side): (P2, K2) 12 times, end P2.
For size Large:
Row 1 (right side): P2, (K2, P2) 13 times.
Row 2 (wrong side): K2, (P2, K2) 13 times.

Work an increase row as follows:
For Small and Medium: (K2, P2, M1) 4–4–5 times, K2, P2, (increase in each of next 2 sts, P2) 3 times, (K2, P2, M1) 4–4–5 times, K2. (64–64–68 sts.)
For Large: Work as above but adding a P2 at beginning and end of row.

Change to #7 needles and establish pattern as follows:
Row 1 (wrong side): Work row 1 of Moss Stitch (*K1, P1*) over next 21–21–23 sts, P1b, work row 1 of Bobble Cable over next 20 sts, P1b, work Moss Stitch (*K1, P1*) over next 21–21–23 sts.

Continue in established pattern for 5 more rows, working the P1b sts as K1b on right side rows, and following Bobble Cable in numerical row sequence.

Row 7 (increase row): Increase 1 st at beginning and 1 st at end of this row, then every seventh row 14–14–16 times, working all extra increase sts into the pattern of Moss Stitch. (92–92–100 sts.)

Work 9–9–0 rows even.

Shape Sleeve Cap: At the beginning of the next 8 rows, bind off 1 st. Bind off remaining 84–84–92 sts, decreasing 5 sts evenly spaced over the 16 stockinette sts of bobble cable as follows: (K1, K2 together) 5 times, K1.

SEW SLEEVES: Measure down 9.5–9.5–10 inches from shoulder seam and mark edges of sweater front and back. Sew sleeve top to body of sweater between markers, matching the beginnings of the rounded edges of sleeve cap to markers. Sew sleeve seams and side body seams.

FINISHING: Steam seams lightly. *Do not press cables!!* Sew on three ready-made pewter clasps.

MEASUREMENTS IN INCHES

A. 20–21.5–23
B. .75
C. 14.5–14.5–15.5
D. 9.5–9.5–10
E. 16.5–16.5–17
F. 2.5

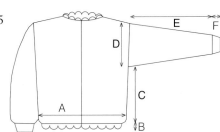

Sources

Venetian Beehives Sweater • PAGE 30

The New Carolingian Modelbook:
Counted Embroidery Patterns from Before 1600,
by Kim Brody Alazar
writing as Ianthé díAveroingne

THE OUTLAW PRESS
160 WASHINGTON SE, SUITE 43
ALBUQUERQUE, NM 87108-2749

Indigo Sweater • PAGE 50

The pattern used on the body of the sweater comes from the Vilani Parish in the district of Rezekne. I found it in the following book:

Latviesu Rakstainie Cimdi,
by Mirdza Slava
Riga: Zinatne, 1992

Published by
THE LATVIAN ACADEMY OF
SCIENCES HISTORY INSTITUTE

The border design is from a Turkish sock pattern I found in another book:

Fancy Feet,
by Anna Zilboorg
LARK BOOKS, 1994
50 COLLEGE ST.
ASHVILLE, NC 28801

Commercial Yarns

The following yarn companies generously sent samples to me so I could compare yarns for suggested substitutions. Their addresses are listed on pages 8 and 9.

Mountain Colors
Heneke Enterprises
Dale of Norway
Beth Brown-Reinsel's Knitting Traditions
Plymouth Yarn Co.
Rowan Yarns
Harrisville Designs
Tahki Imports, Ltd.
Sirdar Yarns

Buttons

All buttons used on sweaters in this book were generously provided by Bob and Phyllis Fishberg, owners of the Wool Connection, in Avon, Connecticut. They do business from their retail store as well as through their mail-order catalog. For information, you may contact them at:

The Wool Connection
34 E. Main St.
Old Avon Village, North
Avon, CT 06001
1-800-933-9665